The Show I'll Never Forget

The Show I'll Never Forget
50 Writers Relive Their Most Memorable Concertgoing Experience

Edited by
SEAN
MANNING

DA CAPO PRESS
A Member of the Perseus Books Group

Contents

1

Introduction
R.E.M.
Madison Square Garden
New York City
November 4, 2004
SEAN MANNING

ON SEPTEMBER 9, 1956, sixty million Americans—a then record-setting 82 percent of television viewers—tuned in to watch Elvis Presley's first performance on *The Ed Sullivan Show*. Ask a hundred baby boomers what, exactly, they saw that Sunday night and you'll understand by the identicalness of their answers why it's impossible for a televised concert to approximate being in the crowd. Nevertheless, due in large part to the DVD boom, the proliferation of DIRECTV, and the advent of webcasting, North American live music attendance continues to decline—roughly 3 percent annually[1] since 2004—without question, one of the most disastrous years in industry history.

That January, the Bottom Line, the Greenwich Village club famous for helping catapult the career of Bruce Springsteen, shut its doors after nearly thirty years. In June, the traditionally thirty–odd stop Lollapalooza festival was cancelled due to poor sales. While Prince bucked the trend with his top-grossing *Musicology* tour, in a sign of the times, opening night at Los Angeles's Staples Center was simulcast in eighty-five Regal Theaters

---

[1] The year-end figure for 2006 was unavailable in time for publication. According to industry magazine *Pollstar*, ticket sales for the first half of 2006 were up 20 percent over the first half of 2005—this despite a corresponding 15.6 percent increase in ticket prices (that's nearly eight dollars more per ticket). Promoters would claim this is evidence that higher prices aren't antithetical to healthy attendance. But all it really proves is that concertgoing, typically identified with community, has, in fact, become a rather exclusive pastime. In October 2006, Lake Group Media—a company that handles list management for promoter-heavyweight Live Nation—put the average household income of Live Nation ticket-buyers at eighty-five thousand dollars. That's almost double 2005's U.S. median income of $46,326.

nationwide to an audience of roughly twenty-five thousand—or five thousand more than the Staples Center's sell-out crowd.

Technology wasn't entirely at fault—a complication, as it were, not the disease. After a three-year recession, in 2004 the economy was finally showing signs of life. But rather than restrain ticket prices to stimulate growth, promoters raced to recoup their losses by charging an average seven dollars more per head. And for what? Concerts felt so inordinately premeditated, even those moments that at first seemed otherwise, such as Janet Jackson's well-orchestrated "costume malfunction" during Super Bowl XXXVIII's halftime show. About the only thing that passed for improvisation was a lip-synching snafu. Take Ashlee Simpson's October 2004 mishap on *Saturday Night Live*—a far cry from Elvis Costello's unscheduled performance of "Radio, Radio" thirty years prior. And yet, these examples only further illustrate the degree to which visual media was altering even my once-stalwart notion of what expressly constituted the concertgoing experience.

All the same, unvarying set lists, obligatory encores, seats so remote you wound up watching the action on a big screen anyhow . . . Might as well stay at home, order it on Pay-Per-View, save the money, and spare the aggravation. Such was the apparent consensus among concertgoers, myself included. Until, that is, something happened to check my cynicism and restore my faith in the life-affirming, life-altering power of live music.

In early November of 2004, I took an unpaid fashion internship with a pop culture glossy. Two years out of a master's program that had sunk me forty thousand dollars in debt, paying seven hundred dollars a month in rent, and working sans benefits as a waiter for a lower Manhattan catering company, I couldn't afford to forfeit three shifts a week. But I'd come to New York to write, not pass hors d'oeuvres. I didn't know Gucci from Pucci, yet figured if I could just get my foot in the door. . . .

My third morning at the cramped Soho office and it was obvious that the sum of my duties would be alphabetizing lookbooks and walking my boss's polyuric golden retriever. That afternoon, K— asked me to run over to a friend's place and pick up her tickets for that night's R.E.M. concert at Madison Square Garden. Sure, I'd pick up the tickets. No problem. Then I'd leave them on her desk with a note counseling in no uncertain terms the method and location most advantageous for their safekeeping.

Five o'clock and already the Empire State Building glowed red, white, and blue. I walked crosstown in the rain, dodging both the spray of passing cabs and obnoxiously oversized golf umbrellas. By the time I arrived at the luxury high rise on West Street, I was soaked through. The scrap of paper I'd jotted the friend's name and apartment number on had bled to illegibility, so that it took some explaining, as well as a thorough inspection of my driver's license, to convince the doorman I wasn't simply looking to wait out the storm.

I was so busy wishing the day would end and feeling sorry for myself that, as I entered the elevator, I hardly noticed the diminutive, bald man exiting. I would've neglected him altogether if not for the road bike he was pushing. I nodded gravely in acknowledgement of the unspoken bond uniting tens of thousands of cater waiters and couriers and freight elevator operators and bathroom attendants—the shared understanding, however scant the consolation, that it's we who keep the city whirring along. He smiled, which confirmed he wasn't a messenger. Still, there was something familiar about him. I'd seen him somewhere; I was positive. Before I could get a better look, the elevator doors closed.

It's trite, but true: there's no more reliable indication that one's a naturalized New Yorker than when upon entering a strange apartment, he or she begins estimating square footage. Without surveying the bedrooms and baths, I guessed K—'s friend's place for a thousand, easy. Big to be sure, with cathedral ceilings and an unobstructed view of the Hudson, presently obscured by darkness and rain. But nothing I wasn't used to catering. Not so quotidian were the bundles of concert tickets strewn across the carpet and coffee table and couch. K—'s friend apologized for the mess, then offered me some tea. I declined.

"Well then, how about a ticket? You deserve *something* for walking all the way over here in that mess."

I'd prefer a byline, I thought as she slipped an extra ticket into K—'s envelope. So that, while only passingly familiar with R.E.M.—of whose thirteen albums I owned none—for the opportunity to ingratiate myself with K—, I was nonetheless grateful.

Of course, in explaining to her what had happened, I acted nothing but apologetic.

"Are you kidding?" K— asked, sounding not at all put upon. "I'd only consider it an imposition if you didn't go."

Getting off the escalator after only one flight, I knew the seats were better than the upper-tier nosebleeds I'd suffered for Prince four months earlier. Just how much better I never imagined.

I turned out of the narrow concourse and walked onto what had, the night before, been varnished hardwood. I gazed up at the retired numbers of Monroe and Frazier, and marveled at the eight-sided, multiton scoreboard's suspension. Near what would've been the jump ball circle, a gray-haired, tuxedoed usher examined my ticket. Then he examined me. My clothes were still sopping, my smile uncouthly wide, my eyes bulging in disbelief while darting feverishly between the surrounding glitterati, among them chef Mario Batali, tossing popcorn into the air and catching it in his mouth. With a look only slightly less dismissive than the doorman's, impervious to my stare of solidarity, the usher led me down the center aisle, flanked by lettered rows of folding chairs dwindling toward the beginning of the alphabet.

K— arrived just as the guitar techs were finishing their tune-ups. She wore a spangled, backless, black halter and her tight, black curls relieved of the ponytail favored around the office. She'd brought along a girlfriend and her girlfriend's boyfriend.

"And, of course, you know my fiancée, D—."

I knew *of* him, primarily as the one person never to disturb with a phone call and whose way interns were collectively admonished to stay out of. But this was the first time I'd actually shaken hands with the founder and creative director of the magazine. In the narrow workplace, its walls lined with computers and fax machines and postage meters whose purchase he had if not outright authorized then at least petitioned for, D— cut an imposing figure, thanks furthermore to the dark-hued sportcoats ostensibly custom-tailored to his power-forward frame. Unaided by the home-court advantage of Prince Street, however, he seemed affable enough. He asked where I was from. I told him Ohio. He grinned and shook his head.

"What were they thinking?"

Had the question not been rhetorical, I might've given D— an abridged history of the economic and cultural polarization that's epitomized the state since the Civil War—or less pompously offered that although Canton's Pro Football Hall of Fame wasn't quite as propitious a terrorist target as, say, Grand Central Station, Ohioans' lives were no less valuable than New Yorkers'; their fear, albeit unsubstantiated, no less real. They were responsible for the election's ramifications, but no more than the rest of us, Democrats and Republicans alike, for allowing ourselves to be so brazenly and shamelessly pitted against one another. D—'s condescension was a prime example.

Suddenly the arena went dark. There followed a cadence-setting snare drum, then a burst of whirling primary colors from the spotlights above the stage. At its edge, dressed in a white suit with a purple blindfold painted around his glistening head, was the man I'd seen in the elevator—though, again, I didn't recognize him at first. He radiated such assuredness, such awe-inducing authority, it was as if he'd grown three feet in as many hours.

> *That's great, it starts with an earthquake,*
> *birds and snakes, an aeroplane and*
> *Lenny Bruce is not afraid.*

The crowd's roar was deafening, its excitement contagious. I jumped up from my seat, beer in hand. Earlier, at the concession stand, I'd remarked to the supremely disinterested cashier about the absurd cost of such a small cup—domestic at that. "Shit, it's not even commemorative!" Now, with half the pricey suds careening up and out, its shallowness was all the more lamentable—especially for D—'s expensive shoes. Fortunately, he was too riveted by the opening number to notice.

> *It's the end of the world as we know it . . .*

It was the first time R.E.M. ever opened a concert with that song, I'd overhear more than once on my way out of the Garden. No doubt, the gesture was intended as *momento mori*. For me, though, the tune was more hopeful than defeatist. It was the end of a figurative world—a world in which pride too often overtook me; a world in which most of the time pride wasn't pride but rather masquerading fear; a world I'd long thought owed me something.

Monday morning, I went into the office and took the golden retriever for its first walk of the day. A month or so later, I got to write a seventy-five-word album review.

Though generally synonymous—as in my case with R.E.M.—your most memorable concertgoing experience doesn't *have* to be the best concert you ever saw. In fact, as the following stories contend, when determining the show you'll never forget, what happened offstage is just as important as the performance itself. How old you were, where you were living, what your job was, whom you'd just started dating, whom you'd just broken up with, and invariably what and how much you had to drink or smoke or alternately ingest before, during, and/or after—these are the prevailing criteria.

As for what standards led to the ensuing assemblage of writers, I had only one: I chose those whose work I admire.

Richard Burgin, in his essay, relates how, as a boy, he'd cold call jazz musicians he esteemed, just to tell them so. While I'll be twenty-seven by the time you read this, my regard for the contributors is not so dissimilar—though, because of my age, I'm not nearly as bold and certainly not as guileless. This project gave me a reason other than mere adulation to keep Harvey Pekar on the phone for forty-five minutes and trade three-in-the-morning e-mails with David Gates. And it gave them and the rest a reason to divulge the biographical marginalia I've long sought to learn of my idols.

The ploy worked to equal effect on my biggest hero of all: my father. For years I've been after him to set down the story of his life (as opposed to "memoir" or "autobiography," which connote an intent to sell and, now more than ever, self-aggrandize). The story isn't wholly unfamiliar—particularly these days with regard to employment history—yet it's this very universality that commends it to the telling: as a teenager, went to work in the rubber factory to pay his way through college and shortly thereafter support his recently widowed mother; wed his childhood friend's sister; rose up from the company ranks to become an executive; tended to my mother after she was diagnosed with Hodgkin's disease, and when she got better and decided she didn't want to be a secretary for the rest of her life, encouraged her decision to cash in her retirement savings and put it towards a nursing diploma; equally in spite and because of a propensity for paralytic guilt courtesy of pre–Vatican II parochial school, dissolved their twenty-one-year marriage; in an egregious demonstration of dickless corporate cost-cutting, laid off at age fifty-four, after thirty-four years of loyal, meritorious service; following a series of middling, mid-level advertising jobs, found work as a part-time mailman for the county school system—a gig that pays half the little I earn as a waiter, yet one which, I remind him constantly, leaves plenty of time for writing.

Still, he's reluctant. Odds are he'd just as soon spend the time in the garden or on the golf course. Or maybe it's too painful for him to recall all those wonderful and horrible things that did or did not happen so long ago. In other words, he'd rather not be reminded he's getting older. Hell, I'd rather not be reminded he's getting older. But that doesn't change the fact that he is. Should I have kids, I want there to be something to help impress upon them—in the event they don't get to discover it firsthand—what an incredible man their grandfather was, something that will leave an image more indelible than the died-too-young, fishing enthusiast his father is to me.

Figuring the daunting prospect of chronicling some threescore years had not a little to do with his reticence, I asked if he'd consider a more modest assignment. It took him four months, but he finally finished.

Elvis was the most memorable concert I ever saw. But why was it I couldn't remember when I saw him, what he sang, or what he wore? Did I see him before my son was born or after? Was I still a copywriter or had I taken the marketing position? Were we still in the apartment or had we bought our first house? Why was I having so much trouble remembering? Was it because I'm sixty-one and showing signs of forgetfulness? Heck, I can remember events from fifty years ago like they were yesterday. How about Lynn Fisher, my first-grade crush? She taught me how to color. I played dumb, pretending crayons were candy, just to be with her. Or what about the three times I flunked my driver's test because I couldn't park the '56 Chevy? No, I can remember back, way back.

At a loss, I thought I'd ask someone who might have went with me—my ex-wife. She assured me we did, in fact, go together. Feeling better, I asked her if we had fun.

"Yes," she said. "Don't you remember? We went with Ted and Karen."

"Ted and Karen?"

"For God's sake—Ted was your best man at our wedding!"

"Oh, *that* Ted and Karen," I replied.

Before long, I started to remember details of the concert, including the fact I was not too keen on going.

Never a great fan of Elvis, I preferred Motown. Smokey and Marvin owned me with their soulful sound. I was thirty at the time, and Elvis was forty, almost over the hill in my mind. Ted, a good friend from Memphis who looked and sounded like the King, was the one who suggested we go. Reluctantly, I agreed. Our wives needed little convincing.

On a hot summer night, July 11, 1975, the four of us left Akron and drove to the Richfield Coliseum. About ten miles from the arena, traffic slowed to a dead stop. When we finally got to our seats, I looked around the sea of faces, mostly women, with a few men sprinkled here and there. The smell of perfume, not pot, permeated the air.

At first, the event seemed more like a circus than a concert. Barkers were hawking the Elvis profile on every item known to man, from toothbrushes to leather jackets. Finally, the lights went down, the music came up, and the women went wild as Elvis walked slowly on stage. Peering through binoculars, I could see him in his famous white-sequined jumpsuit. He couldn't disguise his weight gain or his blue-black hair, but no one seemed to care. Elvis began to speak and the crowd went silent, not to miss a word. His down-home voice welcomed us and promised us a good time. And then he let it rip.

Rock, blues, ballads, gospel—he nailed them all while wiping sweat from his brow with scarves and tossing them to a pool of frenzied females in the front rows. The place was going crazy. During one pause, Elvis asked for the houselights to go up so he could see his fans. He read aloud one sign held by a very attractive admirer: ONE KISS OR I'LL DIE. Elvis snarled as only he could and said, "I can't let you die. Come on down and get your kiss." She raced down the aisle, jumped on stage, and they kissed.

But what I remember most about that evening was the way it ended.

"Ladies and gentlemen, Elvis has left the building."

The words vibrated in my ears as twenty-two thousand adoring fans screamed, "Elvis, Elvis, Elvis." With each "Elvis" the decibel count jumped until again interrupted by the announcer's booming voice: "Elvis's bus has just left the parking lot. Have a good evening, and drive safely."

More than thirty years have passed since then. There have been many changes in my life and in the world. Somehow, I grew older, but Elvis stayed the same.

And now, thanks to your story, so will you, Dad.

2

Miles Davis
The Casablanca
Buffalo, New York
September 21, 1955
ISHMAEL REED

A TRIP TO PARIS and a Miles Davis concert were events that would determine the course of my life. It all started innocently enough. In 1954, I was chosen by the African American Michigan Avenue YMCA to be part of a delegation that would attend a Bible study convention. The money had been raised by the older members of the Y, merchants, professionals, and clergymen who were the informal government of black Buffalo, and who negotiated with the white government that wielded power in the community. I was very active in high school clubs and had used the Y as a second home where I would go and swim and try to set down some chord changes on the piano. There were many eccentric characters who would come to the Y. One was a guy who called himself Lord Johnny. He taught me some blues chord changes that I later learned were the ones that Charlie Parker used. Parker changes.

I hadn't traveled to many places before that. Maybe to Chattanooga, where my mother and stepfather were born. Sometimes to Cleveland, where my stepfather's mother lived. Once to New York, where the highlight of the trip was a glimpse of the boxer Sugar Ray Robinson standing in front of his bar. I was a shy person and was embarrassed by all of the attention paid to those of us who were going on the trip. We lived in the lower-middle-class neighborhood on Riley Street, having moved from East Utica where my parents had rented. We lived in the projects before that.

There was a woman who lived across the street. She looked like a young Etta James. It was difficult to avoid looking into her bedroom from where I slept on the sun porch. She wasn't modest. I had some serious fantasies about her. My interest in women was beginning, but the ones to whom I was attracted were older than me. In Paris, I attended parties attended by the students who lived at the Cité Universitaire. I would be the youngest person there and would survey the French co-eds as they danced with their partners. Walter Dukes, the basketball star at Seton Hall, was studying international law at the time. Just as I was about to hit on one of these French girls, he'd send me to my room. For some reason, he had appointed himself my chaperone.

But he couldn't always be on my case. I'd go to the jazz clubs, sometimes alone, sometimes with some white kids from Long Island with whom I'd begun hanging out. You'd be walking down a narrow street and you'd hear maybe Clifford Brown's "Parisian Thoroughfare" coming from one of the clubs. We once went to a club in Pigalle, and watched nude dancers until we fell asleep over champagne. When we awoke, the club had emptied out and it was dawn. I remember our riding on the Metro and seeing one of the chorus girls who'd performed the night before. She pointed at us. When I got back to my room, my roommate, an older white man from Texas, said, "Some people are out all night." It was my first time of staying out all night.

I have a memory from the proceedings that shows how things were before the drive for civil rights. Kids from all over the world elected me the head of one of the conference's committees. Some of the white kids who were members of the Southern delegation got angry.

When I returned to Buffalo, I was a different person. High school bored me, and so, out of the blue, I told a teacher, who wanted me to be part of a delegation to go to Hyde Park to meet Eleanor Roosevelt, "I won't be here." I dropped out of high school and went to work at a library.

I bought a trombone and began to play with a group of young musicians. I had studied the trombone in high school and had played the violin in elementary school. I took up the violin, again, in high school and formed a string quartet there. We had a band that would play Stan Kenton arrangements. One of those on saxophone was Don Menza, who went on to play with Maynard Ferguson.

The star among the young black musicians was an alto player named Claude Walker. He was a prodigy. Sometimes, he would disappear and we'd discover that he'd been in Rochester performing with the Eastman Symphony. But he liked jazz and was playing hard bop before there was a name for it. Claude later died in a fire. Before that he had a shoot-out with the police. His was a talent snuffed out as a result of being unable to graduate to a larger stage.

One of his friends was jazz pianist Wade Legge, who used to fascinate us with his stories about jazz musicians in New York. He was discovered by

Milt Jackson while playing in a jam session at the musicians' local. Wade died in his twenties. He said that he got fired from the Mingus band because he'd show up late for rehearsals. I still listen to Wade on the only solo album he made from Blue Note. He deserves more recognition.

If our group had a god, it was Miles Davis. People tell you what they were doing when Kennedy was shot or when the Twin Towers fell. I remember being in the house alone listening to a Buffalo jazz show, which was moderated by Joe Rico, for whom Illinois Jacquet wrote "Port of Rico." He played a Miles Davis tune. I'd never heard a sound like that. The sound epitomized where I was and what I wanted to be. I played *Birth of the Cool* until it was all worn out. And so when we heard that Miles was going to perform in Buffalo, we were excited. The night came. September 21, 1955.

We were all standing on the corner when this cab drove up and Miles got out. The black men we were used to were really square. They were working-class types and professionals who were a part of an emerging middle class. Buffalo was, at that time, a backward, dull town where there was little to do. When Jazz at the Philharmonic came to town, there was a scandal at Kleinhans Music Hall because the boppers began to dance in the aisles. Ben Webster was busted for possession of a few joints. It was a conservative town, where people went around assassinating abortion doctors, the Catholic Church being very powerful there. This was before Leslie Fiedler, John Barth, and others came to town. Fiedler also got busted for pot.

Miles was performing with Sonny Lockjaw Davis. Miles played these up-tempo numbers, and Lockjaw seemed to fumble around his keys in an attempt to keep up with him. I don't think he did it out of any kind of malice toward Lockjaw. He wasn't mean like Diz when he did a duet with Satch and tried to show the old man up. I think that he did "Blue and Boogie." He also did some ballads like "Yesterday." We'd heard that Miles was mean and would KO people with whom he had disputes. My friends were scared to approach him. But I had been to Paris. I was fearless and worldly. And so I asked Miles for his autograph as my friends looked on in terror. He obliged. I told him that he was well known in Paris. I wanted him to know that I had been to Paris.

Another incident tested Miles's degree of affability. A man knocked over his trumpet that was perched atop a piano. This guy is going to get it, we thought. But Miles was cool. He inspected the trumpet for damage, and seeing none he continued the break. Rocky Marciano and Archie Moore—

who made his reputation fighting old black men who were in their forties, yet gave Marciano all that he could handle—were fighting that night. Miles paused during his concert to listen to the fight.

When I ordered a drink, *à la* grenadine, which I had begun drinking in Paris, the waitress who served me was the woman from across the street for whom I had eyes. I was flabbergasted. It was like when I was dining at the Hayes Street Bar in San Francisco, and an associate of the San Francisco Opera told me she wanted to introduce me to Kathy. I didn't know whom she was talking about. Suddenly, standing before me was Kathleen Battle, the Diva.

Miles at this club on William Street in Buffalo. I think the name was the Casablanca. (About a mile away was the Zanzibar, where, as a teenager, I caught Kai Winding and Della Reese.) This was the most memorable concert for me, even though I don't remember all of the numbers played. But Miles, in his sharp suit and dark glasses and cool sounds, convinced me that I wanted to be where all of that was taking place. That my hometown could not hold me. That I wanted the world.

3

Jimmy Reed
LuAnn's
Dallas, Texas
April 1958
DAVID RITZ

IT STARTED WITH JAZZ.

For the most part, my early years were spent in metropolitan New York where, under my father's influence, I became a fanatic. I sat in the peanut gallery at Birdland, cover charge a dollar and Cokes a dime. My gods were Monk, Miles, and Mingus. My disdain was directed at anything popular. Bop was high art; pop was slop. I was a pre-teen elitist who could recite the members of all five herds shepherded by Woody Herman. Then, when I was twelve, my dad was transferred. He was a traveling salesman whose product, men's fine felt hats, was a remnant from another era.

Texas was from another era. When we moved there in the mid-fifties, I saw it as no man's land. I was depressed in Dallas, a suburban city with no street life and strict segregation. The teen culture was fixated on football and cars. Country music dominated radio, and jazz clubs didn't exist. Only in the far reaches of black South Dallas, some twenty miles from my home, could you catch an after-hours jam session. The only new music—new for me—that caught my ear was rhythm and blues and gospel. Even though R&B was popular, I couldn't resist its pulsating heart. I liked it in spite of myself. Little Richard and Chuck Berry assumed the stature of Charlie Parker and John Coltrane. My cathedral of high art came crashing down. At the Sportatorium, a cavernous venue used for wrestling matches, I saw Sam Cooke and the Soul Stirrers, the Dixie Hummingbirds, and the Mighty Clouds of Joy. The fervor of gospel, along with the fervor of R&B, got all over me.

In my second year of high school, at age fifteen, I started writing for the *Thomas Jefferson Reveille*, the student newspaper. The faculty advisor saw that I was drawn to non-conventional stories. Soon, she let me pick my own topics. I immediately chose music. I started writing record reviews, nearly all of them positive. Early on, I realized that my natural bent was for cele-bration. I liked to praise. When I didn't like something, I didn't write par-ticularly well. When I loved something, my prose improved. She suggested that instead of writing record reviews, I review a live performance. "Better yet," she said, "you might even interview the performer."

I jumped at the idea. I had long imagined what it might be like to engage Ray Charles or Bo Diddley in conversation—or at least sit in the same room with them. They would be open and friendly, appreciative of my interest in them, impressed with my knowledge of their music. We would become in-stant friends, and they'd invite me on their tours as a special guest. The problem, though, was that this spring neither Ray nor Bo were due in Dallas. But Jimmy Reed was.

Back in the fifties, Jimmy Reed ruled the Texas airwaves. In my mind, Reed bridged the gap between backcountry and big city blues. I had begun listening to Delta masters like Robert Johnson and Charley Patton at the same time I was discovering urbanites like T-Bone Walker and B.B. King. Reed seemed to have one foot in each camp. He sounded primitive as all hell, but the bad boys in my high school with their blue suede shoes had him blasting from their customized Chevys. They weren't blasting Muddy Waters or Sonny Boy Williamson or Howlin' Wolf. But they listened to Jimmy Reed the way they listened to Elvis or Gene Vincent or Jerry Lee Lewis. In suburban Dallas, Jimmy Reed was part of the canon of white teenage rebellion. I was amazed.

Amazement took on new meaning when I walked into LuAnn's on Greenville Avenue to hear Jimmy Reed live. To my teenage eyes, LuAnn's looked like an oversized barn, a cold and characterless dance hall that smelled of Lone Star beer, Fritos, and refried beans. Even on a cool April night, the place was sweltering hot. Hotter still was Jimmy Reed's sound. His sound took off the top of my head—his hypnotic mantra-like groove, his slurry sassy nasty nasal voice, his crying harmonica, his pleading, his hurting, his hallelujah tonight's-the-night jubilation. And then the way he looked: a leopard-skinned guitar at his chest, a gleaming gold harp at his mouth, his slicked-back hair, his razor-sharp moustache, his lime green silk suit, his banana yellow tie, his white buck shoes. He was bathed in sweat, and so was his song—"Got me running, got me hiding . . . Got me up down, down up . . . Baby, what you want me to do?" His song smacked me in the face with a sting I had never felt before. I was awake to some-thing I had never known before. Maybe it was sex; maybe it was the Holy

Ghost; probably it was both. Reed's music was exploding with such force, I found myself dancing without a partner, dancing along with the other hundreds of white kids moving under the spell of the witch doctor, the pied piper of non-stop boogie, the undisputed oracle of an underground under-the-skin sanctified rhythm that was rocking this nation of horny high school kids. "Honest I do," he sang. "Gonna get my baby," he sang. "You don't gotta go," he sang. "Ain't that loving you, baby," he sang. "You got me dizzy," he sang. Song after song he sang, every song sounding the same, but better, tougher, louder, lewder, cruder. I was crazy with his spirit.

When the show was over, I gathered up my courage and made my way to the bandstand. Reed's roadie was packing up while the star was on his way out the door. I had to act fast.

"Excuse me, Mr. Reed," I said, feeling like Jimmy Olsen, the mild-mannered reporter too naïve to figure out Clark Kent's true identity, "but could I interview you for my school paper?"

"Come on," he said, waving for me to follow him.

His attitude was friendly and carefree as he and a voluptuous lady in a blue velvet, skin-tight gown headed towards a long limo. I had arrived at LuAnn's with a group of friends and wanted to tell them that I was leaving, but there wasn't time. The limo was pulling out with Jimmy Reed, his woman and, much to my astonishment, myself, all in the backseat.

I had my list of questions prepared. I wanted to ask him about growing up in rural Mississippi with his friend and guitarist Eddie Taylor, about his relationship with Elmore James, about his moves to Indiana and Illinois, the development of his singular sound, the methodology of his songwriting, the phenomenon of his crossover success. Pen in hand, notepad on lap, I was ready. Meanwhile, Reed fished a flask of whisky out of his suit pocket and brought it to his lips. He drained the flask in a flash, then asked the driver for a beer.

"What about me?" asked his woman. She was young, no more than three or four years older than me, but stunningly self-assured. As she crossed her long legs and locked eyes with him, I felt the heat of her personality.

"Nothing for you," said Jimmy.

"Why?"

"I saw you busy dancing out there," he explained.

"Dancing with the promoter," she said. "Gotta be nice to the promoter."

"Don't gotta be nice to no one but me," he replied before turning his attention to me. "Now what is it that you need to know, young brother?"

"Well, sir—" I started to say.

"That's a bunch of bullshit, Jimmy," said the woman, continuing her line of thought. "I'll be nice to whoever I wanna be nice to."

"Like hell you will," Reed shot back.

"Like hell I won't," she replied.

Before I knew it, Reed whipped out a razor blade from inside his jacket and, in one ferocious motion, cut the woman on her upper arm. Pandemonium ensued. "You motherfucker!" she screamed. She went after him with her fire engine red fingernails, long as short knives, and caught his chin. He smacked her back. She landed on the floor. I scooted over toward the door, determined to avoid injury. Blood was gushing out of her arm. Blood was dripping from Reed's chin. Next thing I knew, the driver, a soft-spoken man who seemed to have it all under control, was calmly pulling up to the emergency room at Baylor Hospital as if this high drama were an everyday occurrence.

While Reed and his lady went in for treatment, the driver and I sat in the waiting room, a dingy area with decrepit furniture and yellowing white walls. We waited. Other patients passed through—a large Latino man who suffered a heart attack, a child who swallowed a bottle of pills, an elderly woman who fell down a flight of stairs and broke her back. There was moaning and crying. Families were praying. Some were screaming in pain. Anxiety was everywhere. Time passed slowly. Finally, at three in the morning, Reed and his lady friend emerged. They were both bandaged and, much to my surprise, they were holding hands.

"Let's have breakfast," said Jimmy.

At an all-night Toddle House, Jimmy, his woman, and I sat in a booth facing a mountain of bacon and biscuits. They doted affection on each other like newlyweds. I was famished. Food had never tasted this good.

"Now, what was it that you wanted to ask me?" he said.

I looked at my list of questions and knew they were no good. I knew not to ask them.

"I guess I just want to know about the blues," I finally said.

Jimmy Reed took a big bite of pancake soaked in egg yolk, swallowed, paused, and then looked me in the eye.

"You don't know about the blues," he said. "You live them."

4

Steve Abbot Benefit Concert
Jordan Junior High School
Salt Lake City, Utah
Winter 1961
RON CARLSON

THE WINTER OF 1961 was strange in Salt Lake City. Look it up and you will find that all of the days of January and February were frigid, and the city was lost in fog. This fog was worst in the cold dawn; it was an airborne, icy mist through which we couldn't see forty feet. It was the first time I saw yellow driving lights on cars, supposed to help penetrate the fog, but they didn't help. There were stories in the paper about cars following the taillights of other cars and finding themselves stopped and honking in someone's driveway. The ice and the pervasive darkness affected everything. I walked alone along the Jordan River in the predawn dark to the mysterious edifice of Jordan Junior High School, and the fog was thickest there at the very bottom line in that western city. It's tough to start a story with the weather, but this was real weather, and I'm not sorry. It was the world of my fourteenth year in and out: dark fog, ice, mystery.

The song that year was "The Lion Sleeps Tonight," which I could not understand anymore than the pull it had upon me. Music had only that season risen in my consciousness, along with feelings unbidden and unnamed, things which most people look back on and smile condescendingly at, but which I do not. These were the first real feelings that had claimed me, and they rang beyond the generic call of adolescence. There was a jungle beyond the village, dense as fog, and there was something in it. I had crawled out of my boyhood into junior high school, and even as I walked in the ice-fog humming that song, which was way beyond my range, I felt there were messages everywhere. For instance, I knew damned well that the lion wasn't really asleep. Hush, hush, the lion's asleep, it says. Oh, he's sleeping. No he wasn't. Not for me that year. The lion had just woken up.

The beautiful Georgian buildings of Jordan Junior High were demolished for homes many years ago, but they stood then elegant and ageless on Sixth

South in a large oxbow of the old river loop, which has also been bladed straight. It had been a confusing place for me, every day of my career there, woodshop and history and chemistry and whatever the hell they served for cheeseburgers in the cafeteria.

My best friends were Terry Hamblin and Marvin Wharton. Terry was a serious guy. He had a job delivering papers and he also worked early mornings at the school on the janitorial crew. Marvin was out of the mainstream, like me, but he didn't mind it as much as I did. The mainstream had been developing for a year or two, and by now it was clear we were not in it. That isn't a bad deal or any deal, and it is a realization I've had over and over in my life, but this was the first time. I thought we were just a bunch of kids in junior high, and then suddenly we were not cool, and that, seriously, was the word that year. It was the same thing with girls. Before, they had been friends and study mates and now they were girls. They had breasts. This was groundbreaking.

Terry had a girlfriend. And there was something else: he could play the five-string banjo. Marvin had a six-string Martin guitar, and he played it skillfully, as well. From time to time over the school years, these guys had brought in their instruments and shown them and played them a little, usually as part of music class with Miss Littlefield, but now with the frosty mist on the city like the end of the world, they were going to be part of the talent assembly fund-raiser for Steve Abbot in the gymnasium of Jordan Junior High School.

The winter of the fog and A-wimba-whey was also the winter that Steve Abbot got shot. Steve was a year ahead of us in school. I had played Little League with him. He was a natural left-hander, and he could hit like a machine. I saw him hit one onto Emery Street once, which is literally out of the park, and I've been waiting to write about that for fifty years. One weekend that fall, he'd been out with some buddies and some .22's and he got shot—in a weird accident—in the skull, right above the eye. He was in the hospital, and every day there was a little announcement on the school PA system about Steve's condition. There was also a recovery fund. I had homeroom woodshop, which was all boys, and we were determined to raise the most money. I'd walk to school in the dark, every streetlamp a circle of icy sparks, the lion somewhere there, too, and fish my lunch money for the Steve fund. He woke up, they said. We waited for him to talk.

One afternoon, Terry Hamblin and Marvin Wharton and I met in Marvin's basement. He lived over by Sherwood Park where the backstop was lined with frost in the gray afternoon. It was all like Planet Frostgloom, and it made crossing the street a surprise every time. Terry's banjo was remarkably heavy, so clearly not a toy. It was an instrument and looked with all that shiny steel like an instrument. Marvin's guitar was impossible to fathom, the way the brass frets were imbedded in the beautiful wood. They played along with the songs we knew, the Kingston Trio and Peter, Paul and Mary. They sang "Tom Dooley," and I sang along, too, as I studied the young Kingston Trio in their striped shirts on the album cover. "Tom Dooley" was a crushing tale of crime and justice and reckoning. Tom Dooley says that this time tomorrow he reckons he'll be hanging from a big oak tree.

And then Terry said to me, "You should play with us." I had already held Marvin's guitar carefully in my lap and it too was alien, so large, and my fingers were idiotic about it. Marvin taught me D7 and C and G, and I made the chords as if I had mittens on. "It doesn't need to be like this," Marvin said. "You could get a four string. For the talent concert."

We talked about Steve Abbot. There was a wicked rumor that he was coming to the concert, that he would be in a wheelchair in the back of the gymnasium, watching. Marvin took the album cover from my hands. "We could get shirts," he said.

They already had matching shirts, short sleeve, button down, madras ones. These were the opposite of what people should wear on Planet Gloomfrost. They were summer shirts. Walking home in the permanent dusk of winter that year in Salt Lake, I hummed "The Lion Sleeps Tonight," and my heart was beating as I considered getting the third shirt.

My father played the accordion. He'd get it out at holidays and play polkas and the like, but it was only once or twice a year. He was a welding engineer and a serious man, but he took me to Sugarhouse shopping district the day I asked, and he bought me a tenor guitar at Beesley Music. The guitar cost twenty-eight dollars. It was a Stella. I told him that Marvin was going to help me learn to play. I did not tell him about the upcoming concert or my hopes for it. I didn't tell him about the Steve Abbot fund. He knew Steve from Little League, and after the shooting accident, my father, a seasoned hunter, made some remarks about guns and carelessness that were meant for my edification. My father didn't know that Steve Abbot had become the theme night and day of Jordan Junior High School.

We practiced in Marvin's basement and in Terry's basement, and I carried my guitar through the thick frost. I worked in the evenings trying to wear calluses in my fingertips. We played along with records and I moved through the basic chord changes. I could strum in time, but the rest didn't come to me or I to it. I loved that music and I admired my friends so much. I saw in those basements that these guys had something that I did not have. I had become a fair athlete, but I could not catch up with music.

The deal breaker was not that I could not play the tenor guitar, which I could not. It was that I could not sing. When Terry, Marvin, and I sang alone, without the record playing, I switched octaves wildly like a child playing in the street. I had always thought I could sing. I sat in front of Jennifer Miles in fourth grade and we sang Stephen Foster for Miss Littlefield, and because I could only hear Jennifer, I thought I was a re-markable singer. Now, when we sang "Tom Dooley," I sounded like Tom Dooley's younger brother wailing from the gallery. My voice was wrong, nutty, and indecisive, and even though Marvin and Terry did not object, two weeks before the concert, I went over to Terry's basement without my guitar and told my friends I was not going to join them. (My brother Bobby, who already played the clarinet, came into my room a day later and asked to borrow the guitar, and though it stood in the corner like my claim on being a teenager, I let him take it. He was in many bands after that and wrote music, and he still does.)

The gymnasium was tiny. There was a small, full court for basketball and on each side the out-of-bounds was exactly the length of my shoe: al-ready size twelve that year. At one end was a little wooden stage and at the other end there was an actual horizontal ladder, wooden, for exercise. You barely see them anymore. The gym smelled of the ages, and it is not a bad smell: layers of varnish and soap and some sweat and the smell of kids in a tight room. And Noxema. There was a lot of Noxema.

Rows of wooden folding chairs were set up on the old wood floor under the wooden horizontal ladder, and all three grades filed in at three o'clock, three hundred kids. They had printed tickets, and a member of the fund-raising committee took mine. The talent show was skits and some pan-tomimes and too many soloists on their violins and flutes. My classmates and I kept turning around to see if Steve Abbot had been wheeled in, but he had not.

When Terry and Marvin were announced they walked seriously out to the microphone in their shirts. Terry picked for a while, and then they sang "Tom Dooley," and Tom Dooley was doomed. Every time I heard it, I thought he might say something like *I didn't do it* or *It was an accident*. I have been waiting my whole life for Tom Dooley to find a way.

I watched them, knowing my own fate: I would never be in a band. I would never understand music, but I would be subject to its mystery and power. I would always prefer ballads over other songs. A little story, so many times sad. I would later develop my own public persona, and I would stand and use words sometimes, but that isn't the same as song, as you know. As I listened to Terry and Marvin sing, I had a feeling in me that I had never had before. I saw that there was another world where I was being asked to go, and it was beyond acing spelling tests and having perfect attendance and getting my history reports in on time. There was something beyond these rooms; I felt it. I felt the limits lift. We would be people next, and very soon, and I was scared in that way which is thrilling. I hung down my head and breathed in the smell of the old gymnasium. We clapped as they retreated and somebody came on to juggle or play the old gym piano.

Steve Abbot never fully recovered. We didn't see him again until the next summer when his folks brought him one night to a Little League game. He was in a wheelchair and his head was distended and his smile was that half smile. After his benefit concert, I left the lighted gym and plunged into the icy dark again. The rules had changed. My heart churned every step home beside the old river through the lonely and persistent mist, and my lion followed somewhere behind. He was with me now for good.

5

The Rolling Stones
The Academy of Music
New York City
May 1, 1965
LYNNE TILLMAN

DURING COLLEGE, I had to invent or reinvent myself every day, create a person who awoke, dragged herself out of bed, and went to class. I was morbidly depressed; life was futile. I had to move from despair and apathy to the shower, then find clothes to put on my naked body, even though for three years I wore a self-fashioned school uniform: baggy chinos and a long-sleeved, all-cotton, black T-shirt. A friend living near me on West 96th Street drove a Bucati, and when I could catch a ride on the back, getting to class was easier. She was depressed, too, but more manic, and sometimes she shouted above the engine and wind, "I want to kill myself." I hugged her waist tighter then and felt my own desire to die tested.

I met my other best college friend in a required Introduction to Sociology class. She had a bad attitude like me, she was two years older, not a freshman, very cool, but then she disappeared for a while. "I dropped out," she told me when she returned. She also told me to take studio art classes, and I did. I listened closely to everything she said, because she knew what was really happening; for instance, she knew the night Linda Eastman and Paul McCartney slept together for the first time.

The Beatles were cute, but they were too fresh and sunny for my dark, youthfully jaded, sort of hip character. The Rolling Stones existed for me and my friend, bad boys for bad girls. The Stones were anti-everything and suited my sensibility. My psychotherapist had asked me, "What do you want to do?" I said, "I want to rebel." "Then," she said, "my job is to make you effective."

The Stones were rebels—at least their songs sounded rebellious—and they appeared effective. They could have whatever they wanted: sex, drugs, cars, houses, more sex, drugs. I didn't question the implications of their being middle-class boys, the Beatles working-class boys, or what rebellion worked in them. I lived inside my troubled mind and each day had to awaken in the same bleak and unchanging world and do what I'd done yesterday or something a little different.

Every night for dinner, I broiled chicken wings and heated up canned, sliced beets. Like wearing the same shirt and pants to school, I ate the same dinner for three years, unless my knowing friend said, Come on, let's eat out, or hear a band, or see a movie. Later, we shared a railroad apartment in the East Village. She fixed up her rooms reasonably, while I ripped plaster from a wall in one of mine, to uncover the brick, but it turned out to be the outside brick, so I stopped. The plaster lay on the floor of the room. I never cleaned it up; I couldn't use the room anyway, because cold air blew in through the cracks.

My friend found out when the Rolling Stones were doing their first concert in New York: May 1, 1965, at the Academy of Music. "Satisfaction" wouldn't come out in the States until June 1965, but we were already hardcore fans. We had to be at the Stones' triumphal entrance into our city.

The Academy of Music was on 14th Street between Third Avenue and Irving Place, where the Palladium would be in the eighties. The first Academy of Music was a grand opera house, built in 1854 on the northwest corner of Irving Place and demolished in 1926. The Stones played the second Academy, erected in the twenties across the street from the original. This one showed movies from the twenties on, but by the sixties, it was mostly a concert hall. Its marquee letters broken, its seats uncomfortable and seedy, its brilliance and glory faded, the Academy of Music was the right theater for the Stones, who were uncomfortable to parents, and seedy and glorious in their own way.

We sat in the balcony, or we sat downstairs; wherever we sat, my sight lines weren't impeded. I'm short and saw everything that happened, and a lot did and didn't. Opening for the Stones, Patti LaBelle and the Bluebelles, which was how she was billed, as a girl band. In their ice blue, space-age costumes and feather headdresses, with Patti's big voice and their choreographed moves, they rocked. But the audience was indifferent. Stones' fans were sullen like the band, and also we were there only for them. Patti must have been onstage an hour, and the audience grew restive. When the set ended, the group received some applause, but they didn't get an encore. They were really fine; we were just lousy for the Stones.

Then nothing, and nothing, and time went by, and no one came on stage, and nothing, and we were waiting and waiting. After a while, someone in the audience roared something, or there was an outbreak of off-the-beat white people's clapping, and a few dispirited, feeble calls for the Stones. Waiting, we turned more sullen.

Where were the fucking Stones.

Forty-five, maybe fifty minutes passed. I don't know how long it was, but still nothing. We were angry already; it didn't take much to make us angrier. Where were the Stones. Where were the Stones. The question was our breath.

People had slumped and settled into their lumpy seats, passive and aggressive both because there was nothing to do but wait or leave, so we were trapped because we wanted the Stones. Wanting was hell, and while existentially waiting was all there was to do, we didn't like it. There was no clapping now, no sudden shouts for the Stones, just enraged sedentary bodies.

Then they walked out. They just walked onto the stage, as if they were going to the men's room. They had no affect. There was no jumping or dancing or mugging. They walked onto the stage and plugged in their instruments and took their positions. They didn't look at us, not once, except for Mick. Mick came to the front of the stage and sort of said, "Hello, New York." He tried a little, but the rest of the band didn't care. They didn't want to be there, and they ignored us. Mick made another pathetic effort, that's all it could be: "Hello, New York."

Brian Jones sat down on the floor. He was stage right, his head down, blond hair splayed over his face obscuring him further, his instrument lying in his lap. Maybe it was his Vox teardrop guitar or a Vox Phantom. He never looked up, the group didn't look at us, they looked bored, and only Mick exerted himself a little, threw off some energy, but he didn't try long. We were angry, deadened, too, and Mick quickly accepted defeat. Listlessly, the Stones started their first number. Probably they were very stoned.

A matron stood at the edge of the stage, on the same side as Brian, but at the top of the stairs, which was the only way up there, except for leaping. She was a heavyset black woman, about thirty—I don't remember any black people in the audience—and she wore some kind of theater or usher uniform. She faced the audience, grim and solemn, with her arms crossed over her chest. The Stones were playing, and Mick was singing, Brian was sitting on the floor, head down, and I don't remember what Keith was doing, but he wasn't crouching the way he does now and uncoiling like a rattlesnake to strike. Charlie Watts was Charlie Watts, steady, imperturbable, playing the drums the way he's always played the drums, and Bill Wyman was himself, unmoving and dour.

There was a kind of stasis on stage and in the audience. Into the third song, a hefty, dark-haired girl made a run for the stage and up the stairs. But when she reached the top of the stairs, the matron blocked her. She gave her the hip. The girl flew down the stairs. One move, down she tumbled. The girl landed on the floor, stood up, and walked back to her seat. That was it, that was our resistance. The matron crossed her arms over her chest again and glared at us. The audience became more frustrated. The Stones hadn't even noticed, and nothing happened again, and not one of us yelled or stood up, either, and soon the atmosphere turned solidly against the band.

The Stones played eight songs, the songs were three or four minutes each. They were onstage less than half an hour. They finished their set and walked off the way they'd walked on. They just walked off. No one clapped or shouted, everyone was fed up, pissed off, let down. We'd become the anti-audience, and rose, grabbed our jackets, left our seats, and filed out. There was no fighting, no talking. We'd all been rebuffed, like the hefty, dark-haired girl. The audience spilled onto 14th Street, a morose confederacy of rebels. It was early evening.

I suppose my friend and I went out for something to eat. Or maybe I went home and ate sliced beets and broiled chicken wings. Life continued, but something had changed: the Rolling Stones had played New York.

By now, the Stones have changed a lot. Brian drowned, murdered, it's alleged, by his assistant; Mick Taylor quit, so Ron Wood plays lead guitar; Darryl Jones plays bass, since Bill Wyman retired; and Mick's, Keith's, and Charlie's faces are cross-hatched and filigreed with event and experience. I've changed, too. For one thing, I have stopped eating wings exclusively, though I eat chicken. I still love beets, but now fresh and roasted, and order them whenever they're on a menu. I still like to wear a uniform of sorts, but now I buy six or seven pairs of the same usually black pants, about that number of the same all-cotton, long-sleeved T-shirts, and many of the same linen, rayon, or silk blouses. I buy everything in different colors. Life isn't as bleak with some variety.

6

The Beatles
Plaza de Toros
Madrid, Spain
July 2, 1965
REBECCA BROWN

ON JULY 2, 1965, in the Plaza de Toros bullfight stadium in Madrid, Spain, when I was nine years old, I saw the Beatles.

My brother and sister were six and seven years older than me and they had bought the Spanish edition Beatles EPs and brought them home and played them. They played them on their little 45 player with the lid that came down and closed like a box and had that kind of stacker that you could stack a bunch of singles on and they would fall down, one after another, and play. They played their Beatles records over and over. They played them all the time. They played them and played them and everything started to change.

My brother had had a flat top and worn loafers and white socks and short-sleeved shirts, but then he started to comb his hair differently then grow it out longer. Then he wanted to get rid of the accordion he had played for years and get a guitar. My sister had worn A-line skirts and nice, round-collared blouses and flat shoes and bobby sox, but then she started to wear blue eye shadow and put stuff on her eyelashes that made them look fuzzy and do her hair like Dusty Springfield. Her skirts got tighter and she started getting this look on her face when my parents said things. I was still in grade school so I didn't have much to change from, but something happened to me, too. Something happened to everyone. Everybody changed.

Earlier in the school year, before the Beatles came to Spain, my third grade teacher, whose name I do not remember because she was an idiot, called my mother in for a conference because she, the teacher, was "concerned" about me. She thought there was something wrong with me because I was—her word—"obsessed" with the Beatles. She told my mother that every time I had to write in spelling or vocabulary class, I wrote about the Beatles. When we had art, I drew their guitars and drums and haircuts and Beatle boots. When we had show-and-tell or current events, I talked about the Beatles.

When we did "Let's Make a Story Together," the names I suggested for characters were John or Paul or George or Ringo. In my "feelings journal," I wrote the lyrics to their songs. Even in math I managed to talk about them—the number of songs on their EPs and albums, their ages and heights or dates of birth.

My "concerned" teacher asked my mother if there was "something wrong at home." I can imagine this idiot woman both pitying my mother as in, "Oh, you poor thing," but also blaming my mother, looking down her snotty teacher nose at her as in, "What's wrong with you and your family?" My mother also realized that this "concerned" busybody teacher was an idiot, but my mother was smart enough not to tell her so. My mother took her leave politely, then came home and told my brother and sister and me all about what she'd said, and all of us laughed at the teacher who just didn't get it about the Beatles. Then, a few months later, our mother got us tickets and sent us all to see the Beatles live.

Our mother had numerous parts of her that were cool. Not trying to be cool, like dressing young or trying to flirt with my brother's friends or compete with my teenage sister, but cool in other ways. One time, before the Beatles came to Spain, my mother, in her capacity as a big Girl Scout troop leader or region representative or whatever she was, went to a big Girl Scout leader meeting in Germany and brought us back the German 45 of "Komm Gib Mir Deine Hand" backed with "Sie Liebt Dich." We were the first people we knew who had it and it made all of us very cool. (I still have this 45 today. It's got a purple paper sleeve on it with all four of them in their collarless gray suits and black ties and the words in German and Paul with a cigarette and my sister's high school handwriting— "BROWN"—because she wanted it to be only hers.) Our mother knew that seeing the Beatles would be a major event in all of her kids' lives.

I remember us taking the trolley downtown to downtown Madrid and then to the Plaza de Toros that night. It was dark when we set out, and I had never been downtown at night before. I had also never been downtown without my parents. My father, though he was not a fan of the Beatles ("Turn that goddamned racket down!" he'd yell when we were listening to them in my brother's or my sister's and my room), had been putting up with our whining and moaning and begging to go to see the

Beatles so long that he finally gave in and let our mother get us tickets. I
think he also hoped to shut us up for a while, at least get us out of the
house for a night. Plus, our father knew he didn't have to worry about our
safety because with the *Guardia Civil*, as he often said, "the streets in Spain
are goddamned safer than the godforsaken streets in the US of A, which is
rapidly going to hell in a goddamned handcart."

My father was a navy man and was genuinely fond of the ever-present
military police that were so much a part of Spain in the sixties. In fact, my
father loved everything about the military—its discipline and uniforms, its
shiny shoes and tidy haircuts, its patriotism and orderliness—so it made
sense he did not like the Beatles and that he did like living in Spain under
the military rule of the man he affectionately called "Generalissimo"
Franco. I didn't see why he shouldn't like Franco. To me, a grade-school
kid, dictator was sort of like just the Spanish word for president. In any
event, it was partly because of Franco's safe streets that both of my parents
allowed my teenage siblings and me to travel to downtown Madrid all by
ourselves late at night to see the Beatles.

They had tried to convert the Plaza de Toros into a giant arena. They had
covered the ground, which I knew, having come to a bullfight there when
we first arrived in Spain because it seemed like a nice thing to do, to take
advantage of this exotic cultural thing, was dusty and blood-and-gut-
stained. I had seen bulls get slaughtered there by picadors and matadors
and the clown guys who cleaned up afterwards. (This was years before my
mother and sister and brother and I all became vegetarians.)

My sister and brother and I were on the eighth row, close enough to
where you could almost see. There were hundreds of rows behind us and
also all the normal, regular bullfight seats way up in the stands. It was the
biggest place I had ever been in my life. It felt even bigger than when it
was just with the bulls.

There were a million opening acts: a steel drum band that nobody white
had ever seen anything like before; a bunch of singers—romantic, croony,
Spanish versions of Dean Martin and Frank Sinatra; women in shiny
dresses that sang to music piped in from somewhere we couldn't see.
There were also a few of the Spanish-language Beatles knockoffs that were
sprouting up everywhere, bands like Los Bravos and Los Brincos, quartets
made up of cute guys with mop-top hair, three guitars and a drum. (The
Brincos' big hit was "Mejor," which came out around the same time as the
Help! movie and its 45 sleeve has a shot of the band standing on a beach,

just like the sleeve of the U.S. 45 of "Help/I'm Down," and one of the Brincos is playing, just like John Lennon in the movie, a hollow body acoustic guitar.) A lot of this was actually good—melodic, danceable, three-minute songs with verse, chorus, and bridge sung in Spanish or English or both.

I sat on the eighth row on the ground between my sister and brother and relatively close as we were, we still had to use binoculars. At first, with the Frank Sinatras, etc., we didn't bother. But when the Beatles came on we did. My brother and I got to use them the most because my sister was screaming and crying so hard, she didn't spend much time actually looking at them. Unfortunately, therefore, as little as we could see them, we could hear them even less. All the girls were screaming, but my sister the most. She screamed so much that next day both the Spanish- and English-language newspapers (*The Stars and Stripes* was the paper for the American military) had pictures of my sister on the front page screaming. All over Europe, in fact, as we learned by friends who sent us newspapers from elsewhere, were pictures of my crying, screaming sister.

I was a girl, too, but I didn't scream. It may partly have been because I was not a teenager, but I would not have screamed anyway. I didn't have the same relationship with the Beatles my sister and most girls did. I didn't participate in the "Who is the Cutest Beatle?" conversations in which my sister and other girls took part. Tomboys like me didn't. Though I hadn't figured out yet exactly why that was, it meant something that I was responding more like my brother than my sister to this whole thing. Of course, I had, like everyone, boys and girls and tomboys, a favorite Beatle—George, the quiet one, who I felt I could have good conversations with—but mostly I shared with my brother the sense that the Beatles were more than just a new kind of music. They were also a calling, a stance, a reason and a way to try to live.

My brother, because he was a guy, got to grow his hair, get a guitar, and start a band. Though I dinked around with—when they were away—my father's ukulele and my brother's guitar, it wasn't like I, a girl in the mid-sixties, was going to get to play guitar in a band. But I did the next best thing. I learned all the lyrics and then bought all the books John Lennon wrote as soon as they were published and then began to imitate, in the private notebooks of my own that replaced my "feelings journal," his writings and drawings, then the writings and drawings of other singers and writers I began to hunt out, learn about, and love.

My brother and sister went on to other things—to pot and the singer-songwriters of the seventies, to acid and acid rock, to Motown and white people trying to dance like black people, to John Klemmer–type mellow jazz and cocktails and knowing what kinds of wine are good and what are not—while I remained true to the Beatles. Not that I did not also listen to, love, and learn from punk, new wave, and everything else, but I never forgot that the Beatles are the Ones.

I still have all the Beatles gear: my sister's 1965 Beatles sweatshirt (they didn't make them in nine-year-old sizes then), which she was going to toss out and which I now keep in a drawer in the house I share with my female spouse the way other people keep their bridal dress or their baby's clothes. I have hundreds of Beatles cards, the kind you got in a pack of gum. I've got a bunch of the toys—the tiny plastic guys, small enough to fit in your hand, playing their little plastic guitars and Ringo with his cardboard drums, a couple of models, stickers. Our preschool and grade school–age grandkids aren't interested in any of these toys, but when they get too rowdy for books or naps, or when they are bored with doing projects, we put on the Beatles' music from way back then and all of us scream and dance.

7

Titans of the Tenor!
Philharmonic Hall
New York City
February 19, 1966
GARY GIDDINS

1.

DOZENS OF CONCERTS live in my memory, the vast majority because they were exceptionally good; some because I saw a legendary figure for the first or only time; others because I had a hand in producing them; a few because they failed spectacularly; a few more because they had great isolated moments; and two because they never took place or ended prematurely. Only the last category may require elaboration.

On a Sunday night in 1975, at Lincoln Center, the musicians' union (Local 802) halted an all-star homage to Charlie Parker's fifty-fifth birthday a few minutes before curtain time because the promoter's checks had bounced on Friday, and he didn't have the cash on hand. The promoter had hoped his checks would not bounce until Monday, by which time he would have collected the receipts and skipped town, paying no one. As far as I know, he's still on the lam. A decade later, there was the hotly anticipated Sonny Rollins concert at Town Hall, which ended midway during an early number as Rollins fainted—falling backwards, stiff as a log. As his guest, Wynton Marsalis, leaned over to see if he was alive, Sonny opened his eyes and said, "Don't worry. It wasn't anything *you* played."

Occasionally, a friend will remind me of a performance I had forgotten, and I'll think, "Yes, of course," but it remains indistinct. Then the friend will offer details, and the event zooms into focus: How could I have forgotten that? Yet splendid as that performance may have been, it obviously failed to generate the lingering impact of concerts (possibly inferior) that live relentlessly in my head. So the determining factors can't be exclusively musical; other dynamics are crucial—especially my own state of mind. In some instances the mnemonic lock may have had less to do with the music than the inspired unity of the audience or the ardor of my companion.

Still, asked to select *The Show I'll Never Forget*, I feel I can choose between only two: two concerts that changed the way I hear and think and, consequently, the way I've lived my life. I am forever paying homage to them in that they aren't really events I can't forget, but rather events I don't have to bother remembering (remembering requiring an act of will or a trigger) because they are always there, like the house I grew up in or the face of my long-deceased father. They took place when I was fifteen and seventeen, and I am pretty certain that not a month—maybe not a week, though how can you measure such things?—has gone by when I haven't thought about one or both.

Neither was aesthetically monumental. I know damned well that had I experienced them several years later, their effect would have been severely reduced, if not negligible. Their generative impact is what counts. Like the lifer who can't forget the crime that did him in, I think of them as decisive markers: the first directing me down an unexpected path, the second keeping me on that same trail. I'm at an age when you look back in wonder at what you've done with your life and why. For the most part, what I've done is write about jazz. That's a lot of stress to put on two concerts that probably weren't exceptionally good.

2.

The first of them took place in New Orleans in 1963, a period when I was looking for something to replace the excitement that rock 'n' roll had given me until a year or so earlier. Had I not happened to visit New Orleans that summer and simply waited out the drought, maybe the Beatles or something else would have done the trick; maybe I would have encountered jazz at home in New York. But there I was, fifteen years old and in New Orleans, doing the touristy thing and going to hear the one band that advertised an afternoon jazz concert during my weekend visit: Emanuel Sayles and his Silverleaf Ragtimers featuring George Lewis. The hotel at which we stayed had segregated lavatories, and a couple of teenage girls had berated me on a Canal Street bus for sitting next to an elderly black woman. So walking into an enclave (the walls papered in red cut velvet) in which everyone, black and white, seemed to know everyone else, suggested not only an enlightened covey in the benighted South, but a leap far beyond my largely segregated life up North.

Musically, the most important aspect of that afternoon—two sets brimming with cheer, plus a conversation with the musicians—was that it awakened my curiosity about jazz, which turned to obsession after I discovered Louis Armstrong's recordings of 1928. I have written about this concert and my initial experience with Armstrong elsewhere (in *Weather Bird*) and won't repeat it here—we all have our versions of Genesis. During the next two years, I absorbed dozens of albums and became an underage *habitué* of the Village Vanguard and the Village Gate, which were then priced to accommodate high school kids strapped for cash and armed with phony ID—I can recall each platter and visit. But the next concert that took off the top of my head happened about two and a half years after New Orleans, and put me in possession of an entirely new set of questions.

Two things ought to be said at the outset about the concert billed as "Titans of the Tenor!" First, despite the participation of John Coltrane and Sonny Rollins, whose public appearances were routinely documented by individuals with hidden recording devices, no record of this performance has ever been released. According to Yasuhiro Fujioka's 1995 Coltrane discography, Coltrane's widow and pianist, Alice Coltrane, has a tape recording, but no one has heard it, not even Fujioka, who, for once, was obliged to write "details are not known." This inexplicable absence heightens the mystery surrounding the concert and puts my memory, vivid though I think it is, on notice: Someday that tape will surface.

Second, although the concert has passed into history and is often mentioned in books about the musicians and the era, these references are almost always strewn with errors. Nor was there much press coverage at the time. I'm aware of only one trustworthy account, a *Down Beat* review by Dan Morgenstern (April 1966), reprinted in his essential 2004 collection, *Living with Jazz*. Dan Morgenstern is a mentor and friend, the jazz critic I most admire and trust. If Armstrong made me a jazz zealot, Dan and Martin Williams made me realize that serious jazz criticism was possible and useful. About "Titans of the Tenor!" however, we have disagreed for forty years.

When I say that his account is trustworthy, I mean that he reported what happened, not that he heard it as I did. He left the hall angry; I left in a state of confused elation. Again, I suspect that had I been a few years older and more knowledgeable my reaction might have dovetailed with his. But a reward of being young and impressionable is that you take what's handed you. With fewer expectations you experience fewer disappointments. Innocence is supposed to enable the child to recognize a naked emperor, yet my innocence was more trusting. Morgenstern saw fakery and betrayal and said so. I took Coltrane at his word: this was what he chose to play and I felt obliged to deal with it. A door of perception had swung open and I had no prior commitments.

3.

A week or so before the concert, my girlfriend Laurie and I were at the Village Gate—more accurately, the Top of the Gate, which, situated a few steps up from street, offered Jaki Byard, Bill Evans, Toshiko, and others for the price of a beer and the discipline to nurse it an hour or two. On this night Byard played duets with vibist Dave Pike, and the between-sets chatter was mostly about two upcoming concerts: "Titans of the Tenor!" on February 19, a Saturday, and Bill Evans at Town Hall, on February 21. The next day, I phoned both box offices to secure tickets. The Monday night concert has also passed into history with a mystery attached to it: publicized as Evans's first major concert, it presented him solo, with a trio, and with a big band arranged and conducted by Al Cohn. A classic album, *Bill Evans at Town Hall, Vol. 1*, was released to rave notices (it represented a triumph for Evans after two years of indifferent work); but the second volume, with the orchestra, never appeared—when Verve boxed its entire Evans archive on CD, it claimed ignorance of the tape's whereabouts.

That was a strange year for jazz, 1966—a crossroads between feast and famine. During the previous few years, an unusual number of jazz recordings had made the pop charts while the avant-garde had rent the audience. Jazz's increasing political anxiety, often tinged with racial redefinitions, became inextricably associated with an aggressive new style variously called "the new music," "the new thing," "free jazz," and "black music." By any name, it alienated those already skeptical of a school of music in which such verities as lyricism and swing were regarded as mutating options. Meanwhile, the redcoats had revived the fortunes of rock, which would lead to a winnowing of jazz labels and venues, chasing many established musicians into studio work or the academy.

The period's lodestar figure was John Coltrane, riding the peak of his celebrity while the other avant-garde leaders, Cecil Taylor and Ornette Coleman, had retreated into low profile or Europe-based phases in their careers. By February 1966, Coltrane had already recorded his major assaults on musical convention: *Ascension, Meditations, Kulu Se Mama, Om, Live in Seattle,* and others. But none had been issued. Except for insiders, fans assumed he was still leading one of the most renowned quartets in jazz history, with pianist McCoy Tyner, bassist Jimmy Garrison, and drummer Elvin Jones—the group that utterly dominated jazz in 1965, thanks to the universally admired *A Love Supreme*. Most everyone filing into Philharmonic Hall on February 19 expected to see that group, along with three other eminent tenor saxophonists: Rollins, Coleman Hawkins, and Zoot Sims, plus, for uncertain reasons, the Clark Terry–Bob Brookmeyer "All-Star Band" (which had no saxophones), and emcee and vocalist Dave Lambert.

The oddness of "Titans of the Tenor!" began with its scheduled time: 11:30 p.m. Laurie and I arrived at Philharmonic Hall shortly after nine, to pick up our tickets and then get some dinner. Later rebuilt as Avery Fisher Hall, Philharmonic Hall was the most notorious botch in the formation of Lincoln Center—an auditorium with the acoustic nuance of a gymnasium. We had suffered there more than once, but were unconcerned this time because our seats were center aisle, second row: surely the sound could travel that far. On the other hand, turning from the box office, we found ourselves imprisoned by a torrential downpour. We stood at the doors, hoping the rain would lighten up, when a bubbly foursome sauntered toward the exit. Seeing us, they explained that they were too hungry for more music and handed us stubs to the half-over eight o' clock concert—Bach, I thought they said—before racing to their limo. We took our seats amid unanticipated peals of laughter. Turns out it was P.D.Q. Bach, Peter Schickele's then newborn Spike Jones–meets-Baroque alter ego. Very funny he was! Perhaps Schickele softened us for what followed.

4.

"Titans of the Tenor!" began with a short set by Zoot Sims, backed by the Terry-Brookmeyer rhythm section (Roger Kellaway, Bill Crow, Dave Bailey); only a breezily inspired "The Man I Love" sticks with me, but Morgenstern points out that he also played pieces by Al Cohn and George Handy and notes that the first was barely audible. As Zoot played, a second harbinger of the weirdness to come (after P.D.Q.) rolled down the aisle in a wheelchair and parked adjacent to me; imbibing from a bottle in a brown paper bag, its occupant provided unsparing commentary on every number. After Terry and Brookmeyer performed "Straight No Chaser" (great musicians, great quintet, but why were they there?), Dave Lambert introduced the incomparable Coleman Hawkins, who had put the tenor saxophone on the map and practically invented the jazz ballad back in 1929.

I had seen Hawkins before, at the Vanguard, playing on a double bill with Rollins, and I'm sorry for a posterity that won't have that chance. If you can see him on film, especially the otherwise riotously corny video *After Hours*, do so. There never was another like Coleman Hawkins. Dressed in silk mohair and looking very much a jazz patriarch with his prophet's beard and mane, he walked out and bent the microphone into the bell of his horn. He opened "In a Mellow Tone" with perhaps the single most unforgettable note I have ever heard: a grainy, weighty suspiration so warm and authoritative that a collective "Ahhhhhhh" erupted from the audience. My wheelchair neighbor raised his paper bag and cackled, "Kill 'em Hawk! Kill the motherfuckers!" He played just the one number and left, imperially refusing to acknowledge stomping applause and pleas for more. Lambert scatted a tune associated with Hawk ("Hackensack") to end the first set.

Rollins was introduced at the beginning of the second half, but a shorter, chunkier, balder man emerged to play with Rollins's rhythm section (John Hicks, Walter Booker, Mickey Roker). Someone seated near us said, "Hey, that's Yusef Lateef." Rollins had apparently invited him as his guest—an unbilled fifth tenor titan. After Lateef soloed for a couple of minutes, Rollins entered: hard to believe he was only thirty-five, carrying himself like a god though dressed head to toe in black street clothes (including Keds sneakers). Holding his horn aloft, he marched to the back of the stage where he played long tones in accompaniment to Lateef and balked at taking center stage. Finally, he came forward and raced through a lightning melody, including "Hold 'Em, Joe" and "Three Little Words" (from his current album, *Sonny Rollins on Impulse*), and . . . split. Lambert sought to soothe a frustrated crowd by announcing that Sonny would return to play with Coltrane. Well, you can imagine the cannon roar. Lambert probably did not know about the unbilled guests Coltrane had invited.

(Note: Morgenstern's account of Rollins's ten-minute marathon differs slightly from mine—for one thing, brown shoes instead of black Keds—and, if I were you, I'd trust his on-the-spot journalism over my recollections after forty years. Still, my memory will not surrender on these points, and I'm obliged to stick with it.)

All hell was about to break loose. Lambert introduced Coltrane, who sent out a phalanx of mostly unfamiliar faces. The first sign that we would not be hearing the Coltrane we knew and loved was the appearance of *two* trap sets. Elvin Jones had been replaced by Rashied Ali and J. C. Moses. Jimmy Garrison entered with his bass, but instead of McCoy Tyner, a handsome woman seated herself at the piano: this was Alice Coltrane, of course. John Coltrane was one of five wind players who took the stage, including two more tenor titans (though at that time, you could have been punched out for claiming any such distinction for them), Albert Ayler—recognizable by a white lightning streak in his beard—and Pharoah Sanders; altoist Carlos Ward; and Albert's troubled brother, trumpeter Donald Ayler. Here is where Morgenstern and I part on every detail. He concluded, "It was not unlike watching Joe Louis wrestle." I felt like a kid at the circus.

The joyful, terrifying noise lasted about an hour. Except for a snatch of "My Favorite Things," melodies were not apparent, though the Rodgers and Hammerstein echo was itself momentous. Coltrane inserted it amid a squalling solo, played with more than a few deep knee bends, and the shock of recognition elicited an explosion of approval. I've given much thought to that quotation, discussed it with fans and musicians who saw him do the same thing at other performances, and I have a theory. When Boris Karloff made *Frankenstein*, buried in makeup to the point of partial immobility, he would waggle his upstage little finger at frightened co-star Mae Clarke to remind her, "It's only me, Boris." I think Coltrane's strenuous yet winking reference to a song that had been a huge hit for him not five years earlier was his finger-waggle, a reminder that he was still Trane, trying something different, but neither a victim of brainwashers nor a turncoat denying his past. With this reference point, he invited us to consider that we would always have "My Favorite Things" and could now try something different.

This was music of massed sonorities. The rhythm section was not a thing apart, providing a swinging foundation, but a collusive force. The collective assault either focused your attention or dispersed it. In the absence of melody and harmonic progressions, it relied on the fever of the players, and while this shattering din could never be the sole future of jazz or of any other kind of music, it could—and, in fact, already did—represent a new way to play and experience music. The sound spread evenly, like the dribblings on a Jackson Pollack, yet the wall-to-wall harangue allowed for plenty of individual details as each player emerged from the ensemble for an *Ascension*-like salvo.

The strength in Coltrane's playing emanated from his spine, as he squeezed out sounds accompanied by calisthenics, his embouchure tight enough to redden his face, saliva flying from his reed. When he wasn't blowing tenor or soprano, he shook percussion instruments, as did the other saxophonists. The part of the audience that was shocked and infuriated retreated into silence or left. The Dionysus of the wheelchair added to the barrage, cheering the players without pause. At one point, he initiated a chant—"COL-trane, COL-trane, COL-trane"—which he kept up for several minutes. Despite the volatile energy level, there were hollows and prominences—each soloist readily distinguishable. Yes, the saxophonists squealed and screeched, but they found individual ways to squeal and screech. I recall Sanders playing for a long stretch with his fingers splayed outward, never touching the saxophone keys, rendering an unholy and unbroken wail, and Donald Ayler offering little more than listless tremolos spaced within an octave's range. Albert's solo was something else: a hurricane of raw emotion and radiant luster. I had not paid much attention to Albert Ayler previously, and immediately resolved to make up for it. The final onslaught was so heavy (needless to say, Rollins had long since gone home) that, despite a chanted wind down, its cessation was followed by an abrupt emptiness, as though we had suddenly been turned back on our own resources. I felt light and giddy and strangely peaceful.

5.

Laurie and I quietly walked up the aisle and were nearly out of the hall before she asked what I thought. I said something to the effect that I couldn't explain why but I liked it. She said, "I did, too." We were so relieved that neither of us thought the other was crazy. Was it really music? Did they know what they were doing? Chalk those patronizing questions to the novelty (it wasn't called "the new thing" for nothing), the adventure, the fear of being taken in, the mystification of getting slaughtered and loving it. I soon realized that it had unscrewed something in my mind in regard to musical indeterminacy. Weeks later, we attended a Broadway musical, and in the moments before the overture, I started to doze and became deeply immersed in a delightful, chattering symphony of sounds—the pit band tuning up. When *Ascension* came out, later that year, I was ready and dove in wholeheartedly, playing it to death. I'm always pleased to meet contemporaries who similarly committed that holocaust of an album to memory— the Rova Saxophone Quartet transcribed and recorded their own version.

We had no way of knowing that the pain in Coltrane's playing reflected his declining health. Within little more than a year, Coltrane died, at forty, leaving a generation of musicians unsure about how to proceed. The front page headline in a French newspaper (I studied abroad in the summer of 1967) translated as: Coltrane Is No More.

The juxtaposition of Coltrane and Hawkins restated something I already knew—about jazz's enormous palette and the centrality of individual expression. Each in his way gave me a kind of pleasure that defied intellectualization. Yet "Titans of the Tenor!" also turned out to be a baptism by fire: afterward, nothing musical could frighten me—appall me, yes, frighten me, no. It had the effect of cleaning the slate of everything I thought I knew about music, prompting me to rediscover the elective nature of melody, harmony, and rhythm, while taking nothing for granted. Music, after all, is where you find it. Aldous Huxley once reviewed a bird singing outside his study. John Cage composed a patch of silence, underscoring the absence of silence. Coltrane licensed communal ferocity as a source of musical ecstasy. For most of us who attended "Titans of the Tenor!" the impact was entirely unexpected—a bucket of ice water, an electric shock, an invitation to madness. Bang! A part of me continues to reverberate, like a gong.

8

James Brown
Boston Garden
Boston
April 5, 1968
DAVID GATES

IN THE PAST FORTY-FIVE years or so, I've been to all sorts of concerts with memorable moments. Thelonious Monk brought onstage by two guys doing a fireman's carry and setting him on the piano bench. Willie Nelson sharing guitar leads with Grady Martin, who played on Roy Orbison's "Pretty Woman" and Marty Robbins's "El Paso," on what must have been Martin's last tour. Charles Mingus and his band coming off the stage to make way for Dizzy Gillespie while playing "When the Saints Go Marching In." Jimmy Martin playing in an icy rain at an outdoor bluegrass festival, determined smiles on his face and the faces of every member of his band. Cecil Taylor's hands poised motionless above the piano keyboard, at the Village Vanguard in 1965, then slamming down to start some forty-five minutes of absolute, exhilarating chaos. John Coltrane, probably that same year, generating even squirmier chaos with a couple of other reed players, one the now-forgotten Prince Lasha. Sonny Osborn of the Osborn Brothers, in a firehouse in rural Virginia, breaking a banjo string halfway through a song, getting another string on and up to pitch while singing harmonies, and playing along again by the end of the song.

I've experienced many moments of musical sublimity from both Bob Dylan and Ralph Stanley. Some ten years ago at the 92nd Street Y, I heard Tatiana Nikolaeva, shortly before her stroke, playing the Shostakovich preludes and fugues; even I could tell she flubbed some of the passagework, but it didn't matter. I heard Rahsaan Roland Kirk, *after* the stroke that paralyzed the left side of his body, playing a tenor saxophone whose keys had been rigged up so he could play with one hand. In the early nineties, at the post-Opry Ernest Tubb Record Store Show, I heard Bill Monroe with about nothing left of his voice; he sang a frail, gentle, unbearably sad and sweet "Wayfaring Stranger." (I'll bet nobody who was there has ever forgotten it, either.) Roy Acuff at the Opry itself, about the same time, on *his* last legs, with spot-on pitch and most of his old power. That same night, backstage at the Opry, I heard Charlie Louvin (playing Stonewall Jackson's guitar) backed up by Acuff's longtime dobro player, Pete Kirby, aka Bashful Brother Oswald. In a hall at Yale, sometime in the eighties, Old and New Dreams (Don Cherry, Charlie Haden, Ed Blackwell, and Dewey Redman in place of Ornette Coleman) kept me spellbound; I also thought Don Cherry was the best-dressed man I'd ever seen.

How reliable are my memories? Well, for years I remembered being transported by getting to see the Stanley Brothers at the 1964 Newport Folk Festival. I was so loudly contemptuous waiting through the previous act— Bob Dylan and Joan Baez—that I had to be shushed. Finally, I heard the recording: it had been a painful, out-of-tune mess. For one thing, Ralph's brother Carter, who died two years later, was too sick to do his usual lead singing. How had I missed *that* little detail?

The concert that hit me *second* hardest, though, I'll still swear was genuinely overwhelming, and a friend who was there will back me up. It was a Merle Haggard show at RPI in Troy, New York, sometime between 1985 and 1987. He was fronting a powerhouse band with three fiddles, a lead guitarist—Clint Strong?—the old Bob Wills sideman Tiny Moore on electric mandolin, good old Don Markham on horns (maybe another horn player, too), and Norm Hamlet on steel. The underrated time machine, Biff Adam—also Haggard's manager—sitting there behind the drums like an Easter Island statue. Haggard was on fire that night: jumping in on lead guitar himself and singing better than even *he* could sing.

But the big one, the one I've probably taken too long to get to, was a piece of history: James Brown, Boston Garden, April 5, 1968. Martin Luther King, Jr. had been assassinated less than twenty-four hours before. I've read several accounts of how it got decided to go on with the scheduled concert. In one, Mayor Kevin White and other "authorities" argued about whether or not to cancel; those who thought cancellation would infuriate the black community further—there'd already been riots all over the country—finally prevailed. In another version, Brown himself did the persuading. White wanted to cancel, but Brown thought it would be smarter not only to go on with the show, but to televise it so people would stay home. The second version is obviously more attractive, and rings truer, no matter how skeptical you are of "authorities." Would a mayor in his right mind *really* have made things worse by failing to involve Brown in the decision? Brown wasn't just an entertainer but a political presence.

I had a decision of my own to make. I'd already bought my ticket, but how good an idea was it to be a young white kid among thousands of justly angry black people? I might well be intruding where I didn't belong; gawking touristically at Mr. Dynamite, the Amazing Mr. Please Please himself, and inserting myself into what must inevitably become a ceremony whose full significance I couldn't fully understand. No matter *how* righteous I might be. (I looked like a hippie, which was better than wearing a blue uniform, but maybe not by a lot.) My choosing to go was partly stubbornness, partly a conviction that it was fucked up not to go—I would *not* be afraid of black people—partly a desire to show my white face in solidarity with them and trust in their good will. And partly because I thought race was, at bottom, an irrelevant construct. That people persecuted because of their race might have a different take on it seems not to have occurred to me.

Boston was a tense, hostile city in those days: working-class ethnic whites, particularly the South Boston Irish, against the working-class-at-best blacks in Roxbury and, God help us, encroaching on Dorchester. And against the hippies: a couple of months after the James Brown concert, I got beaten with a two-by-four for yelling back at a carful of young white locals who'd yelled shit at me. I'd turned twenty-one in January, I'd flunked out of Bard College, snorted crystal meth for a while in New York, got called up for the draft and given a well-deserved 4F, then moved to Boston to join a rock band that fell apart a week or so after I arrived. I forget if I was still working in a stockroom or if I'd moved on to driving a cab for a company whose cars had no radios because the FCC had caught drivers and dispatchers using profanity. I was lunkheaded enough to trade a wonderful Martin D–28 to a pot dealer for a six-foot tall, sparkly red, quilted-and-padded Kustom speaker cabinet. Later that year, I got busted for pot—long story—and decided maybe I'd be less of a danger to myself if I went back to school.

Anyway, I went to Boston Garden, more or less on principle, and didn't get so much as a hostile look: going there, going home, or in the hall. Or if I did, I didn't see it. Boston had no riots in response to the assassination, and it was surely due in large part to that concert—about which I have to admit I remember little but the Cape Routine at the finale. It was Brown's shtick to feign being so transported and so drained that he was in danger of losing his sanity or his life. Someone had to come out, put a cape around his shoulders, and help him off—but just as he was about to reach the wings, he would break away, seize the microphone, and begin his screams again. (Of course, the band kept playing, as if to smooth over the disaster we were witnessing.) Again, he'd be caped and led off, and again he'd break loose. I remember him doing this three times that night; but I've read that he used to do it four times and more. Naïve as I was, I knew this was an act—or was it? Wasn't this getting *too* scary? It worked on me, and apparently everyone else in the house, just the way it should have: I was genuinely anxious about him and, at the same time, enjoying my complicity in the operatically silly artifice.

This probably happened on "Please, Please, Please," but I don't remember a note of any of the songs, nor even what songs were played. (It was surely every hit, past and present, as on the live records that had made me want to see him in the first place.) In fact, little of *any* concert remains, except for Monroe's "Wayfaring Stranger," a heart-stopping "Mr. Tambourine Man" at a Dylan show in Madison Square Garden a couple of bands ago, and "Man of Constant Sorrow" by a voice-blown Ralph Stanley in Tempe, Arizona, in 2000—so honky-tonk that it verged on punk rock. To write about Boston Garden, I borrowed a bootleg DVD from a friend, but I couldn't get the thing to play—on two different computers and with two different players. I'm glad about that now. I've still got it here, and I could look at the back to confirm that "Please, Please, Please" was the closer, but I won't. I'll probably *never* watch it, in order not to mess with the few memories that have survived: Mayor White (I remember thinking how unlucky *that* name was) giving an opening speech designed to mollify the crowd; Brown himself urging people not to "dishonor" King or destroy their own community; the crowd rushing the stage, the cops trying to keep them back; Brown cooling out both the crowd *and* the cops. (I remember not being worried for a second.) All the rest, right up till the Cape Routine, is now (and was the day after) a blur of transcendent exaltation that couldn't be picked apart into how he did this song or that song.

I remember feeling guilty that I—and everybody else, apparently—had lost sight of King's murder as people swayed and danced, hollered and screamed, as if we'd become a single orgasmic organism. I remember being afraid of Brown's power: wasn't this hockey rink–sized secular version of a Holiness service the opium of the people? Shouldn't these black people, shouldn't I, be out there tearing shit down? And I remember thinking that as soon as James Brown took command of the stage, such considerations as race and class went away for all of us. I was probably as wrong as I could be, but I'm afraid I still believe it.

9

Jimi Hendrix and Buddy Guy
The Scene
New York City
1968
GENE SANTORO

BEING A TEENAGER on the loose, prowling New York for music during the late 1960s was like being a young tomcat in an eight-bay, three-story barn full of mice. Each mouse was a unique education, stalked and caught on its own terms. Some were fatter and tastier or harder to corner than others. But all of them fed me and kept me alive, sharpening me in ways I didn't grasp until later, and then only when I needed to.

Which brings me to *The Show I'll Never Forget*. The night Jimi Hendrix jammed with Buddy Guy at the Scene.

First, you ought to know that two 1960s axioms shaped a lot of my life.

One: Just because you're paranoid doesn't mean they're not out to get you. This helped me survive the army, become a Thomas Pynchon fan, avoid serious jail time, and understand Schrodinger's Cat from the Cat's perspective.

Two: If you were there, you probably can't remember what happened; and conversely, if you can remember what happened, you probably weren't there. This two-part postulate underlies whatever understanding I've got of Heisenberg and quantum physics, Buddhism, women, the American legal system, and cultural history.

It also sums up my relationship to my own past. Like *The Show I'll Never Forget*. I'm sure I was there. I'm not sure I remember it.

Slow dissolve to late-1960s New York.

Clubs still dotted the streets of the West Village. On West 3rd Street, Alien Nomads lined up outside bars while at the Night Owl twanged the Lovin' Spoonful—the cartoony electric jug band. Head south down the block on MacDougal, dim and tiny-tabled coffeehouses for folk revivalists: Tom Paxton's smooth voice and wry tales, Eric Anderson's twitchy vulnerability, Dave Van Ronk's outsized roar and unexpected gentleness, his flying fingers and W. C. Fields humor and willingness to leap into the moment at any moment. Van Ronk so completely confused me as he veered from antique folk ballads to raunchy blues to Kurt Weill satire that it took me years to catch up.

Turn left at Bleecker and cross Sullivan for the multilevel Village Gate, pricey with high minimums for a working kid, but worth it for puff-adder trumpeter Dizzy Gillespie—those high-note squeals were literally mind-blowing—and Latin jazz-bugalu.

Across Thompson was the Café Au Go Go, an open railroad flat with its stage jutting into the middle, the band blasting at the wall a few feet away, fans at their flanks. The tix cost a coupla bucks plus a dollar Coke you could nurse through a blurry set of the Blues Project, New York's proto-psyche-delic-blues-jam band, sheared out of the movie *Monterey Pop*. On the corner, upstairs, a shabby theater housed the Mothers of Invention whenever they pulled into town; some nights there were almost as many fans as people on-stage for their satirical cabaret "Ritual of the Young Pumpkin," involving a female doll and vegetables, guaranteed to crack fifteen-year-old boys up.

West on Seventh Avenue, in between train rumbles at the Village Vanguard, Rahsaan Roland Kirk set up his music box and band on the overcrowded stage and blew joyful gusts of life on his three impossible horns, neck swelling, waves washing over him and us, a kind of affirmation I was young enough to revel in but not really grasp. The box ticky-tocked until it ran down, and then Kirk and the band stopped mid-tune so he could rewind it. One of my teen running buddies—call him Ishmael—remembers that at the end of the set, Kirk told the audience to get drunk or stoned. Which anyone who wasn't already proceeded to become.

Across the island at Tompkins Square Park, in the heart of the no-name no-man's-land that was becoming the East Village, I first saw the Grateful Dead on June 1, 1967. (I know that because of a researcher-pal; yes, he's Undeniably True.) I cut high school, walked through the thin blue NYPD line cordoning the park, got blasted on anything anybody passed me in the crowd, and tried to follow the greasy biker with the blues roar, Pigpen, through "Dancin' in the Streets," guitars curling and stabbing, Hammond roaring, neighborhood Ukrainians gathering just outside the thin blue line, trying to bust in and turn the whole thing off. That changed my life as much as *The Show I'll Never Forget*.

Slightly southwest on Second Avenue, the old Village Theater (aka the Anderson Theater) was morphing into the Fillmore East, a College of

Musical Knowledge conducted by Bill Graham. Tickets ranged from three dollars (the upper balcony) to five dollars (primo ground floor). You didn't have to nurse a dollar Coke, nearly an hour's minimum-wage pay, for a set minimum, either.

There was the bracing contrast between the Staples Singers, so like what came out of the storefront churches in the black sections of my blue-collar neighborhood but so much better, and the psychedelic blooz of Big Brother and the Holding Company. The Paul Butterfield Blues Band headlined a show with Charles Lloyd and Tom Rush; Ishmael remembers this (incorrectly) in Central Park, but I can see young Keith Jarrett at Fillmore stage left crawling inside his piano to solo. Sure, I saw the Dead and Jeff Beck with Rod Stewart, the funniest heavy metal band ever. But I also saw Muddy Waters, Duke Ellington, B. B. King, Ray Charles, Nina Simone, Mongo Santamaria, the Preservation Hall Jazz Band—pieces of black America, sometimes (as with B. B. and Ray) with a (for me then, confusing) Vegas overlay on the old R&B revue.

Raw but brutally disciplined and nowhere near Vegas was the Ike and Tina Turner Revue. (I remembered they shared the bill with Janis Joplin, which was gonna be *The Show I'll Never Forget* until ol' Undeniably True dug up Fillmore schedules.) Ike and his Fender, mean and cool, Tina's huge mouth and huger voice, the Ikettes, the sharp-creased horns and conks and shiny suits, miniskirted legs and bump-and-grind choreography. It was clear from the tenth row these people wanted your ass and weren't leaving till they nailed it. Which in my case, they sure did.

The vibe was different but not completely with Jimi Hendrix. I saw him more than I saw anybody, judging by this essay, including at the Fillmore with his Experience paired with Sly and the Family Stone. Here were two new versions of black culture (I was aware of this) feeding back into white America but (I knew this, too) rejected by black radio and communities. I saw Hendrix, the Experience, Band of Gypsys. Everywhere. Even on Randall's Island, the former boys' prison now again a concert site where Dave Matthews jams. Seeing Hendrix nearly always changed my life. Especially at *The Show I'll Never Forget*.

There were shows at the Fillmore nearly every week that I'll never forget. Some nights the lines stretched to St. Mark's Place, where the Velvet Underground were screeching and yowling to a handful of strobed-out fans who would over time, thanks to wannabe memories, multiply into thousands.

By 1970 or so, most of this scene would be gone. It just couldn't compete with the new scale or economics. The music industry was committed to "the youth market." After Woodstock, festivals proliferated, and promoters searched for venues to funnel eager youth into shows.

They found them in the damnedest places.

Out in Queens sat Singer Bowl, an open-air oval with a rotating stage left over from the 1964 World's Fair. The Doors and the Who took turns on that weird set one humid August 1968 night. Then Hendrix headlined a bill with the Chambers Brothers and Soft Machine, so much of the music's body-slamming power dissipating into the darkening skies, most of the audience at any given time staring at their backs. The undisclosed "extra feature attraction" turned out to be Joplin with Big Brother, their last NYC gig ever. (Ishmael, who was there, wasn't sure Joplin was, but U.T. confirmed it.) It was awesome, though, the Unisphere and New York State Pavilion looming over what became the home of the U.S. Tennis Open—another concert that changed my life, even if it's not *The Show I'll Never Forget.*

Starting in 1967, Schaefer, a long-gone New York brewer, sponsored summer evening shows at the Wollman Rink in Central Park. For two dollars, after standing on line (New Yorkers didn't stand "in line" in those pre-Web days), if you got to the window before the gig sold out, you got to file into the orchestra and bleacher seats. When it rained, the band cleared off-stage, and you waited until it stopped, or you gave up. If you didn't get in, you could park on the benches and boulders outside. You could hear OK, and if it rained you had a shot at tree cover.

I heard Nancy Wilson's sleek Vegas jazz and hated it—took me decades to get over it. Ella Fitzgerald and Lionel Hampton sounded old school to my too-young ears. Ravi Shankar droned microtones and jabbed microrhythms for hours, inducing meditation among trippers. Dave Brubeck (with Gerry Mulligan and Paul Desmond), a double-bill with Chico Hamilton, was jazz I knew. And, naturally, there were rockers aplenty. The series was a dirt-cheap window on the music world until the rich folks living around the park finally forced it to relocate (too much noise! too many kids! drugs and debris!) over to the West Side piers, where it died quietly in the mid-1970s.

I sort of knew this was a world on the cusp. By 1970 or so, I even sort of knew the modern music business was evolving in front of me. But I sure didn't know what that meant. Any more than I'm sure now that I ever saw *The Show I'll Never Forget.*

The Scene survived a while longer than most clubs. Way off the beaten track on West 46th Street between Eighth and Ninth Avenues, it was run by Steve Paul, Johnny Winter's manager. It was a basement dive, a windowless warren of small open brick rooms surrounding a stage. It was also a sonic nightmare. That didn't matter. The crowd mixed jet-setters (Paul Newman, Andy Warhol superstars) and groupies and hippies, who came to drink and dance and hear about-to-break acts, like the Doors. WOR-FM, New York's first FM rock station, came on the air in 1967, the same year the club started, initially for one afternoon hour; Scott Muni DJed album cuts of non–Top 40 rockers and pattered. As rock elbowed classical music off its airwaves, WOR did live broadcasts from the joint.

A tall, filthy longhair with a big nose lived in the storage room; he was the janitor and all-purpose opening act when he wasn't reading the Bible and lecturing about morality to kids like me. He'd clamber on stage with a paper bag, pull out his ukulele, and do one-man schizophrenic duets like "Hey Paula," call-and-response in a warbly tenor and wild falsetto vibrato that made Buffy Sainte-Marie's seem tame. His name, the world would learn, was Tiny Tim.

Jimi Hendrix raised these caverns to the aboveground map of music history, even though there's little documentation—Undeniably True and I snagged a few (disputed) recordings, wisps of reportage preserved online or buried in archives and morgues. When my editor asked for ticket stubs or memorabilia for possible visuals for this book, I burst out laughing. (Luckily, we were e-mailing each other.) I explained (online, after a decent interval) that I didn't have any: I didn't keep that kind of stuff in those days, and if I did I'd just forget where I stashed it. I didn't know it was history, you see. It was just my life. Which was in the moment. Which was one key thing all these concerts and the life around them were definitely teaching me.

Hendrix was living at hotels and recording at the Record Plant when he started hanging out at the Scene. All over that part of town, actually. Colony Records, Manny's 48th Street Instruments, which would shut when he came in, so we'd press up against the plate glass to watch him fiddle with new toys. The Scene became part of his orbit; he fell by to dance or armed with a roadie and a high-end reel-to-reel deck, a Marshall, and a Strat, so he could plug in with the band and tape whatever happened.

Like he did during *The Show I'll Never Forget*, the night he jammed with Buddy Guy. If it ever happened.

Time at last to recall our axioms and get down to biz.

I remember being there. Ishmael remembers being there. Buddy Guy told me he remembered being there when I asked him years ago. The best guess is 1968.

This was the peak of the Electric Blues Revival, which was helping shift the storyline of some cultural history. Though I didn't exactly understand that then.

The Folk Revival recast Lightnin' Hopkins and Muddy Waters as acoustic artists. The Blues Revival let Muddy strap his Telecaster back on and lead a hard-driving band that blasted young white kids with a deep blues mojo, his incantatory power, and showed us why the Rolling Stones named themselves.

Buddy Guy showed up at the Scene out of Chicago, not yet a Fillmore semi-regular. He was Muddy's godson, an urban-blues hitmaker and bandleader, the guitarist whose stinging, quavering, behind-the-beat licks filtered into Eric Clapton and Jeff Beck, Mike Bloomfield and Jimi Hendrix. But Ishmael and I didn't exactly know how—Buddy Guy records weren't easy to come by—until we saw him.

Like the Ike and Tina Turner Revue at the Fillmore, Guy didn't know or care about crossover audiences. He just did who he was onstage.

"He was wearing a shiny sharkskin suit, right?" Ish says. "This totally black look and attitude. He walked over to tables during the set and just picked up people's glasses and drank from them. And he was picking his guitar with his teeth, and behind his back, and I thought, 'He's stealing all this stuff from Hendrix.'" He pauses. "Then I found out I had that backwards."

Exactly. Me, too. Little wonder.

Like I say, every Hendrix concert changed my life even more than most others. Even if it was just by getting caught up in the sheer exhilarating gusts of power blasting from that wall of Marshalls, the soundshaping swirl of his hands and sonic effects tripping in my head. Even if it was just from staring at the size of his hands, that huge thumb wrapped around the guitar fingerboard climbing up and down bass strings through hammerons and pulloffs, the fluid chordings and arpeggios out of Curtis Mayfield and Chuck Berry. Even if it was at Hunter College Auditorium, one of those weird venues of the time, where I saw Hendrix (he blew out his stack of amps for a forced intermission) and Cream (Clapton seemed lost and frustrated during the endless "Spoonful" jam, maybe at his imagination's limits, maybe hemmed in by speed freak drums and jazz-rock bass on steroids).

So Buddy Guy at the Scene looked like Hendrix through the wrong end of a telescope. Conked hair, slick suit, semihollow Gibson hanging from him like he was Chuck Berry, its thin sound as he tortured notes and fanned arpeggios like a flamenco player swallowed by the Hammond organ and the Scene's eccentric acoustics.

He almost certainly played "Stone Crazy" and "When My Left Eye Jumps." These were his greatest hits, the intensity he'd gleaned (he'd tell me later) from Guitar Slim and Elmore James burning through the bad sound and cigarette and joint smoke. Awesome. Confusing.

And then out ambled Hendrix. He jacked-in to his single Marshall and they kicked into a Muddy Waters tune, I think "Hoochie Coochie Man." As the jam rolled and they traded licks, Hendrix's overdriven space-blues devoured Guy's increasingly buried if frantic comebacks. It got to be like watching a mime show through billows of standing wave blasts.

Or so I remember. See, Ishmael and I disagree about whether Hendrix showed up.

I thought about calling Buddy Guy. But then I thought of Schrodinger's Cat in that closed box, simultaneously enjoying all possible states of being between life and death, until someone lifts the lid and he collapses into just one—the act of measuring reality altering it irrevocably.

So I decided the hell with it. Just once, thanks, this old cat would rather keep the lid on his box of memories.

10

Woodstock
Max Yasgur's Farm
Bethel, New York
August 15–17, 1969
SIGRID NUNEZ

SOMETIME IN THE MID-EIGHTIES, I believe, I heard myself say, "I am so much a woman of my time, I went to Woodstock on the back of a motorcycle driven by a Vietnam vet who was on acid and with whom the following summer I lived on a commune."

To be absolutely truthful, however, the man I'm talking about—Steve—wasn't on acid on the way *to* Woodstock but on the way home.

It was the summer between my freshman and sophomore years, and I was working as a typist in a bank in lower Manhattan. I told my boss I needed that Friday off. I don't recall what reason I gave; I just know I didn't say I was going upstate to a three-day festival of peace and music. But when I came back to work after that weekend, there was no way I could keep to myself that I'd actually been part of this thing the whole world was talking about, and which also happened to be my first rock 'n' roll concert ever. The people I worked with were shocked. "Don't tell me you were in hippieland!" my astonished but forgiving boss said.

I'd met Steve the fall before, when I'd just started at Barnard College, and he'd just come home from the war. A friend of a friend of my roommate's, Steve was from Morristown, New Jersey, and it was from there we set out that Friday morning, the two of us and about a dozen of his friends. Some were on bikes like us, but in our cavalcade I recall there was also a car or two and a Volkswagen van. We weren't on the road very long before it became clear we should have set out at least a day sooner. We must have been among the last people to reach Bethel before the New York State Thruway was closed. By that time it was the middle of the night, and the concert had been going on for hours.

Of that first night I remember the feeling of having arrived in the wake of some natural disaster like a flood or an earthquake: hordes of helpless, raggedy, freaked-out folks churning about in a daze. We were nowhere near the stage, but we heard—uncannily, as if the sky itself were singing—the voice of Joan Baez cutting through the night like a knife. In our group there were other Nam vets besides Steve, and though they were all fiercely antiwar themselves, I remember how, when Joan Baez sang, they booed.

The first day of Woodstock was over, we had missed it, and now here we were, stranded in the middle of some field. At that time, I'd never been "up the country," and I wasn't used to that much dark. We had sleeping bags but no tent. It had rained earlier, and the grass was wet and cold. We hadn't brought a tarp or anything like that. We hadn't brought any kind of rain gear or even warm clothes. We hadn't brought food or water. But as we liked to say: as long as there's dope, there's hope.

After we'd passed out, some girl stumbling about in the dark stepped on my stomach, and I must have cried out. Steve, soldier instincts still keen, shot upright, grabbed the girl by the throat, and pinned her to the ground. Someone came to her rescue. She was hysterical, but my stomach hurt too much for me to feel sorry for her.

I remember we went back to sleep thinking the next day we'd get back on the bike and ride out of that mess. But come morning the sun was shining, and everything looked different. I got up first and went off by myself, feeling like a character in a fairy tale. I came upon a guy sitting on the tailgate of a station wagon, selling baloney sandwiches for a buck. A local kid, but he was the one who looked weirdly out of place in his crew cut and khaki polyester shirt. As if we didn't speak the same language, I spread my hands to indicate I had no money. He nodded and, also without a word, held out a sandwich—gingerly, as if he were feeding a deer. I hadn't eaten anything in almost twenty-four hours, and before I unwrapped the sandwich, I put my arms around him and kissed him.

I don't remember worrying about food after that. It was part of the enchantment of the place: whatever was needed would be provided. And somehow, just as you got thirsty, a huge jug of water would appear, and you'd take a sip and pass it on. And food—to this day I can't figure out where it came from, or how it could possibly have been passed like that, from hand to hand, over all those acres, enough to feed everyone: a true loaves-and-fishes miracle. We would spend that day and most of the night stuck on the same spot of ground we'd managed to claim, still pretty far from the stage but very much part of the audience. Trapped, is what we were, though that was no way to think about it.

I was the baby of our tribe and had been given to understand I wouldn't be tripping with everyone else. Steve, who'd turned me on earlier that summer, said I didn't have enough experience to drop acid in a crowd that size and under such unpredictable circumstances. Also, I was a puker; I always threw up when I peaked. I was disappointed, but there was no point in arguing. Besides, no one was saying I couldn't get high at all.

I remember while I'd been walking along, eating the baloney sandwich, I passed a couple of guys sitting outside a tent sharing a breakfast pipe and having some kind of argument. "Say what you want, it's still fucked up. Look around, man. How can you call it Paradise, when our black brothers are left out?"

Actually, we had a brother with us. His name was Bruce, and he'd never tripped in his life. Somehow, those same wiseheads who'd agreed I should not take acid that weekend decided it would be fine if Bruce did. Not just fine: *great*. Bruce was into heroin, and Steve and his friends had a notion that once Bruce experienced the enlightening effects of LSD, he'd want to kick that nasty habit. The immediate effect, however, was distinctly horrifying. For one thing, he didn't know who any of us were, but whoever we were, we'd better not touch him. We decided the best thing was to let him be—not that we had much choice. I remember at one point he started undoing his belt. We figured he was just taking off his clothes, but then he pissed down the back of the girl sitting in front of him. (Not quite as bad as puking, perhaps, but still.) Later, I remember this incident would keep being brought up as an example of just how groovy Woodstock was: how, after Bruce pissed on the girl, she stayed cool, and her old man sitting next to her stayed cool. And how, though Bruce was standing up most of the time blocking people's view of the stage and in other ways making a nuisance of himself, no one freaked out and no one got violent. Everyone just wanted poor Bruce to be okay. Which, in the end, he was. But he never took acid again, as I recall, and his heroin habit got much, much worse.

And this was the way Woodstock would be talked about for years to come: how what could easily have been a major disaster with scores of casualties had turned out to be a miraculously happy and peaceful event, and all because we'd been kind and loving to one another, and rather than every man for himself, it was every man looking out for the next—and wasn't there a lesson here for the whole world and for all time? This was what people would remember about Woodstock, as much as—if not more than—the music.

And what about the music? What with so many problems—the mother of all traffic jams, crowd control, recurrent storms, and various technical glitches—causing endless interruptions and postponements, there was no way performers could know exactly when (or even if) they'd be going on or under what circumstances, so it's no surprise that not everyone was in top form. Some were clearly unnerved by the unprecedented size of their audience. It was later reported that several performers were unhappy with their sets. Janis Joplin was one of those said to have been dissatisfied, and yet I remember being blown away by her, as I was by Sly and the Family Stone, Sylvester flashing up there like a sequin from where I sat. (I stand firmly by this memory in spite of having seen at least one account that has Sly performing on Friday, not Saturday. On the other hand, for years I remembered Ten Years After's electrifying set, but now I know that by the time they came on, Sunday night, I was already gone, and what I'd been remembering, almost surely, was seeing them in *Woodstock*, the movie, the following year.)

Santana was one of the lesser-known bands performing at Woodstock, but they gave the people what they'd come for, and then some. The Who seemed to play twice as long as everyone else—not that anyone was complaining. As no one complained when Pete Townshend whacked Yippie activist Abbie Hoffman with his guitar for taking over the stage and attempting to interrupt the program to bring us a political message.

One of the main reasons anyone wanted to go to Woodstock was to see Jimi Hendrix, billed as the festival's grand finale, and scheduled for Sunday night. In fact, things were running so late that Hendrix didn't come on till well past dawn Monday, when I believe less than a tenth of the audience remained. By that time we were long gone. We'd been rained on one too many times (we'd spent the better part of forty-eight hours soaking wet), we looked like mud people, we desperately needed a hot bath and some warm, dry clothes. And who knew how many hours it was going to take to get home. It was a late decision, though, catching Steve not yet down from the acid he'd taken sometime that day. But: "I think I can drive," he said, and off we roared. Once we were safely home, he told me the only real scare he'd had was with traffic lights, those sudden explosions of red and green—"like fireworks"—which, he confessed, had actually been pretty cool. And which reminds me: once, the following summer, when we were living on the commune—not far from Woodstock, the town—riding around late at night, I fell asleep on the back of that motorcycle.

Though some had tried hard, none of my Barnard friends had made it to Woodstock, so it was quite a distinction when I got back to school. For a while, it was something you could be thrilled about, could even gloat about, while other people kicked themselves for having missed it, our generation's biggest party, especially after the movie came out. And then time passed—not slowly, whatever the song said—and what did having been to Woodstock mean? It meant you were thirty. It meant you were thirty-five, forty. It meant—shut up about it. Why remind people you were that old now?

In 1996, while I was on a book tour, I caught some of the movie on my hotel room TV, and what I saw brought up more embarrassing feelings than sentimental ones. The flower generation came across pretty silly and obnoxiously self-congratulatory and, in some cases, painfully dumb. Somewhat later, I happened to be teaching at Amherst for a semester, and some students insisted on taking me out for a drink—with an agenda: "We want to hear about Woodstock." And I told them about watching the movie in that hotel room (in San Francisco, by chance, that counterculture mecca) almost thirty years later, and how uncomfortable I had been. I didn't really want to talk about it. I've never been big on reminiscing about the sixties. I am nostalgic for my teens—it should be a crime ever to have been so young—but I have no deep yearnings for that era or that lifestyle, and I don't ever listen to the songs of my youth anymore.

Sometime in the late seventies, I went to see Bruce Springsteen at Madison Square Garden. I went against my will. I liked Springsteen all right, but I didn't like Garden-sized crowds; I didn't want to be part of a huge audience of screaming kids. But my boyfriend (not Steve, of course) had come by some tickets, and he really wanted to go. I had misgivings about the people we were going with, which included my boyfriend's *mother*, for god's sake, a woman in her forties, the only gray head in the whole damn crowd. None of us was high. We were totally out of place, anyone could see that, and to me, at least, there was something creepy and even shameful about it. And I remember thinking how different this crowd was compared to the half a million of a decade before. These people were young, but they didn't look young to me—or at least not in the same way.

These were the *working* young, not the hippies and dropouts and summer-ing college kids we had been. They were enjoying themselves to the hilt on this hard-earned night out, but the spirit was utterly different. Everything was different, I remember thinking. And a third of my life was gone.

I'm sure it was a terrific concert, but I had a miserable time. Not that I could ever forget it either, though: the last time I heard rock 'n' roll live.

11

Nina Simone
The Village Gate
New York City
Winter 1970
LINDA YABLONSKY

MY FATHER DIED AT 5:34 in the morning on a Wednesday. Yesterday. The call came at 5:39 and woke me. A little while later, the sun became visible in the sky.

My father's name was Irving, but everyone called him "Irv." He was a singer, though not by profession. I resented him for that. I wanted him to be on the stage, but he didn't have the imagination or ambition, which I did not understand. He started singing as a boy, when his voice was still soprano. He sang in a boys' choir from a synagogue on the Lower East Side of New York City. The choir performed at weddings and bar mitzvahs and Friday night Sabbath services in different parts of town. My father was paid five dollars more than the other boys because his voice was so sweet, and he always had a solo. Twenty-five bucks was a fortune in those days, even before the Depression.

One of the first things I knew about my father was his singing. He often did vocal exercises in the morning when he strapped on the leg brace that he wore for several years after the Second World War. Shrapnel from a bomb dropped by a German plane had shredded his right leg. The bomb should have killed him. This happened on a day in 1945 when my father was hiding in a foxhole during a standoff with a German soldier who was shooting at him from another foxhole in an otherwise open field. I don't believe my father had a weapon on him. He was a medic and had gone out there to pick up the bodies of dead American soldiers. The driver of his jeep had been shot. That's why my father was alone.

The Nazi soldier must have called in the air attack. It probably did kill him—or he simply ran off. My father was attached to General George S. Patton's armored tank division, and when a few of its soldiers found him, some hours later, they put him on the back of their tank and took him to a field hospital.

Surely, the back of an armored tank is no kind of comfort. The journey must have been unbearable, but because my father was a medic, he had morphine in his kit and kept injecting himself to endure the pain.

He was sent back to the States to a makeshift hospital that the U.S. Army had set up on the boardwalk in Atlantic City. By that time, his leg was not so much a leg as a moat of gangrene. It was scheduled for amputation. As luck would have it, his surgeon turned out to be the starving man whose life my father had helped to save in France, just after D-Day. The surgeon had not forgotten. He was determined to save the leg. The operation took a number of hours, as he cut through the gangrene, bit by bit, and when he was done, all that remained was the central nerve, a bit of muscle, and the bones. But it was a leg all the same.

Because my father had to stay in that hospital long after the war ended, convalescing from the surgery and getting off the morphine, my mother wrote letters to the army, to General Eisenhower, even to the President—Truman, I guess—pleading with them all to transfer my father to a hospital in New York. Before the war, they had moved from the Lower East Side to an apartment in the Bronx, by the Jerome Avenue El. My mother was working in the mid-Manhattan garment district as a secretary to a furrier. Furs were not exactly a wartime commodity, but I think she did pretty well. She certainly dressed well. In photographs from that time, she looks quite fashionable.

Once, when I was twelve or thirteen and was rummaging around our attic for something else, I found a box of letters that included replies from the army generals and the White House concerning my father's prognosis and sympathizing with my mother's frustration. Fascinated, I emptied the contents of the box and found a few packets of mail bound with string: letters that my mother had exchanged with my father while he was overseas. Most of his had lines blacked out by U.S. Army censors, who did not want soldiers to reveal from what part of the world the letters came or what those soldiers were supposed to be doing there.

It embarrassed me to see the censors' handiwork, as these were love letters and I had never read anything like them. I had often seen my parents nuzzle each other, but I never knew them to express themselves the way they did in those letters. Even vandalized by censors, they were my first real clue to the nature of love and longing, to the durability of love. I wish I had those letters now.

My father threw them out in 1973, after my mother died. I did not like him much for that. (I did not like him for many reasons, except for his singing.) Those letters were private, he said. I had no business reading them. To him they were not pieces of an eloquent history that would otherwise go unrecorded. They were just papers, old things that no longer had any weight.

My father was the person who introduced me to show business. I must have been four or five when he took me along to the public school auditorium where he was rehearsing with a community group he had joined, people who sang well or liked to perform but had to work a day job and raise a family. They were putting on an operetta, *The Merry Widow*, I think. (He did that show more than once.) We were living in northeast Philadelphia at the time, in a neighborhood called Mayfair, after the one in London. It had row houses that looked a little like those in London, because they had little gardens in front.

All I can remember from that rehearsal is the empty auditorium and my excitement at being there. I had a baby brother and my mother was at home with him, so I was alone with my father. Perhaps that's why I'm remembering this. I think the auditorium was actually a gymnasium with a proscenium stage at one end. At least, I don't recall any permanent seats, only folding chairs. All of this is rather fuzzy.

I do recall sitting on the bench of a baby grand piano, because there wasn't anywhere else to sit. I remember plinking out a tune: "Silent Night," the only song I could think of, for some reason, though we were Jewish and never sang it at home. There was someone else on the bench with me, probably the rehearsal pianist or maybe the piano tuner. Whoever it was, he took an interest in my playing. I remember him telling my father that I seemed to have a natural "ear," and feeling happy about it. I think it was not so easy to get me away from the piano after that, so the rehearsal could begin.

A year later, my parents moved us into a much bigger house with trees and a real lawn. It was in a brand-new suburban development called Levittown, Pennsylvania. It had cookie-cutter home designs but didn't feel so much like a suburb because it was in a rural area that was mostly dairy farms and stables. My parents bought a Knabe baby grand (that's a good one) from a secondhand dealer, and arranged lessons for me with a woman who lived somewhere near. The idea was that I should learn to play the piano well enough to accompany my father's singing, so we could go around and give recitals for money.

In the beginning, this seemed a fine idea. Then we started having problems, mainly of perception. My father was a lyric tenor; he sang operas by Puccini, Verdi, Bizet, and Tchaikovsky. I thrilled to the sound when he nailed the high C in the Rodolfo/Mimi duet from *La Boheme*. The trouble was that I grew up with rock 'n' roll, with the Coasters, Frankie Lyman and the Teenagers, with Elvis, Little Richard, the Isley Brothers, with Motown, Ricky Nelson, the Beatles and Stones. And I liked all of them better, partly because it was easy to sing and dance along.

Though my mother had the radio on all day, listening to programs that played Billie Holiday, Rosemary Clooney, and other big band artists, my father always tuned the car radio to an easy listening station and bored my brother and me to death. To our parents, rock 'n' rollers weren't singing. They were shouting. They were screaming. Of course they were. To us that was still singing. It was vocal expression, anyway. (Better than singing!)

Musical theater was the one passion I did share with my parents, at least for a while. They bought Broadway show albums, like *My Fair Lady* and *The Music Man*, which was also the first show I ever saw in New York. We made it a family outing and sat way up in the second-to-last row of the upper balcony at the Majestic Theater, a dizzying height.

Now I wanted badly to be in the theater, but my parents were less enthusiastic. Even so, they went along after I won a New York University scholarship as a drama major, and when I told them I had taken an after-school job in an off-Broadway play, they were just glad I was earning my own money—my own twenty-five bucks.

The year was 1967 and the play was *MacBird!* It was a big hit off-Broadway, and I was its wardrobe mistress. It was a very clever parody of *Macbeth*, involving the Vietnam War–era politics of the Lyndon B. Johnson White House. Robert Kennedy was a character in the play, "Bobby Ken-O'Dunc," the opposition force after the John F. Kennedy character was bumped off. Though it was a kind of silly romp, the play hit all the right points about the wrong-headedness of the war and the rivalry between LBJ and RFK.

There were thirteen in the company, and we were like family. Stacy Keach played MacBird, Rue McClanahan was Lady MacBird, and William Devane was the Bobby figure. All three would go on to big success on television. Another actor, Joel Zwick, became the director of TV's *Laverne and*

Shirley, and Cleavon Little later starred on Broadway in *Purlie*, and on screen as Black Bart in *Blazing Saddles*.

Cleavon had the tiniest apartment I had ever seen. It was on the north side of Houston Street, near Sullivan Street, not far from the theater, the Village Gate, on Bleecker Street. We all joked around quite a bit before the show, while the actors got into their fairly elaborate makeup, and almost every time I went into the men's dressing room, Cleavon would tease me by saying I'd never had real southern fried chicken until I'd had his. I laughed, because he came from California, but I soon learned he was right. I went over to his place a couple of times and still remember that chicken.

Cleavon played a minstrel as well as one of the three witches, a harbinger of all tidings. He was clearly the token black in the show, but he had a sense of humor about it, and may even have been proud of it. I was proud of our friendship, partly because it was uncommon in those days for a young single woman to be just friends with a young single man. And it helped get me over my upbringing.

Levittown may have welcomed Jews, but its developers came up with all sorts of ways to keep black people even from looking at homes, much less buying them. Relations between the races were not much better in New York—or anywhere else in the 1960s, when the Civil Rights Movement began to make a difference, and riots regularly inflamed big cities across the country. Harlem was not a neighborhood I would have visited then, but the Village was different.

All kinds of people went there, all colors and sexual preferences, all ages, everyone. But I still had to get over my upbringing. My parents were not bigots—my mother was something of an activist—but they didn't encourage mixed socializing. They didn't want me going out with Christians, not just blacks.

Becoming friends with Cleavon meant I had really stepped away from my parents' thinking and was beginning to have a life of my own—but who was analyzing anything then? I was happy when Cleavon hit Broadway and then did the film. And then he died—I don't remember what from. He was still young. It had been a long time since I'd seen him. I don't know why or how we lost touch, but in New York—in life—paths cross and diverge this way all the time.

Sex is part of it. While working in *MacBird!* I had a few flings, one with an actor in the show who was married at the time and had five children, and another with his replacement, who would go on to play the sniveling villain in *Dirty Harry*. It can get this way in long-running shows, when you see each other every day and reveal yourselves, in body and speech, in the dressing rooms before each show and eat and drink together after. Eventually you sleep together; in such close quarters, it's hard *not* to fall in love.

The Village Gate was an enormous place that took up the basement and first two floors of a cheesy transient hotel on Bleecker between Thompson and Sullivan. The main bar was at the front of a restaurant with a large, L-shaped dining room on the second floor that had red-flocked walls and wood-beamed ceilings and looked something like a bordello. This was the Top of the Gate, and it was dedicated to live jazz by top-caliber musicians—Ornette Coleman, Charles Mingus, Thelonius Monk, Gil Evans, Miles Davis. A narrow, street-level bar area was called the Terrace, and served beer and burgers. It was really just a way station between the action at the Top of the Gate and the shows in the basement cabaret.

The whole operation—restaurant, bars, theater, talent—was run by an impresario named Art D'Lugoff. Art had opened the original nightclub in the basement in 1958. He loved all the jazz players and they all loved him, a portly white guy with dark hair and a beard who looked something like Francis Ford Coppola, but less bear-like.

He also gave gigs to comedians like Dick Gregory and Richard Pryor. Once, I even had a drink there with Pryor. He was hanging out at the bar in a tall, white fur hat and was not in the best of moods. This was during his down period, before he developed into the comic genius he became. Still, he regaled everyone around with a nonstop monologue made up on the spot. Sam Shepard worked in the Gate's kitchen for a time, at the beginning of his playwriting career. I remember other men whose careers were on the want—one novelist, in particular—who would be at the bar every night wondering how they could be at the center of so much activity and still have to watch it pass them by.

To get to the dressing rooms before each show, I had to go through a trap door in the floor behind the Terrace bar and down a narrow flight of stairs that came out in the tiny backstage area, where I would help the actors do quick changes during the show. Or I would go through the main entrance and down a grander flight of stairs into the theater itself.

The room was pitch-black and seated something like four hundred people. Long, dark, narrow wooden tables were set in diagonal rows along the lines of supporting columns that stood at intervals throughout, running from the back walls to a thrust stage that pushed out into the audience like the prow of a ship. I think one of these columns ran right up against the apron of the stage and represented Birnam Wood, among other things. Cocktail waitresses or waiters—I don't remember which, maybe both— served drinks before the show and at intermission. Everyone drank and smoked everywhere in those days.

Bigger music acts sometimes played late shows in the theater after the curtain came down. I saw Dizzy Gillespie there once, and he was as claimed, a very cool cat, hip to all the shit you could name. But *The Show I'll Never Forget* came after I'd left *MacBird!* for another, lesser play that was at the Circle in the Square Theater across the street.

One Saturday night, I had nothing much to do after my show and so went over to the Gate to hang out with Art, who took me downstairs to see Nina Simone. I think I was the only white person there, besides Art and some of the waitstaff. This was unusual in that black performers routinely drew mostly white audiences in mostly white neighborhoods. But this was the Village, and the Gate.

I had seen Nina Simone perform once before, when I was still in high school and she appeared at a summer theater where I was working as an usher. Anyone who grew up in the 1960s and heard Nina Simone sing "Pirate Jenny" or "Strange Fruit" or "Mississippi Goddam" got caught up in the Civil Rights Movement. She vented all the anger of the age, and, black or white, you could feel it—not the anger so much as the depth of her understanding of what was behind it. I knew enough piano to see she was a virtuoso player, though she was better known as a chanteuse, a songstress. She had a husky, sultry voice that was capable of great booming declarations and aching loneliness. She could sing those songs of rage and then turn around and do "Plain Gold Ring" or "Don't Smoke in Bed"— torch songs that made her sound both ominous and wounded—or a rocker like "I Put a Spell on You" and make it sound holy.

That night at the Gate, she performed two back-to-back sets. The first started at ten or eleven and went two hours, and then she did the other one, playing into the night. The place was packed, with an audience that included all sorts of music luminaries. I remember Max Roach was there, a sinewy figure in a suit. And maybe Dizzy was there, too. And Philly Joe Jones. No, maybe it was someone else, someone surprising. I wish I could remember who: Harry Belafonte? No, and not Miles. Someone else. A guitar player? No, wait! It was Buddy Rich! (I'm pretty sure.)

Art sat me close to the stage. The audience glittered in their Saturday night best. I don't actually have a mental picture of what Simone was wearing—I seem to recall an African print dress—but I do remember her face, mostly her eyes, and the way they took us all in, first with suspicion, then welcome, then they seemed to scan some inner landscape that had the power to alter the outer one.

She performed all of the most popular tunes from her peculiar repertoire, love songs and protest songs and gospelly blues, everything everyone wanted to hear. But she and her band also jammed with a succession of the other musicians who had come to see her.

There is something about watching musicians improvise that is close to lovemaking, the way it teases and caresses and jolts you. In a live performance, in an intimate room, you can almost see the music move between the players. It's like the weather, the way it rises and falls and storms and grows dark or lets in some light, so inevitable and yet unpredictable—a very physical experience. You don't get this from a recording; you can hear the exchanges but you don't see them, and that is what makes all the difference.

I remember watching Roach go at his drums as if they were the pages of a book of joy and madness that he was reading and writing at the same time, and that Simone picked up to add color and meaning. Yet, even with all that other talent on the stage, it was hard to take my eyes from Simone's face as she listened to the sound around her, so absorbing was the quality of her attention and pleasure. In the audience, it was as if we all took the same drug at the same time, so easily did we become a single body instead of four hundred. When Simone did her version of "Pirate Jenny," I think we all heard her deliver it the same breathtaking way: that resentful Brechtian hotel maid had grown into the world's scariest domestic, a pronouncedly black American who had had enough of service and was about to turn the world on its end, killing off her masters one by one, burning cities behind her. Never did a song seem more like an anthem of revolution, not with actual cities burning around us, after the murders of Bobby Kennedy and Martin Luther King, Jr. Who wouldn't feel pushed?

But "Pirate Jenny" was not the song that really got to me that night. It was Simone's version of Hoyt Axton's "The Pusher." This number had become a chart-topper in the rock world when Steppenwolf's cover was fea-tured on the *Easy Rider* soundtrack. That song touched a nerve, even though it came at least a decade before I ever had a need for a pusher my-self—or indeed became one. There was something in the raw, unmediated, self-hating need in Simone's rendition that ripped at my throat: God-*damn!* The *pusher-man!* I can still hear the grief and agony in her voice, still see her long fingers hang over the piano keys poised for the kill. I was afraid of her. I was amazed by her.

After the set was over, Art asked me if I'd like to meet Simone. He took me backstage to her dressing room—the one where I'd spent so many nights in *MacBird!* We shook hands. She was still sweating from the perfor-mance. It was a tiny room, very hot and crowded with people, and I re-member feeling surprise at how gentle she actually was and pleased by her taking the time to listen to me stumble through my appreciation. Then she had to change and get ready to do the next set. She invited me to stick around and hang out. I wanted to stay but felt intimidated by all the musi-cal giants around me, Roach and Gillespie and the rest. I was acutely aware that I was a guest in this house, where I had spent every night for two years. Or maybe I was feeling self-conscious because it was late, and I was alone, and everyone else had a date.

Simone was a woman alone in a man's world. All of her sidemen were men. She was the strong one, the one with the voice everyone heard, the player everyone else followed. They took their cues from her. Yet it was her attention to them that was at the heart of her performance. That attentive-ness is what I never had in any conversation with the singer who was my father, because it demands humility.

He died yesterday, and he never knew about any of this.

One of Nina Simone's best songs was "Ne Me Quitte Pas," the Jacques Brel composition that was Edith Piaf's signature tune in my father's youth. *Don't quit me. Don't leave me alone.* It's a love song, but it's also a life song. When people know they are dying, know the end is near, know there is nothing more to be done, one might expect them to lose heart, to face the inevitable, give up. That is not what they do. They hang on. If you hold out your hand, they hang on tight. And they will stay until you let go.

My father lived to be eighty-eight, almost eighty-nine. His birthday was in August. He died on May 31. They called me from a hospital in Philadelphia at 5:39 a.m. The doctor recorded the time. I didn't have to answer the phone to know what it was about. When the phone rings at that hour of the morning, it is always for sad news. But I thought it was my alarm ringing and didn't reach the phone before the voicemail kicked in.

The doctor left a message. She said my father had taken a turn for the worse. She said it was serious. In fact, he was dead, but they never tell you that if they're leaving a message. She said I should call her back. When I did, she was matter-of-fact. My father had just stopped breathing, she said. She thought it was his heart. They had worked over him for several minutes, but it did no good. He was gone. He had left.

I had been to see him two days earlier, drove all day from New Hampshire to get there after speaking to him on the phone. He said, "I wish you were here." First time he ever said that. My family was there when I arrived: my father's companion and her adult sons, my brother, his wife, my niece and nephew. The nurse was very kind. She explained what was happening. Kidney failure. Heart failure. *I'll never go home from here*, my father said. The nurse spoke to him sharply. *That just does not have to be true*, she said.

In fact, he didn't look so bad, not counting the rivers of plastic tubing running from his arms and his neck and his kidney. Both arms had many bruises, but his color was good. He was considerably more diminished in size than he had been two weeks earlier, when I had seen him last, after the heart attack.

His hair was snow white and thin. When I was alone with him, I touched it. I touched his hair for the first time in my life. It was very dry. That surprised me. It wasn't what I expected. It didn't feel real, or the way I think real hair should feel.

When I was a child, my father had a full head of dark, wavy black hair. He brushed it vigorously every day, the way his father must have taught him. Now I forced myself to touch it, stroked it away from his forehead. I put a kiss to his forehead. I had never done that, either.

For most of my life, I recoiled from my father's touch. Didn't like it. Didn't want it. I don't know why. He wasn't rough. He didn't beat me. It's just that I didn't like my father. For a long time I hated him. He was the enemy. Whatever I stood up for, he was against. Whatever I knew, to him it was wrong. Whatever I suggested, the answer was no. Then it was my turn. I became the opposition, stonily refusing to give him an inch. Now, at last, the fighting was done. I touched my father's hair. I stroked his head.

I held his hand in mine. His skin was cool. I rubbed it. I held his hand a long time.

"I'm glad you're here," he said, his voice a whisper. "I love you very much."

My father was a singer. Whatever he was as a father, he had a beautiful voice.

12

Bill Evans
The Jazz Workshop
Boston
January 1971
RICHARD BURGIN

IN MY EARLY TEENS, I had an unusual hobby. Whenever the urge grew strong enough to overcome my basic diffidence, and whenever I didn't think it would show up too badly on my parent's phone bill, I used to make long-distance calls to different jazz musicians I admired. From the safety of my home in Brookline, Massachusetts, I'd tell them how much I liked their music and then ask such typically journalistic questions as, "Who influenced you?" and "Who is your favorite jazz pianist?" It would be much more difficult to do this in today's world, but back then in 1960–61 (right in the middle of what I still regard as the golden era of jazz, when Duke Ellington, Thelonious Monk, Miles Davis, Bill Evans, Cecil Taylor, John Coltrane, Lennie Tristano, Charles Mingus, and Ornette Coleman were all at the height of their powers) unlisted numbers were almost unheard of. I knew from regularly reading *Down Beat* that most jazz musicians of stature lived in New York. It was simply a matter of asking the operator for their phone numbers and *voilà*, I would be speaking with Taylor or Tristano.

I was fired up—dying to communicate with people who had communicated so much to me. I think it was this enthusiasm and curiosity that gave me the ability to sustain these conversations that sometimes lasted as long as a half hour. I remember that Tristano was especially loquacious, referring to Monk as "the dissonance kid," praising Cecil Taylor for being "more adventuresome" than Monk, and also expressing admiration for Bill Evans. I don't remember any of the conversations going badly or any of the musicians ever hanging up on me. They were giving people, who perhaps were flattered by the unexpected attention, for while they were my heroes, they were still largely unknown to the public at large and even among so-called lovers of music.

When the calls were over, I'd go running and jumping around my large home where my parents, both quite successful classical musicians, were probably either practicing their violins or else giving lessons. When I stopped celebrating I'd call my best friend Randy, a fellow jazz aficionado, and repeat as much as I could of the magical conversation that had just ended.

By the time I was fifteen, though my love of music, including jazz, had substantially deepened, I'd stopped making these calls. For the next nine years, in fact, I talked to just two jazz musicians—both times face to face. The first was with pianist Randy Weston, after his gig at the Music Inn in the Berkshires. I was with my best friend, Randy, who was arguing the merits of Dave Brubeck to Mr. Weston, who called Brubeck's music "pretty," but not important. It was a surprisingly long and invigorating conversation that ended up pleasing all three of us, I think. The other talk I had was with pianist Martial Solal on a ship to France where he was playing piano. (Yes, the piano was and is my favorite instrument.) My talk with Solal went well enough, though I think I annoyed him when I asked if Bill Evans influenced him.

Evans was my new god of jazz, in general, and of jazz piano, in particular. His influence on me was incalculable, and I assumed he had—or should have—influenced the rest of the world the same way. After all, Evans had introduced a new language for the piano featuring a kind of lyrical introspection never heard before in jazz, with a harmonic language and rhythmic conception never heard before in any music. Moreover, his excruciating sensitivity and fiercely concentrated demeanor completely bereft of any pandering to the audience made him seem unapproachable—someone I could never dream of speaking to.

I first discovered Evans through his LP *Everybody Digs Bill Evans*, then the great *Live at the Village Vanguard* albums, made with the exquisitely inventive bassist Scott LaFaro and the best of Evans's drummers, Paul Motian. Next came Evans's majestic solo achievement, *Conversations with Myself*, which even impressed my classically trained mother. She was the first of many women (and a number of men) to whom I proselytized about Evans, no doubt boring more than a few of them in the process. Unbeknownst to Evans, he had an unpaid publicist in me apt to strike at any time or place.

As I grew older, it was inevitable that I began to hear Evans live, first at the Village Vanguard in New York, later at the Jazz Workshop in Boston.

Just as so many of my contemporaries would be reminded of important times in their lives by different Beatles' songs and albums, Evans performed that same function for me. On the night when I lost my virginity, for example, I made sure my girlfriend first listened to *Undercurrent*, the brooding but lyrical album of piano and guitar duets Evans made with Jim Hall. Two years later, at a turning point in my relations with the new love of my life, Phoebe, we went to Evans's 1966 Town Hall concert in New York (from which an album was eventually made). There was also a whole summer I spent in Tanglewood, where my parents went each year to perform with the Boston Symphony, that I can still bring to life in Proustian fashion by listening to the moody "Elsa" from Evans's album *Explorations*.

By the winter of 1971, when I was at one of my peaks of loving Evans (and just beginning to more seriously compose some of my own music), I was also at one of the seemingly bottomless valleys in my love life. I was twenty-three, teaching English at Tufts University and in the midst of the agonizing dissolution of my relationship with Jane that was so horrible I couldn't talk about it with anyone. Everything that had once been so beautiful had become appallingly painful—that kind of relationship.

On this January night, however, I afforded myself some relief by going to hear Evans's new trio with the always excellent Eddie Gomez on bass and Marty Morell on drums. They were playing at the Jazz Workshop, a wonderfully intimate club (that now no longer exists) in downtown Boston between Copley Square and Arlington Street, where I'd previously heard Coltrane, Tristano, and Horace Silver. For me, the most successful venues for music, or for anything else you love, are those where you aren't aware of time or space. The Jazz Workshop had no clocks, but even if it did, it would be too dark to see them. You entered from the street, but the music itself was performed below street level, which removed you from the outside world by another welcome degree. It was not a large space, but because it was dark enough with the lighting focused on the simple but functional stage, space melted away like the ending of an Evans's song. As a result, it attracted first-rate musicians and was a place where people listened quietly and seriously to the music as if in a concert hall instead of a nightclub.

All of Evans's virtues were amply displayed that night, from his silken touch on "Nardis" to his uncanny arpeggios on "Spring is Here" to his otherworldly chord voicings on "Blue in Green." In my hypersensitive state, every note dug into me, delivering its bittersweet message about the elusiveness of love and the inevitability of loss. Normally not a night owl, I sat transfixed for the first two sets. But I wasn't completely frozen. I did manage to move my arm up towards my mouth to deliver a few drinks. By intermission before the third and last set, when it was already after midnight, I was pretty loose. Incredibly, I noticed Evans sitting alone at a table near mine. I must have been high, because the next thing I knew, I'd walked over to the table and started talking with him. I'm sure I began by telling him how much I loved his music—that was all I thought I really wanted to say. But for some reason Evans invited me to sit down and started asking me about myself.

Almost immediately, I began telling him about my breakup. It was odd; there were still more than fifty people in the dark room, but there was no sign of anyone else waiting to speak to him. It was as if a magical space and time were created where I could speak alone to the man whose music I had listened to almost every day for seven years. And with this undreamt of opportunity to ask the greatest jazz pianist who ever lived anything about music, I was telling him about my girlfriend, make that my ex-girlfriend.

Mercifully, for Evans's sake, I skipped most of my history with Jane and concentrated on our final catastrophic date on New Year's Eve, which culminated with her reaching for a bottle of quaaludes, which unfortunately were legal at the time and had been prescribed to me for my insomnia.

Evans watched me closely behind his glasses. He had one of the most earnest and sympathetic faces I'd ever seen, like the way one wished one's psychotherapist would look.

"Did she OD?" he asked.

"No," I said, feeling a moment's shame—but only a moment's—before I forged ahead for at least another fifteen minutes. I told him how she was taken to the hospital, but was all right now. I told him about meeting her parents in a restaurant and how her father said he wanted to kill me. I revealed still more horrible details, about drugs and jealousy and obsession, including how much I wanted her back.

To all of this, Evans listened as intently as if he were listening to music he had to occasionally accompany with an appropriate chord or fill. Frankly, no one had ever listened to me that way before or ever has since.

I knew that Evans himself had drug-addiction problems throughout his professional life (which explained why one hand had swollen to almost twice its natural size). That's why I knew he could understand and not be shocked by my story. (I didn't know then how many loved ones he'd lost or would lose to suicide, including his ex-wife, Elaine, nor that Evans himself would die only nine years later of drug-related causes.)

Finally, I concluded my self-indulgent horror story and transitioned to music again. I asked him how he liked playing with Gomez and whether he would ever record again with his previous bassist, Gary Peacock. Evans, of course, said that he admired both musicians and hoped his trio with Gomez would last. I told him that my favorite albums of his were *Sunday at the Village Vanguard* and *Conversations with Myself*, and that my favorite compositions of his were "Time Remembered" and especially "Re: Person I Knew," neither of which he'd performed that night. He thanked me. He was unfailingly polite, gentle, and sincere. Fortunately, I didn't say anything particularly embarrassing except near the end when I said, "Don't sell out," to which he smiled but said nothing.

The next day, when I thought about it, I was sorry that I remembered so few of his exact words. Were I to have another chance to talk to him, I'd ask all the questions and listen much more carefully. Of course, I'd already done that in a way, I thought, consoling myself. I had listened and would continue to listen to his musical "conversation" for the rest of my life, and surely that was what Evans cared most about. It was just that, on the night that I met him, I needed his listening even more than his music, and for no discernable reason other than his own humanity, he had given it to me.

The first song he played in the next and final set was "Re: Person I Knew." I was touched. He had remembered. I prefer to end this little story here, with the Jazz Workshop still in existence, with my young and tormented heart touched and momentarily fulfilled, and with Bill Evans—his head bent over so close to the piano while he played, as if he were a doctor examining its heart.

13

Led Zeppelin
St. Louis Arena
St. Louis, Missouri
May 11, 1973
DIANA OSSANA

I WAS ATTENDING COLLEGE in Portales, New Mexico, in 1971 when Led Zeppelin scheduled a concert appearance in Albuquerque. I was young and newly married, and my husband was in the air force, stationed at Cannon Air Force Base in Clovis. When we heard about the concert, he was scheduled to leave within a few weeks for a tour of duty in Vietnam. Though desperate to see them in person, we had neither the time nor the money to make the trip.

After my husband left for the war, I moved back to our hometown of St. Louis, Missouri, found a job, and counted the days until he would return home.

I was at the airport an hour early the day he was scheduled to arrive back in the States. The plane pulled into the gate, and as the men hurried out of the Jetway, I stood there with the other wives, girlfriends, children, and mothers, watching for my husband. He was nearly impossible to miss at six feet two inches with wavy blond hair, sky blue eyes, and a smile so appealing it made women's knees buckle. He weighed a muscular 195 pounds when he left for Vietnam, but it was his wry humor, generous spirit, and strength of character that I had missed the most. I could hardly wait to see him.

The gate area was packed solid with people hugging and crying. I stood there, thinking he had missed the plane somehow. I had begun to panic, when I felt a hand on my elbow. I turned around and found myself staring into the face of an emaciated stranger. He tried to embrace me, but not recognizing him, I pulled away.

Then he spoke—and I knew that this gaunt young man was my husband.

The man who stepped off the plane at Lambert Field in late 1972 weighed just over 140 pounds, and was so changed from the person who had left the year before that I had walked right past him.

We went home, hoping to resume our life together.

As the days passed, and then the weeks, I came to the tragic realization that my beloved husband—a strong, funny, open, affectionate, brilliant light of a man—had left himself in a country halfway around the world, back down the months, across the canyon of time. What emotional wounds he had suffered in that place had severed him from his self—the self he had been the day he left to go to war. I could remember the person, the excellent human being that he had been, but no matter how hard I tried, no matter how much or how long I loved him, I had to accept, finally, that he would never be that person again.

We separated, then divorced in 1973.

I grieved for the loss of my husband, my marriage, and I withdrew from any life outside of work. Friends tried over and over to pull me out of my funk, but I was in no mood for fun and spent weekends by myself, reckoning with my past and contemplating a lonely future.

The morning of May 11, 1973, two of my buddies dropped by unannounced for a visit. They were in a great mood, and when I asked what was up, one of them flashed something in my face: three tickets for the Led Zeppelin concert being held that day in the St. Louis Arena. If anything might get me out of the house, it would be Page, Plant, Bonham, and JPJ, they explained. I wavered at first, but they were relentless. I finally agreed to go.

My love affair with music—which continues to this day—began when I was a little girl growing up in St. Louis. I remember sitting in the backseat of our 1962 Valiant listening to AM radio with my mom as she sped around running errands, listening as she sang along with the Shirelles, Elvis, Marvin Gaye, Smokey Robinson and the Miracles, the Drifters, Bobby Darin, Eddy Arnold, Marty Robbins, Gene Vincent. I sat there looking out the window, memorizing the melodies and words to those songs so I could sing along, too.

The Beatles arrived in my life in 1964: four high school freshman girls sat around our tiny TV set waiting for John, Paul, George, and Ringo to arrive onstage at *The Ed Sullivan Show*. We had heard their songs on the radio and liked them well enough, each of us acknowledging our favorite (mine was John, the "intellectual" one), but we had all rolled our eyes at news stories of teenage girls flinging themselves at these four "older" men. We would never be so uncool, we thought, until Ed introduced them and they appeared in all their long-haired, black-and-white glory. We jumped off the couch and promptly flung ourselves at the television en masse, peppering the screen with adolescent kisses. After the show, we daydreamed aloud about what it would be like to see them in person, and how we might simply die right there on the spot if we were ever to be so lucky.

I had many boy friends—as opposed to boyfriends—in high school. Independent even then, I preferred the ease of friendship over the complexity of romance. On Saturdays, we would ride around until the sun peeked over the horizon, listening to KATZ radio in St. Louis and blues music broadcasts from East St. Louis, the only all-night music stations on the air in those days. Most nights we would pool our money and hit a late-night barbecue joint on North Kingshighway, feasting in the car on a mess of ribs and thick pieces of greasy toast while listening to the dusky world of the blues: Buddy Guy, B.B. King, Thelonious Monk, Lou Rawls, Robert Johnson, Muddy Waters.

In 1968, it felt like serious rock 'n' roll FM radio came to St. Louis, and AM radio became passé. I traded Top 40 tunes for Derek and the Dominos, Emerson, Lake & Palmer, the Allman Brothers, Pink Floyd, and the Band.

In 1969, the big news among me and my friends—and a chance to have our first "live" music experience—was a plan for a gathering on a farm outside a little town in upstate New York, Woodstock, which was to be the biggest free live concert event ever held in the United States. The words "free" and "live" made it sound like rock 'n' roll paradise; all a person had to do was figure out how to get there. We bought a road atlas and decided to hitchhike east, but our hopes were dashed when we made it as far as Chicago and heavy rains hit the Midwest. When no one stopped or even slowed down, we crossed the highway and pointed our thumbs back towards St. Louis.

Not long after, a friend from high school who "dropped out" after graduation (a term synonymous then with becoming a hippie) had returned from a road trip to San Francisco, raving about a new band she had seen there, a second-tier act on a playbill with Country Joe and the Fish and Taj Mahal. I was intrigued, since I was familiar with the guitarist, who had played with a group I liked called the Yardbirds, but other than that I knew nothing about them.

One Sunday afternoon, she brought over their first two albums, and we played them over and over, deep into the night. They were, like *Sgt. Pepper's Lonely Hearts Club Band*, all of a piece, and it felt wrong somehow to play them any other way than straight through from beginning to end.

Their name was Led Zeppelin, and like the Beatles and Rolling Stones, hailed from England, but Zeppelin's music was more complex, more bluesy and soulful than Lennon/McCartney or Jagger/Richards. "Babe I'm Gonna Leave You" made us shiver, and we agreed that Robert Plant's voice was the sexiest we had ever heard. "Your Time Is Gonna Come" introduced me to how a Fender pedal steel should be played, and we pronounced Jimmy Page the best guitarist on the planet. "Whole Lotta Love" made us feel as if we were listening to something forbidden and seductive. I was jealous that my friend had seen them live, and I told her so. Would a band that ballsy ever come to the Midwest, we wondered.

Three years later, I no longer had to wonder—they had come to St. Louis, and I was about to see them live. My friends were so revved up that we left for the concert four hours before it was scheduled to begin. When we arrived at the Arena, folks were already lined up by the hundreds. They were dressed in wild seventies garb: huge bell-bottoms, the shortest miniskirts, platform shoes on both the women and the men. One of my friends wore Frye boots, adding another three inches to his six-foot-three-inch frame. The other wore a full-length leather trench coat that concealed two hip flasks of straight gin. I wore my best pair of patchwork Levi's bell-bottoms, pieced together from a hodgepodge of used jeans bought at Value Village (they still live on the top shelf of my clothes closet), a hand-crocheted top given to me by a waitress friend at my favorite vegetarian restaurant, and a pair of my hippest platform sandals.

When they opened the doors to the Arena, we made our way inside, scoring seats twenty rows back from center stage. As the lights went down and the appetizer act came on, some folks settled in, while the rest visited with each other and drank and lit up. The sweet odor of pot wafted through the auditorium. My buddy took a swig off one of his hip flasks and passed it to the girl next to him. The fellow to my left had a pistol stuck in the waistband of his jeans. He caught me looking at it and smiled. Three girls sitting in front of us were barely sixteen. Wide-eyed and curious, they giggled nonstop until the opening act wound down and the music ended.

The stage went dark, and the audience became silent. Then the light show began, and we saw them in the flesh for the first time.

I no longer remember the order of the songs, but I vividly remember moments: the descending chords and metal slide on "Whole Lotta Love"; the slow build and release in "Ramble On"; the crowd's collective surge towards the stage at the first chords of "Stairway To Heaven"; Plant's despairing "babe, babe, babe . . ." on "Babe I'm Gonna Leave You"; the complex rise and fall of emotion in "What Is and What Should Never Be." Everyone stood; then we stood on our seats. I fell in love with Jimmy Page that night, full, fast, and hard.

After the collapse of my marriage, a kind of protective mechanism must have kicked in because for a long time I was simply numb. I cast off family and friends, music—the things that mattered most to me, that made up the fabric of my young life—and in the process I somehow lost the ability to *feel*.

So in revisiting the memory of my virgin live concert experience—Led Zeppelin's 1973 visit to St. Louis—what stands out for me are the *physical* sensations their music evoked: the heat of Robert Plant's sexually hypnotic vocals; the startling genius of Jimmy Page's chill-inducing guitar riffs; the fierce, singular drum work of John Bonham, resonating in the pit of my stomach; and the rumble of John Paul Jones's bottomless, heart-thumping bass racing up and down my spine. I felt more alive than I had in months.

Afterwards, none of us wanted to go home. We wanted to hold onto the experience of that live music as long as possible. My friends and I left the concert hall and drove around listening to our eight-track Zeppelin tapes deep into the night, on and on, until the sun rose over the Mississippi River.

14

Three Dog Night

San Diego Sports Arena
San Diego, California
Autumn 1974
JOHN HASKELL

THERE I WAS, at the San Diego Sports Arena, waiting for my first rock 'n' roll experience to begin. I'd just started high school, and along with the incipient experience of independence, or the hormones of independence, there was also the anxiety of isolation, and in an effort to forestall that anxiety I'd gone with a circle of friends to this concert. I was sitting with them in the upper deck, getting slightly high, waiting for Three Dog Night to start playing. It was these friends with whom I'd begun to experience, not so much the world of independence, but the world of drugs, and by drugs I mean marijuana. I remember sitting in someone's house, someone's parent's house, when a song by Three Dog Night started playing from the speakers. Three Dog Night had a couple of hits—"Eli's Coming" and "One (Is the Loneliest Number)"—and because I was looking for meaning, and because I thought lyrics had meaning, when someone told me that "One (Is the Loneliest Number)" referred to the first marijuana cigarette you'd ever smoke, I believed it. In San Diego, at that time, "reefer" and "doobie" and "joint" and "number" all referred to the same thing, and the song was saying, so I was told, that the first one sometimes didn't have much effect, but that the more you smoked, and the better you got at smoking, the more you could feel the high. And I thought that made sense.

Quite a few years after high school I was living in Chicago, near the now-defunct Cabrini–Green housing project, and to bike from my house to the theater where I worked I had to pass that particular project. Which usually wasn't a problem. Except this one time. It was the middle of the day, and as I was coasting down the slight incline of Ogden Avenue I could see a group of kids crossing the street in front of me. They were young kids—not even teenagers—and I thought of them as children. I didn't think a child could be dangerous. And maybe one individual child

79

wouldn't have been dangerous, but this was a group, and because they were standing in the street, not moving, I slowed down and got off my bike. And that's when they began throwing rocks. I didn't know where they got the rocks, but they were throwing them at me, and I remember one stone hitting my leg and several hitting my bicycle. But I still wasn't afraid because I thought of them as harmless kids. I thought they were harmless until, like a mob, they started coming after me, about eight of them, young and yelling, and I probably said something to them, something naïve like "I did nothing to you" or "I'm a friend," something peaceful like that, but they weren't in the mood for peace. And it wasn't that they hated me; they were part of a group, and the mentality of that particular group united them in an unthinking allegiance to whatever momentum had gathered, and as it continued to gather, that particular momentum was bent on my destruction. I got back on my bike and began to pedal as fast as I could, hoping to break through their ranks, and I remember rocks passing by my head, and I remember hearing laughter, exuberant laughter, as they chased me down the street, still throwing rocks, and although I did manage to ride out of range, and out of the project, I remembered that mob, and the mind of that mob, blind to anything other than its own exhilarating logic.

So there I was at the Three Dog Night concert, the opening act playing on the stage, and although I'd never heard of the band, I didn't want to be a sedate observer. I wanted to get up off my seat and be part of the ecstatic, enthralling experience that a rock concert was supposed to be. This was sometime in the 1970s, but I wanted the freedom and loss of restraint that I imagined existed in an earlier generation. The 1960s meant liberation to me, specifically liberation from the self. I was a teenager, but to the extent that I had a sense of self, I wanted liberation from the isolating aspect of that self. Beneath the constraint and inhibition of my normal life I could feel a freedom percolating inside my chest, and I wanted to release that freedom. I left my circle of friends, jumped a barrier and walked down the aisles to an area closer to the stage, slightly to the left of the stage, where people were standing on their seats, arms waving, voices yelling, and I joined this group. If music was a way to discover something greater than me, not that I even cared that much about the music, I wanted it, wanted the intoxication the music might bring. And then it happened. To some extent it did happen. By doing what everyone else was doing I felt the general intoxication that was either around me or in me. I felt part of a trancelike exuberance, and I remember turning to the person next to me, a long-haired guy who was flinging his hair from side to side, and I was flinging my own hair and waving my arms over my head. And by doing it I felt, not only lost in the moment, but connected to a larger community. Of course an aspect of my consciousness, because I was trying to be lost in the moment, was having trouble being lost. But I continued screaming and jumping with my fellow screamers and jumpers, hoping that if I concentrated hard enough and yelled loud enough I would feel the liberation I wanted.

Years later, I was living in San Francisco. I'd gone to Golden Gate Park, to a Jefferson Airplane concert, or maybe by then it was Jefferson Starship. Either way, it was a free concert, and since I didn't have a circle of friends at that point I went to the concert by myself. If I wanted to relive the spirit of the 1960s this was the place, sitting on the grass on a sunny day with hippies dancing on blankets and people sitting and lying on blankets, and the band was singing all their hits, about revolution and white rabbits, and I happened to be sitting behind a girl who had a blanket and long hair and it's possible she had flowers in her hair. I'm almost sure she had a wreath of flowers, and as the momentum of the concert built, we were all standing on or next to the various blankets, and this particular girl was dancing, and I was dancing, not so much to the music as to her. Although she didn't know it, I was moving my body in rhythm with her body, and because she was alone I thought . . . I didn't know what I thought, but it had something to do with the song the band was playing. "Don't you want somebody to love?" Yes, I thought. "Don't you need somebody to love?" Yes, again. The lyrics were in sync with my desire, and the girl in front of me, I saw her as a way to achieve my desire. And because her body language seemed inviting, I danced a little closer, trying to lose my isolated self in the mob of swaying bodies, and I almost did. I was hoping to join in what I thought of as the spirit of liberation, and the only problem was, I wasn't liberated. But I wanted to be. And what I remember is not my failure to relive the spirit of free love with the girl in front of me, but my desire to be part of that spirit, of liberation or love or actually a spirit of anything.

When I was living in Copenhagen, I used to go to an area of town called Christiania. It was created in the 1960s by idealistic hippies, and for years it had functioned as an alternative city, but then the hippies got old, and although there was still the community food store and the cooperative bicycle shop, the project they'd created had turned into something else. Drugs had come and commerce had come, but more importantly, nostalgia had set in. I remember being there during a demonstration against what is now called the First Gulf War. There was a march and a collection of speakers at the end of the march, and because I didn't speak Danish, I stood near a building slightly removed from the speakers. I was standing next to a dog, and next to the dog was a bench, and the men on the bench were slightly older, and because it was hot, even in the shade, some of the men had taken off their shirts. I noticed, first of all, that they were very tan, with the kind of tan that comes from years of standing in the sun, and because their bodies weren't young, the skin was hanging on their bodies like a layer of loose leather. They were drinking beer and probably had been drinking for a while and now they were getting excited, not by the speakers who we could hardly hear, but by the movement—that's what they called it—by the sense of community they still desired. One of the men, with a thick mustache, stood up and began shouting something about Woodstock. It started as a single voice, and then a few other voices joined in, invoking Woodstock, chanting that Woodstock was still alive. And clearly it wasn't, but they were chanting it. And that's the second thing I noticed, that although it was more than thirty years after the event, the people who were chanting were still, in their enthusiasm, trying to relive—not reinvent but relive—the time in which, presumably, they'd felt alive.

There I was, slightly to the left, looking down on Three Dog Night as they played their songs, and at a certain point, as the momentum of the music became more frenzied, I couldn't stand it any longer. Even though I was swaying and dancing and shouting with the circle of people around me, I saw that other people were swaying and dancing and shouting with more exuberance. They were the people standing in front of the stage, and so I left my seat and squeezed past the writhing bodies and past security guards into the pulsating heart of the crowd. It took a while, but when I got to that heart and stood beside the large, black speakers I could feel my heart beating, and I could feel the pure noise vibrating from the speakers into my chest, but most of all I felt the movement of bodies. And I was part of the movement, sweating and dancing and looking up at the colored lights flashing on the stage. We were all together now, the band and the music and the dancing, no him or her or me dividing us, and it wasn't dancing exactly because it was too crowded to dance, but it was union, both with the music and with each other, and the reserve I'd felt before actually disappeared. I remember calling for an encore, shouting, "One is the loneliest number" into the general cacophony surrounding me, and I was part of that cacophony, part of the world, part of the surging mob uniting everyone with everyone. My sense of self was sucked away, and without that isolating self I had a sense of being part of something larger, and I was left, at least momentarily, in the state of being I'd been desperately trying to find.

15

Television
CBGB
New York City
Winter 1975
BRUCE BAUMAN

NOT LONG AGO, my wife Suzan asked me if I was upset because CBGB, the monument to despair and hope and youth, officially announced that its doors would soon close. I said, "Nope, the time is right to say bye-bye." She seemed a bit taken aback because she knows I go gooey-eyed over the dirty, dank, and blissful moment, in the winter of '75, when I first stepped into CB's.

An aspiring misanthrope, I remember cursing at the body-slashing winds as I hustled down Bleecker Street, wondering why I had left my bedroom in my parents' apartment. Dave Schulps and Ira Robbins, two friends who, as teenagers, had started the seminal *Trouser Press* magazine, dragged me to this "club." Dave, a supremely low-key guy, told me about this "amazing" guitar band; maybe there'd even be some girls hanging around. Well, there were only six of us, *all guys*, in this dimly lit, smoky, smelly bar when we arrived that Sunday night. The one waitress was surly as hell, which was a great sign. She had a future at the Second Avenue Deli if things didn't work out in her acting career. I slipped and almost broke my leg on the mix of sawdust and undetermined slop covering the floor.

I don't remember the opening bands that night except for one lead singer who seemed to have missed the auditions for *Godfather II* and ended up at CB's instead of the local social club—he kept glaring and gesturing at us threateningly when we didn't applaud loud enough after each song. The last band was Television led by Tom Verlaine, who seemed to embody a contradictory mix of a Gary Cooper–like laconic power and tubercular frailty. In my youthful arrogance, I thought they seemed kinda old—maybe twenty-six or twenty-seven. They had a new bass player, Fred Smith, who had recently replaced the not-yet-renowned Richard Hell. Smith kept his

head down, sometimes glancing at drummer Billy Ficca and Verlaine. I figured this was the reason that it took them forever to tune up. Suddenly, the
dueling guitar sounds of Verlaine and Richard Lloyd soared and lifted me
out of my angst and desire to be home in bed and took me to the home of
rock 'n' roll dreams. But it wasn't only the guitars that got me; it was
Verlaine's often anguished and sly lyrics.

> *How I fell?*
> *Do you feel low?*
> *Nah.*
> *Huh?*
> *I fell right into the arms of Venus de Milo.*

But more than anything, they were oh so cool.

I went back some weeks later to see them again. This time the pre–Jerry
Harrison Talking Heads played, as well. I thought they were awful, and
yet, they too had "the aura" of stars-to-be. That night, Patti Smith came by
and left quickly. I saw her play soon after, and like many others, I envisioned her as a Dylan for this age. In one of my next forays, I first heard the
One-Two-Three-Four chants of the Ramones. I was a street kid from Queens
and, as they made it to the stage in their leather jackets and torn jeans with
their edgy yet confident bop, I imagined myself as one of them. They hit
the perfect note of the snotty, working-class dorks gone hip. We knew
something was happening, and we knew what it was.

It wasn't only the music scene that gave energy to downtown New York
in the mid- and late seventies. The near bankruptcy of the city, the end of
the Industrial Era, the death of the printing plants all started to give way to
lofts and galleries. Walk-up apartments were affordable, even for those
with a minimum-wage job. You could score a whole building on Greene
Street for what you'd now pay for a bathroom. Those cheap rents allowed
the seventies downtown music and art scenes to be born.

As the Dictators—a savagely funny band fronted by Handsome Dick
Manitoba—would say, it was manifest destiny that soon six people at CB's
became sixty, and then six hundred. John Rockwell of *The New York Times*,
to his everlasting credit, started coming down and pimping the scene. In
time, the A&R record company people arrived—which was what everyone
wanted. The bands were making music to be heard. I thought bands like
the Planets would get contracts but never did. I still don't understand why

the Dictators didn't become the NYC version of the Mothers of Invention. Still, bands like Blondie emerged and hit the big time. Patti got written up in the *The New York Times Magazine*. The legend had begun.

Around this time, I was working as a gofer at an ad agency when I was able to parlay my ability to get coffee into a free ticket for a Christmas catalog shoot in London. I quit the job after the shoot, saw Eddie & the Hot Rods at the Marquee Club, then headed out to Paris and points east 'til my money and health ran out—ending up in the hospital suffering from one more of my lifelong bouts of chronic ulcerative colitis. When I got healthy, I moved out of my folks' place to a rent-controlled railroad apartment—with bathroom in the kitchen—on Second Avenue and 84th Street that I shared with Dave. Total rent: 134 bucks a month. After I got my strength and got out of my misanthropic funk, I left the apartment for a night at CB's. I couldn't believe the crowds; the New York hipguard had arisen from the ashes of the demise of the Dolls and the Mercer Arts Center and found 315 Bowery.

It was on one of these nights when I saw Television at their all-time best. CB's still smelled awful, and now it was packed—a fire marshal's wet dream. It seemed as if every single person was smoking something. I was scared the place would burn down. I thought about leaving until I had a few beers and my neuroses calmed down.

It was probably around one or two in the morning when Television finally made it to the stage. As now had become their trademark, their tuning up lasted longer than a full set of the Ramones. I don't remember what they opened with, but they hit their stride with "Prove It." Verlaine ended the song not with the familiar "Case closed," but as he opened and shut his eyes with those long, feminine eyelashes he took his time as the last chords vibrated, and then whispered almost ominously, "Case . . . still wide o-pen."

Somewhere in the fifteen-minute improvisation that was "Little Johhny Jewel," Verlaine started spinning slowly in place, tangling the wire that ran from his guitar to the amp around his torso and neck, and just as we thought he might strangle himself—with all the grace of a ballet dancer pirouetting on a snowflake—he started twirling in the opposite direction. Lloyd snapped a string on his guitar but never stopped playing as he and Verlaine matched solo for solo and took us to that mythical land where guitar gods go to die and be born again. The band's mix of almost hippie-dippie jamming, the guitars' razor blade thrust of existential danger, and

Verlaine's pain-voiced straining like a drowning bird produced that night a sound melodically tortured and pure. This was Pollock becoming the canvas, Kerouac becoming that one, long roll of paper that is *On the Road*.

I still get chills thinking of that night and how music can make me feel. They played the 13th Floor Elevators' "Fire Engine," their own masterpiece, "Marquee Moon," and finished with "Knocking on Heaven's Door," which is what I think we all felt like we were doing when we left CB's somewhere near four a.m.

I drifted in and out of the scene for some time. With a group of French friends—because downtown had become Eurochic hot—I attended *Punk* magazine's "wedding" of Debbie Harry to Joey Ramone. I watched as John Cale and Lou Reed "made up" one more time, and Lou lived up to his claim to being as good a guitar player as Hendrix—at least for one night. I shook my head as Johnny Thunders puked on Richard Hell—or maybe it was the other way around. And I veered my gaze away from Lloyd as he shot up in the back by the CB's bathroom. It was a helluva time.

Soon, my life took another path, and I drifted away from the scene. I continued on my uncharted road as I wandered through years of traipsing around the world, long stays in lonely hospital rooms, numerous crappy jobs, and, almost inexplicably, ending up a writer and teacher, happily married and living in L.A.

My longer, unsentimental answer to my wife's question is that CBGB's moment, which was spectacular, lasted three decades. It wasn't started to last, and it wasn't meant to. It rose spontaneously out of a need for people to pound their guitars and wail their neurotic visions. The legacy of CB's is the bands it produced and the music they made. We are not talking Chrysler or Flatiron buildings, here. What made CBGB's a name known around the world are the sounds that shrieked and shook the walls inside the building and reverberated from New York to Paris to New Delhi.

A couple of years ago, I did a reading at the Bowery Poetry Club across the street from CB's. After everyone had gone home, I darted around the cars and taxis and crossed the Bowery. It was early March, and, once again, the harsh winds ripped down the streets. I stood alone outside CB's for I don't know how long, trying to decide whether or not to go inside. I realized Thomas Wolfe was right. He was also wrong. Because even after you do leave home, you don't. There's not a day—or more accurately an insomniac night—that goes by when some sound or vision from that time doesn't pass through my memory cells to stir a laugh, a regret, or more often than not a remorseful peace with my New York past.

Sure of what not to do, I turned away and started wandering up the Bowery and suddenly, unexpectedly, I smiled. I knew right then that long after CB's is closed, the sound of Tom Verlaine falling into the arms of Venus de Milo would haunt the New York night. Forever.

16

The Sunshine Festival
Anaheim Stadium
Anaheim, California
September 28, 1975
KAREN KARBO

THE RECOLLECTION—or rather attempted recollection—of my first rock concert, a certified high point of my youth, has left me rattled. Not nostalgic for simpler times; not inflicted with that weird vertigo you experience beginning around age thirty—or the first time someone in retail calls you "Ma'am," whichever comes first—when you look back on the past, and it seems so long ago it makes you dizzy. Nothing as easy as that. In realizing that I can't remember an event I consider to be a seminal moment in my teenage life, I have fallen into an authentic existential funk. What the hell? How can this concert be one of my fondest memories when I can't even remember it? I hasten to add that I am not that old, i.e. I don't have pre-senile dementia—I don't think.

The paltry details, as I remembered them, without help from Google or an old boyfriend I drunk-dialed to see if he'd been my date to the concert (he hadn't):

1. It was 1975.
2. It was the Eagles.
3. It was Anaheim Stadium.
4. It was during the day. (Could this be true?)
5. I was wearing a pair of huaraches, which I'd purchased recently in Tijuana—the kind with the thick rubber soles made from Uniroyal tires.

I can just about conjure up the image of myself swaying blissfully to the folky strains of "Lyin' Eyes" (then, a new release) in a sunburned stoner haze. I can feel the sun on my arms and scalp. My hair smells like Herbal Essence shampoo. There are thousands of people around me, similarly swaying in peaceful easy groovitude. I can tell you without knowing for sure that I'm also fretting about my hair. Then, as now, board-straight blonde hair was the height of feminine beauty. I had thick, wavy, reddish-brown, madwoman hair, riddled with cowlicks, bleached orange by the sun.

Was the concert in April? July? October? One peculiar downside of growing up in Southern California is the weather rarely serves as a door-way into memory. Even though the early spring mudslide season is brought about by Bangkok-like rains, I don't ever remember popping open an umbrella or stomping through puddles. Instead, the sun is always drowsy above smoggy, lemonade-colored skies, the evenings smell like star jasmine, and I am leaving wet footprints on a succession of concrete aprons surrounding dozens of swimming pools.

Our seats were not good. We were eight hundred miles away from the tiny stage. We were so far away there was actually a sound delay. That's impossible, isn't it? We were seventeen or so. I don't think we understood the concept of acoustics, that a huge baseball park was not a good venue for bands that trafficked in cozy harmonics.

For these were the high-mellow "Tequila Sunrise" Eagles, the pre-stressed-out "Life in the Fast Lane" Eagles, the band with whom every girl I knew wanted to sleep with in the desert tonight with a million stars all around, though I sort of doubted they or the Eagles themselves had actu-ally ever slept in the real desert. I mean, on the hard, parched ground of the Mojave, where you need to check your shoes in the morning to make sure there are no scorpions.

I cannot recall the concert, and I cannot remember the Eagles, except to say they were four very small guys waaaaaay far away down on the stage—really you only could tell who was who by what instruments they were on—but I can easily summon up a clear image of all my Eagles al-bums stacked on my turntable in my orange and pink bedroom in our tract house in the semishitty suburb of La Habra (which I now hear is actually a desirable place to live), waiting to drop with a soft creak onto the disk be-neath it. I can hear the snick of the needle on the edge of the vinyl, feel the seconds of anticipation before the peppy twang of "Already Gone" com-menced—my private anthem for getting out of La Habra, and never look-ing back, which I did, and I did.

Our family also owned a summer house in Laguna Beach (something a middle-class family could still do in the seventies), where we always spent the month of August. I would drag my huge speakers out onto the deck, in order to blast our length of beachfront. "Desperado" was one summer,

"On the Border" the next, and "One of These Nights" the next after that. It was all Eagles, all the time, the summers of my high school years. Even now, whenever I hear them on some classic rock station, I can smell the Bain de Soleil and Mr. Zog's Original Sex Wax, and hear my mother hollering over the crashing waves and Glenn Frey, "Turn. That. Down. Before. They. Arrest. Us."

A clue:

On eBay, I found an unused ticket from the concert. It was called the Sunshine Festival, and also featured sassy Linda Ronstadt as well as the prematurely elegiac Jackson Browne. The tickets were $10 in advance, $12.50 the day of the event. Anaheim Stadium, now called Angel Stadium of Anaheim (as if it's a five-star Hawaiian resort and not a ballpark hemmed in by freeways), was then called the Big A.

It was the date on the ticket—September 28—that unlocked the depressing secrets of the past. The reason I couldn't remember who I was with is that I barely knew who I was with. It wasn't a gaggle of childhood friends or an adored boyfriend, as I'd imagined, but a boy I'd worked with that summer at Knott's Berry Farm (known in modern times as Knott's Berry Farm Adventure Theme Park).

I worked at a snack stand called the Chow House. We served hot dogs, chili, nachos, pizza, boysenberry turnovers, soft drinks. "No, we don't have root beer." I must have said that eight thousand times a day. No one wanted to work at the Chow House. Every day we punched in hoping, like farm team infielders, to be called up to the big time: Mrs. Knott's Famous Chicken Dinner Restaurant, where on Sunday night you could pull down $40 in tips.

The Chow House was staffed mostly by girls in their late teens. We wore red and blue calico aprons over our white waitress dresses. I made friends with three blonde Pi Phis from San Diego State. I idolized their shiny hair and sweet natures. They were very Californian and untroubled. I was a Californian, too, but I was grouchy. I liked to poke fun at people and complain. My mother blamed it on my Slavic blood, which—she never failed to discriminate—did not come from her side of the family. The Pi Phis (they were adorable, really) could tell our customers we had no root beer until their tongues dropped out of their heads from sheer exhaustion, and it didn't seem to affect their impression of the intelligence of the human race.

They did not have a full-on stand-up act like I did: *"You'd like a root beer you say? Let me ask you something. On that huge menu above your heads, do you* see the words, 'root beer'? No, you do not. Do you see the words, 'Ask about our root beer, which is not listed here'? No, you do not. That is because WE DON'T HAVE ROOT BEER. We have never had root beer. We will never get root beer. Now, please, I beg of you, eat shit and die."

The only boy who worked at the Chow House was named Vince. He was older but not by much. He was a lifer, a community college dropout. He still suffered breakouts on his chin. There was a rumor that he was caught, you know, doing it in the walk-in freezer with a girl who got fired because of it. Why didn't Vince get fired? Another mystery. And given what I now remember about the Sunshine Festival, I don't think I want to know.

Vince was also the resident Chow House pot dealer, and an expert on how to steal money from the register at the Timber Mountain Log Ride Icee stand, which was part of Chow House operations. The stand was the size of the bathroom on a jumbo jet, and stuck on the far edge of the park between the log ride and the stables where the stagecoach ride horses were boarded. There was no air-conditioning, a billion flies (the horses; the sticky sweet boysenberry Icee mixture) and an eight-hour non-stop soundtrack of WHEEE-OOOOHHHHH-EEEEEEE! as every thirty seconds a log full of happy park-goers plummeted into the pond at the ride's end.

Pulling Icee stand duty was like getting sent to Siberia. One day a few weeks after I started, our boss, a lady from Alabama with a nest of iron-gray hair named Iona Platter caught me doing my "no root beer" act for the other girls, and told me she did not cotton to my attitude. Out to the Icee stand I went, to serve my sentence for the next three months.

It was the summer before I went to college, the summer the movies always portray as a halcyon time of blowout fun, tender love affairs, or poignant coming-of-age experiences. Instead, in my memory, it is the summer of learning that if I couldn't be blonde and sweet-natured, at least I could save myself some grief by keeping my big mouth shut. It is the summer of sticky elbows, sticky hands, swarms of biting flies, the smell of horse manure, and the pocket of my calico apron jingling with pilfered quarters. Driving home in my VW Bug, the Eagles were always on the radio, already gone. Often, I wept out of pure boredom.

Vince heard about the Eagles concert on the radio, which is where you heard about concerts then. He bought a block of tickets—for the Pi Phis, a girl named Laurie who also worked our shift and was getting ready to go off to Princeton (which struck us all as very exotic) and Vince's best friend Rob, who worked over at the Pan-for-Gold attraction. While Vince was someone you could tolerate while imprisoned at the Icee stand, Rob was someone you might want to know outside of Knott's Berry Farm, a swimming champion from Newport Beach headed for Stanford.

I played it cool. "Yeah, sure, the Eagles, totally." But really I was bursting with excitement. The thought of finally seeing the Eagles in person—*in person*—made me feel as if finally my life was going to start. I had never been to a concert before. In the mid-seventies, in that part of the sprawling suburban world, there weren't a lot of venues. If you wanted to see anyone you had to drive into L.A., which most of our parents forbade. (Where I currently live in Portland, I can walk to the Rose Garden, where there's a worthwhile band playing about every seventy-two hours. My thirteen-year-old daughter has already seen Green Day there twice.)

In my well-cloaked delirium, I didn't think to ask Vince about the details; nor, apparently, did anyone else. No one thought to find out the date of the concert or when classes started at our respective colleges. Vince didn't have to worry, of course.

I went off to USC the last week in August. It was far enough from La Habra to seem as if I'd left home, but not so far that I couldn't go to the Sunshine Festival; the Big A was only forty miles away, give or take. Anyway, I had already paid for my ticket with my embezzled change.

No one showed up but Vince. Just Vince and me and empty seats on either side of us. Even though he'd brought enough weed for seven of us, there somehow was not enough to obliterate our mutual feelings of disappointment. He was not Rob, and I was not one of the Pi Phis.

Still, this strange boy and I were desperate to make it one of those crazy old nights. In the parking lot after the show, we crawled into my VW Bug and made out. Vince was extremely sunburned. His tongue—I can't believe I remember this—was as rough as a cat's. He kept hauling me towards him, jabbing the gearshift into my belly. I wish I could report this was a euphemism.

After a few hours, we lost interest. Is this possible? That a nineteen-year-old boy and a seventeen-year-old girl, alone in a car on a warm California night, can lose interest in one another? It is one of life's little-told stories. Certainly, the Eagles never sang about it.

As I sped back down the freeway, back to my dorm room and my new life, I must've thought about how things never turned out the way you imagine them to, or how life was not, in the end, like a rock song. Or, more likely, I just turned on the radio and sang, already gone.

17

Queen
The Capital Centre
Landover, Maryland
November 29, 1977
TRACY CHEVALIER

IT STARTED WITH A champagne toast and ended with a limo pulling away into the night. In between these two gestures symbolizing glamour and sophistication, I lost my virginity. Not in the technical sense (that would take another few years), but in other ways. At my first-ever rock concert—going with four friends to see Queen at the Capital Centre in November 1977—I got an eye-opening peek at elements of the adult world, with its power and its limitations, its glittering artifice and dirty reality, and it demonstrated how little I knew and how much I had yet to learn about life.

I was ripe for it; overdue, really. I had turned fifteen the month before the concert, and though people often thought I looked older than I was, I was remarkably naïve and unworldly at that age. Perhaps we all are at fifteen; perhaps we should be. You would think I'd have been more sophisticated, though. I grew up in Washington, DC, with its brainy government types, international diplomats, and substantial black population creating a heady, diverse mix. Moreover, my father was a photographer for *The Washington Post*, taking pictures of all the presidents, covering Watergate, bringing home news of the outside world. Yet little of that registered with me. I don't think I truly grasped that we were at war in Vietnam throughout my childhood until long after it ended. The assassination of Martin Luther King, Jr. simply caused riots and an inconvenient curfew for DC residents. Watergate was confusing and boring and kept Dad working late.

Despite a few character-building events in my childhood—the death of my mother when I was almost eight, the experience of being a minority in DC public schools—I was so unsophisticated, so unaware of the world, that I didn't even realize Queen was an English band until lead singer Freddie Mercury appeared in a tight white cat suit on stage at the Capital Centre, raised a glass of champagne at eighteen thousand screaming fans, and toasted us with, "Good evening, Washington," in a fruity English accent. I was stunned. Then, I started screaming.

I had been a Queen fan for a couple of years. *A Night at the Opera* was the first LP I ever bought, and I could sing every word of every song. I don't remember how I was introduced to Queen—though I do remember hearing their biggest hit, "Bohemian Rhapsody," on the radio and being impressed by its audacity. It sure beat the hell out of the Beatles, Bob Dylan, and Neil Young, which had been my older sister's staple music diet. By fourteen, I was trading Queen lyrics with a boy I had a crush on in algebra class and daydreaming of guitarist Brian May kissing me.

The concert was part of Queen's *News of the World* tour. While not a great album, especially after the double whammy of *A Night at the Opera* and its follow-up *A Day at the Races*, it did produce two of their best-known songs, "We Will Rock You" and "We Are the Champions," which dropkicked them firmly into stadium anthem territory. Appropriately, the concert began with the lights going down and the primitive, effective, impossible-not-to-join-in-with BOOM-BOOM-CHI, BOOM-BOOM-CHI, BOOM-BOOM-CHI intro to "We Will Rock You" rolling over the audience. Everyone immediately jumped up out of their seats and began to stomp and clap along. I, too, stood and stomped and clapped, watching in awe as people began flicking their Bics, a gesture I had never seen before. What, were they going to set light to something? I had tried not to act surprised earlier when people nearby started smoking grass in public, but now was there going to be a riot? What other illegal things would go on that night?

Then a spotlight picked out Freddie Mercury, who began to sing, "Buddy you're a boy, make a big noise, playin' in the street, gonna be a big man someday . . . ," and I thought, "Jesus H. Christ, that is the loudest noise I've ever heard! Is *that* legal?" The wall of sound terrified me, and I wanted to cover my ears, but I didn't dare, as it would have been a very uncool thing to do. I think I looked around for the exit, wondering how many people I would have to climb over to escape the sound. It was just so goddamned loud—exhilarating, yes, but painful too, dangerous and overwhelming. I wavered between loving it and hating it, but knew it would be uncool to hate it, so I'd better try to love it.

Towards the end of the song the single note of an electric guitar began to hum louder and louder under the chorus we were all shouting, and Brian May stepped into the light to add his distinctive sound, ending "We Will Rock You" with low, long-sustained, three-part-harmony chords, overlaid with a high melody he made fuzzy and metallic by using a coin as a guitar pick. I adored Brian May. He was the reserved, straight guy (literally) to Freddie Mercury's camp high jinks—tall, dark, good-looking, with long, curly hair and a melancholy pensiveness that made every teenage girl want to comfort him. At this concert he was wearing a silvery white jacket with long, pleated wing sleeves; that combined with his mop of curls should have made him look effeminate, but instead he was deeply sexy.

I loved Freddie, too, for his outrageous antics, his riskiness, his joy at performing, and his glorious indifference to how ridiculous he looked wearing glittery leotard jumpsuits, eyeliner, and a mullet, prancing and strutting and posing, twitching his hips, smacking his lips, and otherwise hamming it up. But even without being conscious of Freddie's sexual preference—I hadn't yet met anyone who was openly gay—I instinctively sensed he was not to be lusted after. For all his extroverted, welcoming stage presence, he was clearly playing a part, which served to hold us at arm's length; whereas Brian May's taciturn moodiness was clearly himself served up raw.

Thank God for Freddie, though. Without him, no one would have moved onstage: Brian May was not a dancer, John Deacon, in time-honored bassist tradition, stood solidly in one place throughout, and Roger Taylor was trapped by his drum kit.

To set us at our ease, after "We Will Rock You," Freddie toasted us with a glass of champagne—"Moët et Chandon, of course," after the reference in the hit "Killer Queen." My friends and I heard this and screamed and clutched one another. He mentioned Moët et Chandon! That was our champagne! He was acknowledging us! I swear he made eye contact with me, two hundred yards away and over the heads of thousands.

For we had done what we thought was the most original and extravagant gesture (for fifteen year olds) a fan could make: we had sent a bottle of champagne backstage. We'd pooled our money and gotten an older sister to buy it for us—the same sister who had been obliged to drive us all the way to the Capital Centre, smirking at our overexcited fandom. We'd even made our way to the stage door down a loading dock at the back of the arena and reluctantly handed over the precious bottle to a bored roadie, who said he would take it to the band. We'd had our doubts about his reliability, and his jadedness had dampened our enthusiasm a bit: had we really blown all that money—twenty dollars, which in those days meant twenty hours of babysitting—to have some unshaven jerk with a beer belly swill the precious liquid? But, clearly, the roadie had pulled through for us, for there was our champagne in Freddie Mercury's hand, and he was referring to Moët et Chandon in his pretty cabinet, the lyrics we had so cleverly quoted in the note we sent along with the bottle. We were sure we—among the many thousands—had managed to get through to the band.

If we had bothered to look around rather than feast our eyes on Brian and Freddie (I'm afraid John Deacon and Roger Taylor never got a look-in from me), we probably would have seen other clusters of fans also screaming and clutching one another during Freddie's toast. But we didn't look around or harbor doubts, or we ignored them. It was only much later that I allowed myself to consider the veritable champagne lake that must have existed backstage at every Queen concert. Tip to rock stars: want a free truckload of champagne wherever you go? Sing a song that mentions some—preferably name-checking a more expensive brand to ensure better quality—and watch it pour in backstage every night from adoring fans. There must have been a hundred bottles from fans back there, not counting the stash the band may well have brought with them in case Portland or Houston or Detroit weren't so generous. No wonder that roadie looked so bored—he'd probably been put on champagne duty that night.

Freddie's toast worked its magic, though, giving me the connection I needed to negotiate a place within the strangeness of the concertgoing experience itself: the weird, scary power of a crowd; the mixture of exhilaration and embarrassment at collective participation; the physical discomfort of standing for two hours when there's a perfectly comfortable seat behind you. It is one of those tricky, unresolved tensions at concerts: are we there to listen to the music or actively respond to it, participate as a group or answer our needs as individuals? It's an issue I've never entirely resolved—from Queen onwards I have spent concerts going in and out of myself, losing myself to the music and spectacle one minute, the next minute overly conscious of myself clapping or singing or screaming, or shuffling my aching feet and wondering why concerts have to be such an uncomfortable physical ordeal. As a teenager the conflict felt even more acute, as everything is during adolescence.

I was taken aback by the sound of Queen's music live: not just the volume, but the familiarity and yet also the strange rawness of the songs. Studio albums have all the mistakes airbrushed out, the layers added in, the balance between players carefully calibrated, like clever dialogue in a play without the awkward pauses and unfinished conversations you get in real life. Queen albums were highly produced, multilayered affairs. Live, the music was necessarily stripped of a lot of the choral mixing, more raucous, simpler, and much messier.

The band wisely didn't dare attempt to reproduce in its entirety the long, baroque confection that is "Bohemian Rhapsody." For the infamous operatic middle section, the band members left the stage as the studio recording played. Freddie and Brian then changed costume, and, at the word "Beelzebub," all four men popped out of a door in the stage floor and joined live again for the heavy metal section, fireworks going off, dry ice pouring out, everyone going berserk, me in tears of excitement. It was one of the best live moments I've ever witnessed. Indeed, I was spoiled by seeing Queen play live before anyone else; for sheer exuberant theatricality, no one else has come close.

The concert ended with an instrumental version of "God Save the Queen" and once more the flicking of the Bics, which, no longer the virgin concertgoer, I understood now as a gesture of tribute. My friends and I weren't finished, though. Emboldened by Freddie's toast, we decided to go to the stage entrance again and say hello. I still choke with embarrassment when I think of it. When we got there, a black limousine was pulling away, our heroes and their entourage inside, and we were left with the detritus: older, dolled up, hard-bitten groupies who had followed the band around and not made this night's cut. I stared at one, at her long, bleach-blonde hair, her miniskirt, her blue eye shadow liberally applied, her bright red lipstick. She glared at me briefly; then her face went slack as she dismissed the idea of me being any sort of competition. In fact, I had not really taken in that there was a competition, that the girls (and I?) were here to spread our wares and catch the attention of one of the men, and then . . . And then? I hadn't thought it through at all. I wouldn't have known what to do with such a man as Brian May if he even so much as looked at me. All I knew was that I was way, way out of my depth, that even if I had eluded the roadie minding the door, there was no way I was ever going to get past a woman like this.

The contrast between the sparkling theatricality of the concert and the gritty reality of the backstage, with its dirty concrete, anonymous faces, and unfulfilled dreams turned my stomach and almost ruined the night. I wished I hadn't seen it because it reminded me that the show was a fantasy, while it was my aching feet and the roadies' boredom and the groupies' hard desperation that constituted real life. As I stood watching the limo pull away and the unsexy women stand about, licking their wounds, looking for a ride to the next city and another chance, I felt as if a door had been kicked open a crack onto a world I knew nothing about: the seamy underbelly of the concertgoing experience, a mix of sex and power and exploitation, of cigarettes and poorly applied makeup and long, cold nights waiting to be noticed and defining yourself by someone else's attention. If that was grown-up life, I didn't want to know about it. I wanted the champagne toast but not the limo. Not yet.

18

Mink DeVille
The Paradise
Boston
Winter 1978
NICK FLYNN

WHAT FOLLOWS is a story I've told many times, and if it works it is because it ends with me in jail.

Sometimes I tell it as if I've never been set free, and then it works even better.

Some background: Legend has it that only a miniscule number of people bought the Velvet Underground's first album, but that each one of them went out and formed their own band—such was the reach of their influence, or so the story goes. I can think of no one who formed a band after buying Mink DeVille's first album. All traces of their influence, if there were any, are lost. Still, their eponymously named debut album, from 1977, is a masterpiece, but most people have never even heard of it, or only vaguely if they have.

The story: I saw Mink DeVille at a club in Boston when this album was still on display at the front of the record store in the mall, the mall a half an hour from my house. A worker there must have liked it, for it occupied that front rack for months, though it went unbought and unknown, at least in my hometown, except among my small gang of friends, and this in part was what attracted us to it. My friends and I were the only ones who knew how perfect it was, and each song ("She's So Tough," "Spanish Stroll," "Cadillac Walk," "Mixed Up, Shook Up Girl"—a handful more) was ours alone. Perhaps the appeal of the underdog was part of our devotion, for we were, or at least felt we were, misfits.

On the cover of that first album Willy DeVille's gaunt face stares out from an orange background in three-quarter profile, his cheekbones jutting like wings beneath his deer-in-the-headlight eyes, outsized eyes, junkie-gaunt, hair slicked back. *Mink DeVille* became the soundtrack to our last year of high school, and that same winter they played the Paradise in

Boston, which seemed the center of a certain smoky bleary universe, and which it was easy to drink in with my brother's ID. We drove the hour in from the suburbs, and in that hour we drank, and this drinking continued in the club, so much so that I knocked over some tables every time I stood up, and I stood up at the beginning of every song, so I knocked over many tables, upended many drinks. We had a table in the front, and midway through the set Willy DeVille gestured once to me, for a sip of my beer, and I handed it up to him, and he tilted it to his lips and passed it back.

Understand, we were kids stranded in the teenage wasteland of the suburbs before it was pharmacologically transformed into the daydream nation of the eighties, before traces of Prozac were reported in the drinking water, before we as a country decided to accept the unacceptable and watched as our children stepped over bodies sleeping on the streets on their way to school. Then Mink DeVille appeared, with their weird hybrid of punk dischord and soul, a harmonic wail from a doo-wop street corner. It's odd to imagine it was once considered punk in any way, so distant from the hardcore that would soon become my breakfast of champions. Willy DeVille didn't sing politics like the Clash, he was clearly an anachronism, the last stop of innocence as Reagan's limousine rolled down Pennsylvania Avenue into the White House for the first time. We still felt safe in our leftover sixties haze; we had an army amassed on the border that would easily defeat him—John Frikken Lennon. Bob Freakin Marley. Marvin Fucken Gaye. Yet Reagan rolled in, and one-by-one they died.

Of course, there were the reservists: Patti Smith, PiL, the (aforementioned) Clash. Yet one-by-one they simply left the room, decided to unplug. Maybe drugs were involved, probably cocaine up a mule's ass—the country was awash in drugs. When Patti walked away everyone noticed, but she never said she'd return, never said wait, she just stepped off a cliff, and we figured she'd risen up but it was just as likely she sank straight down. Or became a vapor. Or was reborn as Kurt Cobain. Or Michael Stipe. Or Cat Power. She transformed. A penny we passed and didn't pick up and blamed for our bad luck from that day on. It was all our fault. We had nothing to do with it.

After that, some stood before us onstage but were no longer there, not really. The last time I saw Johnny Rotten, in the mid-eighties, he was drunk, staggering around the stage dressed, appropriately, as a clown, following in Basquiat's floppy shoes, Basquiat who by the end had, tragically, exchanged his crown for black face. But where the hell did the Clash go?

Was it just a coincidence they all decided to pass on 1980s America? Others replaced them. But did any threaten to change the world?

Willy DeVille had never threatened to change the world, but on that first album he was at least awake. Like any great art, it is both transforming and eternal, contains both matter and anti-matter, being and non-being, self and non-self—it embodies duality. And listening, it was clear that all us sleepwalkers could also awaken. We didn't know he was already strapping himself into his duct-tape time machine, flying backwards into the land of nostalgia and string sections, into boogie-woogie and tin pan, so that when he disappeared he didn't exactly go, but he didn't exactly stay, either. Always both coming and going—that was part of his greatness. He seemed to suggest he'd be back in a minute, like when a concert ends and we stand applauding and yelping. But it went on for hours, then years, and the lights never came up, the doors never opened.

I said this would end with me in jail. Here I am. It is cold, and they have taken my belt and coat and socks and shoes and the cell has a metal bed and cinderblock walls and a broken window. Snow falls on me as I try to sleep. My other friends are in adjacent cells, but we can't see each other. We can talk, but we are still drunk, and what is said is not important. At some point in the night someone screams from another cell that he's fallen and cut his head. He is not one of us, wasn't in the car with us after the concert when we were pulled over and handcuffed and tossed in the back of separate cruisers. He screams for hours and hours it seems. The guards tell him to shut the fuck up. He screams that he's bleeding to death. We saw him carried in earlier and heard that he was on angel dust. After an hour of screaming he pries the toilet off his wall and smashes it against the bars, and water slowly begins to fill the cells. We don't have our shoes, remember, so if we step down our feet get wet. We all begin yelling, and the guards come, and they drag the screaming guy out and bring him back hours later, his head shaved and stitched up, wearing a straightjacket. In the morning, we are shackled together in a line and led into a van, which brings us to a court where we will stand before a judge and be given fines. I am shackled to the screaming guy, who is still in his straightjacket. When we are finally set free we have to ask what town we are in, and we have to ask where our car ended up and how to get to it.

19

Patti Smith

Winterland	Or . . . Boarding House
San Francisco	San Francisco
May 13, 1978	August 1979

JENNIFER EGAN

THERE WAS A LEADER, OF COURSE. I'll call her V: a scholarship student at our private high school. She'd moved to San Francisco recently from Alaska and lived with her mother in a small downtown apartment. V's mother was not like the mothers I'd grown up knowing: she was in her mid-thirties, divorced, worked full time.

One afternoon in the fall of our freshman year, I climbed with V to the roof of her apartment building and smoked my first joint in the cold punching mix of sun and fog that any San Franciscan knows in her bones. Then we went downstairs to V's apartment, where she slept on a mattress and box spring in the living room by a window overlooking the bay. We listened to Patti Smith. V and her mother had *Horses* and the new album, *Radio Ethiopia*. I had never heard anything like the crooning, menacing wildness of that voice. By the time I took the bus home, I felt like I'd crashed through a false bottom into *real life*. It was something I'd been debating: was reality the inside of my stepfather's Jaguar, where I sat with my little brother in the backseat during night rides home from downtown, Neil Diamond's "Hot August Night" playing on the tape deck? Or was it what I saw outside my window as we drove toward the Broadway Tunnel: hookers, strip clubs, addled sunburned hippies, spidery young people with chopped hair and ghostly skin who were clearly in extremis—orbed with a glow of duress even when they were laughing?

This was 1976.

At fourteen, I began a secret life. It tunneled underneath my old one, which looked the same to the untrained eye, but was revealed, now, to be the insubstantial thing I'd always guessed. The entry point was V's apartment, where I went for weekend sleepovers, thus avoiding (for a while) the suspicions of my mother and stepfather. But brownie baking and late-night

TV figured nowhere in these odysseys with V and L—another girl from our class who had joined us. I knew L from the girls' school where I'd gone until that year; she played the violin. She told outrageous lies with a straight face.

Our nights began with the taking of various drugs—pot, acid, mushrooms, quaaludes, all of which we bought on the street—followed by prolonged nocturnal wandering: to the fancy Nob Hill hotels near V's apartment, whose halls and gilded bathrooms we haunted, then down a fall of hills to Ghirardelli Square and Fisherman's Wharf, where we bought ice cream and spied on tourists. When it got to be two or three in the morning, we unearthed our cans of spray paint and left hurried, cryptic scrawls over sidewalks and buildings. It felt important to leave our mark on the city. Once in a while, driving with my mother in daylight, I would see something V and L and I had written, and my stomach would do a little flip.

There was a soundtrack to all this: Patti Smith. After school, the three of us lay side by side on the grayish white wall-to-wall carpeting in V's living room, and listened to Patti sing. We knew every note, every phrase; we sang along with her, and in the course of our school day, we muttered lines to each other:
"Boy was in the hallway drinking a glass of tea."
"From the other end of the hallway a rhythm was generating."
"Another boy was sliding up the hallway."
"He merged perfectly. With the hallway."
"He merged perfectly. With the mirror. In the hallway."
"The boy looked at Johnny. Johnny wanted to run but the movie kept moving as planned . . ."
And so on, until Johnny is raped by the second boy, who may or may not be Johnny's own reflection, and a throng of imaginary horses is unleashed. Patti heaved up these horses from somewhere in her chest. She panted them out. She was doing more than singing—she was showing us a way to be in the world: fragile but tough, beautiful and ugly, corrupt and innocent.

There was a cotton-mouthed sleepiness to Patti's voice, as if her passions had exhausted her. We understood this, virgins though we were. She was entranced, hypnotized—like us. We were her girls.

I stopped combing my hair after I'd washed it, let it tangle and frizz into a glorious ratty mane like Patti's. I wore my stepfather's old shirts loosely tucked, unbuttoned to my breastbone like Patti in the famous Mapplethorpe photo. Like V and L, I put pen to paper as I listened, stoned, to Patti sing, trying my best to capture the monumental swerving of my brain. V and L were better at this. They expected to be famous and believed it of each other. L would be an artist, V a writer. But really, they would be rock stars, like Patti. I made no such claims, and no one made them for me.

I've written about this time in my life again and again. I can't seem to leave it alone. Part of the attraction is a sense that I remember it all perfectly—like it's still there, a long swoony continuum, waiting for me to step back in. But when I push against the memories, they disintegrate. How many sleepovers was I allowed to have at V's house before her phone was turned off for nonpayment and my mother and stepfather stopped letting me go? It could have been as few as three. What I'm left with are fragments of perception, of sensation: the fluorescent glare inside the Stockton Tunnel, where men howled at us from their cars; the seafood stink of Chinatown's sticky streets (where we often walked barefoot); V's waist-length hair and tanned, double-jointed fingers. I loved her so much.

And Patti Smith. For a long time I couldn't listen to her music. And when I finally did again, recently, for the first time in more than twenty years, the words were still in my head along with every pause, every breath. As if I were the one who had sung them.

None of it came naturally to me. I was the quavery one, afraid to take the first hits of LSD we bought from a sniffling guy who walked us from Union Square to a nearby alley before handing them over. But after we'd cut the small yellow pills with a knife, I swallowed my share, then spent hours sobbing out the phrase, "I don't think she knows." I must have been talking about my mother. At night on lower Broadway, I turned my head away from passing cars as V and L and I moved among the barkers outside strip joints. I was afraid someone from my old life would recognize me. I felt as if my "good" self was gone forever—as if she'd died, but no one had noticed yet. A mourning ache suffused my adventures with V and L, despite the fact that I'd killed her off myself—the dutiful girl I'd always been—at my first opportunity. My qualms made the other two impatient, and at times V and L assumed the roles of fed-up parents to my stubborn, fainthearted child. We were all still children, of course, but this was lost on us. We reacted with cool nonchalance to old men masturbating in corners, although none of us had ever kissed a boy.

After the school year ended, I exchanged feverish letters with V from Chicago, where I'd gone for my annual visit to my father and his new family. I spent my days volunteering at the day camp where my young half-siblings went, wondering if a letter from V would be waiting for me when I got back to my father's apartment. She wrote to me on construction paper and enclosed shells and leaves and feathers. She'd lost her virginity to a man her mother brought home. She and L had briefly become lovers. I read with awe, with envy. Over the strong objections of my mother and stepfather, I made plans to transfer into public school that fall. This was an act of great determination on my part, but its source is mysterious to me now—and maybe was then, too. Somehow, I knew I had to get out. It was my first clear break with the world that had made me.

I still saw V and L after that, but not to smoke pot in Alta Plaza Park during free periods. Now we met mostly on weekends, when we'd take the ferry to Angel Island and sunbathe on the rocks. V and her mother moved to a new apartment with an outdoor deck, where they raised a crop of sinsemilla. Inside, they grew opium poppies under fluorescent lights. V read voraciously; she planned to compress her four years of high school into three. She planned to become a chemist and invent new psychedelic drugs. She planned to study in England. She had a boyfriend, a hippie she'd met on a visit to a commune with her mother. He seemed like an old man to me, which is to say that he was an adult, with a bushy beard and thick yellow toenails. I watched him sit with V on her bed, one of her double-jointed fingers stroking his leg through his jeans. I couldn't stop looking at her hand, wondering how it was possible to touch a person that way.

All this time, Patti Smith continued her ascent. People were starting to know about her. Her third album, *Easter*, contained an actual hit, "Because the Night," which she'd co-written with Bruce Springsteen. Now we heard Patti on the radio and in stores and occasionally even in the Jaguar with my parents. In some mystical way, her rising popularity seemed to bode well for us, her girls, as if she could take us with her, lift us out of our lives into something better. And when it was announced that she would come to San Francisco in concert in the summer of 1978, we arranged to go together.

I don't remember the name of the venue, but I think it was south of Market Street, which in the late seventies was still somewhat desolate.

I don't remember if she sang "Land," our favorite song, with its stampede of imaginary horses. I want to think she didn't—it seems impossible that I could have forgotten that.

Here's what I do remember:

We were close, almost directly in front of Patti, all three of us wearing hooded sweatshirts. We held hands and looked up.

My gut disappointment at realizing that Patti didn't recognize us or even see us—that our years of devotion were lost on her.

The miracle of her sheer proximity—seeing her alive, breathing, flicking sweat from her tangled hair—which finally washed away that initial disappointment.

Patti wrapping herself in an American Flag.

Becoming separated from V and L as the concert went on. At one point I noticed L holding a man from behind as she danced, her arms around his waist.

My thirst. It was something I barely noticed at first in the sweaty hall, but gradually it overpowered me, until my need for cold water crowded out everything else, even Patti Smith onstage, and made me wish for the concert to end. Would this be the last song? Would this? I prayed so. I fantasized about the feel of water in my mouth—one glass would change everything. That's my strongest memory of my night with Patti Smith: how thirsty I was. I can't remember ever having been thirstier in my life.

L left with the man I'd seen her dancing with. The next day, she would come to my house, trembling, and tell me she'd been gang raped. True or not? I wasn't sure. Within another year, I would watch her shoot heroin with a room full of punk rockers she'd moved in with, all of them sharing a needle, then nod off against my shoulder for an hour. Sometime later she would tell me, in a tone more boasting than confessional, that she'd robbed my house. I remembered the break-in, of course; it had happened when we were on vacation. I'd lost the few pieces of jewelry my father had given me over the years, the most precious being a necklace with my grandmother's engagement diamond in it. L said she'd talked our cleaning woman (who knew her, of course) into letting her into our house while we were away, and sold my jewelry for drugs. True or not? I still don't know.

V and I left the concert together. In my memory, fog is spinning in the cloud of fluorescent light outside the late-night corner market where we sprint to buy a gallon of orange juice. V is as thirsty as I am, it turns out. We pass the carton back and forth, gulping the cold sweet juice until it runs from our chins and soaks our sweatshirts. We drink the whole thing, panting and gasping.

V will graduate from high school a year early, as planned. For her thesis, she'll write a book on Willa Cather, copying two hundred pages by hand in a series of drafts. She and her mother will move back to Alaska, where V will get straight A's through two years of college, six courses a semester, and then drop out. She'll become addicted to cocaine and finally get clean. In our late twenties, we'll lose track of each other.

But I don't want us to go our separate ways yet. I want to stand outside the corner market a while longer with V, surrounded by fog, the two of us holding our empty orange juice carton and talking about how it felt to see Patti Smith right there in front of us, how beautiful she looked, how small, how strong she is and how we want to be like that, too, strong and fierce, how we want to do big things in our lives, like Patti. How we can feel it— the rest of our lives—coming up underneath us like a huge, unknowable shape. But I'm making this up—I don't remember what we said. I don't remember if I drove V home in my mother's boxy blue Fiat, or if we both took the bus. I don't remember if I could drive yet, which is another way of saying I don't *really* know whether this concert happened in 1978, when *Easter* came out, or the next year, to promote *Wave*, the last album Patti Smith released before her long hiatus. I should know these things—I should remember everything—but I don't. When I push against the feeling of standing there with V, the moment blows away like the fog that may or may not have been out that night.

20

Bruce Springsteen
Madison Square Garden
New York City
August 1978
DANI SHAPIRO

I WAS SIXTEEN when I first saw Bruce Springsteen play Madison Square Garden, and that night is up there on my small list of accessible memories between birth and leaving home. If you were a Jersey girl growing up in the 1970s, you had a certain soundtrack to your life, a soundtrack that made the endless gray turnpike unfurl like a magic carpet, made the thick, throat-closing smoke from oil refineries along Routes 1 and 9 somehow heady and romantic. *Bruce.* On the soundtrack to my teenage years in New Jersey, in the music blaring from the tape deck of my high school boyfriend Chip McGraw's VW Bug, I was Mary. I was Rosalita. I was every Springsteen heroine whose dress brushed against her bare legs in the summer breeze.

> *'Cause down the shore everything's all right*
> *You and your baby on a Saturday night*
> *Nothing matters in the whole wide world*
> *When you're in love with a Jersey girl*

But I wasn't that kind of Jersey girl—not the kind Bruce sang about. I grew up in a leafy suburb in northern New Jersey—a neighborhood that could easily have been in Westchester or Connecticut, but wasn't. It was halfway between Newark and Elizabeth; the most exciting thing that happened in our part of the state during my childhood was the construction of Newark Airport. It would be an understatement to say that I had no pride of place. I think I can speak for most of us—children of Hillside, New Jersey, in the 1970s—when I say that all any of us wanted was to get the hell out.

Bruce!!!! In the halls of our prep school, inside the cars we drove around in aimless loops, we would scream his name at the top of our lungs.

Bruce!!! It was a wail, a plea, a battle cry. *Save us from our pathetic, powerless teenage existence! Make us proud to be from this fucked-up, boring place!*

Bruce single-handedly made it cool to be a girl from New Jersey—if *cool* and *New Jersey* could even be joined together in the same sentence. Bruce made me morph—at least in my own mind—from a confused, sweet-faced blonde girl with chubby thighs and a tendency to blush at the slightest provocation, a girl who lived in a red brick Colonial with a sprinkler system and wore pom-poms on the backs of her tennis socks into an angular, sinewy, don't-fuck-with-me femme fatale who knew exactly who she was and what she was doing.

I owed a debt to Bruce—I knew it even then. Even without the particulars of my own childhood, to grow up in New Jersey was to develop, over time, a constant, nagging sense of inferiority.

Kiss her where it smells: take her to New Jersey.

Why are New Yorkers depressed? Because the light at the end of the tunnel is New Jersey.

But Bruce paid the jokes no mind. He had taken his corner of the world—the crumbling boulevards of Asbury Park, the sticky summer nights, the bored, the disenfranchised, the kids gunning their engines with nothing better to do—and turned it all into something magnificent.

Our parents (well, at least my Jewish, book-loving parents) had Philip Roth as their poet of New Jersey. We had Springsteen. His Jersey was our Jersey. When he sang about unwed mothers and thundering cars—

> *You can hide 'neath your covers*
> *And study your pain*
> *Make crosses from your lovers*
> *Throw roses in the rain*
> *Waste your summer praying in vain*
> *For a savior to rise from these streets*

—he was singing about us. No matter that our streets were treelined cul-de-sacs with names like Surrey Road and Nottingham Way. No matter that our summers were spent on the diving boards and tennis courts of North Jersey country clubs. Even though we had never set foot in Asbury Park, even though we were overprivileged preppies who had never known a moment of financial worry—Bruce was talking straight to us. We were sure of it.

Okay, so—the concert. I remember the escalators going up, up, up. The thousands of kids streaming in from Penn Station—boys with shaggy hair wearing polo shirts, girls with grosgrain ribbon belts tied around the waists of their jeans. The smell of spilled, watered-down beer, even in the stairwells. Our seats—purchased at Sam Goody in the Livingston Mall—were so high up that the stage itself appeared to be floating in the middle of a sea of thousands of tiny people. Of course we pretended—even to each other—to be cool and unfazed. We had our Bic lighters, our packs of Marlboros, a few pre-rolled joints tucked between the cigarettes. We were tough, regular citizens; we had been around the block a few times. *The screen door slams/Mary's dress waves*. I leaned into Chip's hard shoulder and listened to the crowd roar as Bruce strutted on stage.

Waving hands reached up for him. The flames from Bic lighters all over the Garden like so many fireflies in the darkness. And while it's true that I was stoned out of my mind, the buzzy, numb feeling I remember—the feeling that life was going on all around me but I couldn't quite join in—had nothing to do with being stoned. I was a lost girl-child pretending to be a woman, a blurry, unformed kid who wanted to be a dark, mysterious creature with a sullen mouth and gleaming shoulders. A girl who had songs written about her. A girl who knew who she was.

A few years later. I had fled New Jersey and hadn't once looked back. Chip McGraw and I were no longer an item. I had gone to college in Westchester, and was living—finally!—in *the city*, and was in a brief, lunatic phase of thinking that I might become an actress. The pom-poms were gone, and my thighs were no longer chubby.

I got a call from my agent one day about an audition.

"It's for Springsteen's new music video," my agent said. "They liked your headshot."

Bruce!!! I hadn't thought about him in years. I had renounced him, along with everything about my New Jersey childhood, shedding it all like a second skin. *Bruce!!!* It all came roaring back. Had he looked at my headshot himself? Was I the right kind of Jersey girl after all?

"Three o'clock tomorrow," my agent said. "At One Fifth Avenue."

"One Fifth?" It wasn't the address of an ad agency or casting director's office—the usual places for auditions.

"Brian De Palma's apartment," said my agent. "He's directing the video."

I always got nervous when I was auditioning. I hated people looking at me—not a very promising trait in an actress. But this was worse than usual. I don't think I slept all night. I mean, this wasn't an audition for Hostess Twinkies. This was *Bruce*.

In the foyer of Brian De Palma's apartment, there were just two of us waiting. Me and a pretty girl about my age with close-cropped, dark hair and bright blue eyes. There was no script for this audition, and my agent hadn't known what they were going to ask us to do.

"There are no sides?" I asked the girl.

She shook her head.

The casting director poked his head out of a large room where, through the cracked-open door, I could see a half-dozen people and a video camera set up on a tripod.

"Courtney?" The casting director called. "Courtney Cox?"

She rose from her seat with a wide, easy smile, and disappeared behind the studio door. She was in there for what seemed a really long time. It may have been fifteen minutes, or twenty—much longer than a usual audition. I sat there with nothing to do—no sides to study—getting more and more terrified. My palms were damp. My heart jumping around in my chest. I wanted to bolt, but fleeing wasn't an option. I had to go in there and grab hold of a piece of my past. I had to own it—to make it mine. I tried to do a sense memory exercise: Chip McGraw's VW Bug, feet up on the dashboard, eyes closed, radio blaring.

Finally the studio door opened, and Courtney came bouncing out. Her cheeks were flushed.

"They ask you to *dance*," she whispered.

Fuck.

"Dani?" The casting director emerged once more. "Come on in."

I felt everything inside me stiffen as I walked into the studio. I scanned the room, the people folded languidly into comfortable chairs. A couple of older women. A bearded, heavyset guy I took to be De Palma. A younger guy with glasses.

"Okay, so the idea of this is that you're a girl at a concert—maybe a girl from Jersey—"

"I *am* from New Jersey," I managed to say.

A nanosecond of a pause.

"Cool. So anyway—you're in the front row of this concert, and you're dancing. That's all there is to it."

All there is to it. I took a deep breath. Tried to summon Madison Square Garden, 1978. Stood there under the bright lights, waiting . . . waiting . . . still waiting.

"Any time you're ready," a voice said from the darkness.

"Isn't there music?"

"Not today."

Even *with* music, I wasn't the world's best dancer. I closed my eyes for a second—preparing. And then I started to move, but I knew how awkward and tense I must have looked.

"All right, that's fine—" one of the voices said, putting me out of my misery. "Now Springsteen has just chosen you out of all the girls to come up on stage and dance with him. Show us how you feel about that."

I smiled painfully, mimicked excitement—it's hard to even write these words—reached up my hands and pretended to be helped on stage. I shook my hips from side to side, waved my hands in the air.

"Thanks, Dani," the casting director said. "I think we've got what we need."

I was in and out of there in less than three minutes. Courtney emerged from the bathroom just as I was collecting my things.

"How'd it go?" she asked. I detected a hint of a southern accent.

"I totally blew it."

"Oh, I'm sure you were great."

We took the elevator downstairs together, then walked out onto the street. She—the future television star, small and adorable, tomboyish in her denim jacket. She—a kid from Alabama who would be cast as the Jersey girl plucked from the audience in Springsteen's "Dancing in the Dark" video. And me—the future non-actress, the future novelist. The summer sun beat down on our heads as we walked and talked. I knew one thing for sure—and I remember knowing it: I had auditioned for the part of a Jersey girl—just as I had been auditioning for the part of a Jersey girl all of my high school years—and I hadn't been remotely what they were looking for.

21

Billy Joel
Madison Square Garden
New York City
December 14, 1978
ELIZABETH CRANE

FOR THISBE!

December 1978. I am seventeen. My mother is an opera singer and my father is a professor of musicology. They dig all things classical. In spite of this, I listen to WABC-AM on my red plastic Toot-a-Loop (*it's an S, it's an O, it's a crazy radio*) beginning around fifth grade, and establish my strictly pop-leaning musical tastes right away.

The Captain and Tennille is one of my first records, if not the first. Diana Ross and the Pointer Sisters are the first two 45s I ever buy with my own money, and my collection will later include "Seasons in the Sun" by Terry Jacks and "Afternoon Delight" by whoever the hell that was by. Elton John precedes Billy Joel sometime during seventh grade, and I suffer great pain because some of the other kids in my class get to go to his show at Madison Square Garden, while I am declared too young by those heartless, single-minded classical people I bunk with. My longstanding love for piano undeterred, it naturally follows that when *Streetlife Serenade* and *Turnstiles* fall into my hands, I fall into love.

Witness this testimony, from my diary of February 20, 1978: "I love him and think I'll die if I miss his concert . . . dammit he's married + 28 years old. Oh, well." What the, "Oh, well," refers to here, the twenty-eight or the married or possibly me not caring about either, or the likelihood that I'll actually meet him, eludes me now (although I suspect it isn't the latter because meeting future celebrity husbands has never seemed unimaginable to me). Fortunately, I do not have to find out if I would, in fact, have fallen dead of this Billy Joel–concert-missing, because at the decrepit age of seventeen, my best friend Nina and I, along with her boyfriend Gary, score tickets to an upcoming show of his *52nd Street* tour at the Garden. I am beside myself.

Nina and I convene prior to the concert to coordinate our outfits, which, naturally, involve ties. (At this time, Nina takes an inexplicable joy in us dressing like twins, a joy I do not share, but which for this one special occasion I decide to tolerate.) Gary's best friend Stephen joins us. Nina and I are seniors at Columbia Prep; Gary and Stephen go to another private school nearby.

The promise of many firsts resulting from this single evening are almost unprecedented. I have never had a boyfriend. I have never been kissed. I have never had a date if you don't count the unfortunate blind date with Nina's then-boyfriend's best friend in Canarsie in tenth grade, which I never did, because neither would you and let's just leave it at that. I have never had a cocktail—if you don't include the Irish coffee I ordered one time thinking it would be like a cappuccino. I have never been to a rock concert, and I am practicing my signature as Mrs. William Martin Joel even though I also really, really like this other guy who goes to Stephen's school, Christian Parker, who, not coincidentally, sings and plays piano. Stephen is, I suspect, only in attendance because he thinks I'm cute. We'd met when a bunch of us had been to the Paramount to see that Anthony Hopkins movie where he plays a scary ventriloquist, and I am not averse to Stephen's presence. He and Gary are both really funny and smart and Nina and I have had lifelong plans to meet and marry best friends. So this will work out.

We start with pizza across the street before the show. Nina observes in her own diary, "The atmosphere outside is strange—drugs!" For two self-proclaimed sophisticated city girls, we are alarmingly, you know, not. Case in point, I cannot be distracted from my primary purpose this evening: to sing along with every last word to every single song as loud as I possibly can, which isn't something I generally like to do in front of people I don't know very well, but in this case, I will let nothing, not even hope of a boyfriend, stand in my way. We find our seats, on the absolute farthest end of the Garden from the stage, if not at the highest tier. I crack a joke about us being "half a mile away." Joke is well-received and seeds are planted for possible first boyfriend.

Stephen and Gary are both vocal about their preference for Springsteen, which I do not much appreciate. I am a year away from having any appreciation at all for Springsteen, as I am still in some respects my parents' child and am not yet able to understand that his raspy voice is, well, anything anyone would ever want to submit themselves to. I am strictly about melody at this point (about a year away from understanding that Bruce's melodies are in any way equal), and although it's arguable that Billy's voice isn't technically more beautiful, all I can say is I'm feeling it.

In fact, I have the sense that I'm the female counterpart to Billy Joel, vocally. No, seriously. I copy all his inflections when I sing along, occasionally harmonizing, and as I do, I feel that, musically, we're one. That should the time come, as I expect it will, when he wants to record a duet, I will be the only possible choice, and he will know of my existence simply by feeling this symbiosis psychically, feeling the inexorable pull of my female Billy Joelness and finding himself suddenly in front of my apartment building on West End Avenue, where my mom answers the door and, praise God, remembers that his name isn't actually "Billy Joe," inviting him to sit at our piano where he busts out a melody featuring minor keys and I lay some sweet rhymes on top of it, generating what will become the best-selling duet ever, of all time, and we win all kinds of Grammys and then, after he gets divorced from his first wife, but before he marries his second and I'm of legal drinking age, we begin a famous affair that ends when I leave him for my new boyfriend, Robert Downey Jr. (In reality, my stepfather will meet Mr. Joel at a restaurant sometime during the Christie Brinkley years. Billy overhears him singing some aria and strikes up a conversation, which results in an autograph I keep in a frame for a good, long time. When I ask my stepdad if he thinks I might have a future with Billy, his reply is something like, "Not likely.")

At the time, Billy's sendoff catchphrase is, "Don't take any shit from anybody." This is profound to me, at seventeen. I think about using it for my senior quote. I'm not sure what kind of shit I think I've been taking in my cushy, Manhattan prep school existence, but it resonates just the same. Maybe I'm thinking preventatively, maybe I just think anything Billy Joel says is deep. Instead, I choose this quote from "Honesty": "If you look for truthfulness, you might just as well be blind/It always seems to be so hard to give." A self-described Very, Very Late Bloomer, I always sang the line, "Hardly anyone has seen how good I am!"—from "Rosalinda's Eyes"—just a little bit louder than the rest, and this might've been a more appropriate choice. "It's either sadness or euphoria," from "Summer, Highland Falls" still kind of kills me, even though I hover way closer to the euphoric end of the curve these days. Billy proves our psychic connection by playing these and most of my favorite songs, including "Vienna," "Scenes from an Italian Restaurant," and the apocalyptic "Miami 2017" in which the Yankees are spared from the total destruction of New York and which elicits that kind of loud cheer that spreads through the audience whenever the name of the place where you live comes up.

After the show, I write down what I can remember of Billy's set list for the night, and Nina and I discuss plans for how Stephen is going to be my boyfriend. She will ask Gary who will ask Stephen, which in reality morphs into something slightly more complex, along the lines of Nina asks Gary who asks Stephen who asks Gary to ask Nina if I'm sure who asks me if I'm sure and then it goes around a few more times before Stephen finally calls me and we date for a while until I'm sure he really, really likes me, at which time I decide to break up with him on our two-month anniversary without much of a reason besides I don't want a boyfriend, calling the "Honesty" quote into question; if I can't have Billy Joel, I want Christian Parker, although our love never amounts to anything either, foiled as it is by a certain other girl Nina and I make the mistake of introducing him to. Making matters worse, I do this after Stephen's gone and scored me a copy of *Cold Spring Harbor*, Billy's first album, which was famously recorded at the wrong speed (which don't make no nevermind to me; I play and love it anyway). I might like to add that for a decade or two, as I remain single, and notably, always the breakupee and never again the breaker upper, I am convinced that the gods are punishing me because the first one they sent me was such a great guy and I passed him up.

Less than a year after Billy at the Garden, I pile into a rented car with nine other people from my dorm to see him at the Capital Centre in Washington, DC, and less than a year after that, Nina sets me up on another blind date with a friend of her then-boyfriend, who has connections at the Garden, and these connections bring extra chairs out just for us to see Billy in the eighth row, which makes us feel extremely special at the Billy Joel concert and where we can actually *see him* see him, and the boys pay for dinner, which is another first for me.

I spend a good portion of my college years pining for a very cute, green-eyed stoner from Hicksville. At our local bar, he flirts with me by serenading my virginal self when the DJ plays, "Only the Good Die Young": "Virginia don't let me wait/You Catholic girls start much too late." Nevermind that I'm not Catholic. Eventually, I stop making him wait, and swipe his tattered Hicksville sweatshirt, which is as close to the real Billy as I ever get.

Subsequently, I attend two or three more Billy Joel concerts, each tied into some romance or another, each with its own potency in my memory banks, except for the one that may or may not have happened. I've kept a journal index for decades now, with loose notes about which books hold details of which events, and one listing for 1990 reads, "Billy Joel with Greg," about which I have no memory and which I cannot find in said diary. Greg, when contacted, also has no memory, although as he thinks about it he says, "Well, maybe we did. I can sort of picture it," which I suggest may be like when people suddenly remember their abusive childhoods.

It should be no surprise that although I am now married, my new boyfriend, Ben Folds, has kindly stepped in now that Billy's gone to the classical side, and I've already seen him twice in the same year. Some things never change.

22

X/Levi & the Rockats
The Whisky
Los Angeles
1979
ARION BERGER

IN 1969, MY PARENTS snagged the top floor of a duplex at the corner of Fairfax and Melrose Avenues—what was to become punk rock's ground zero in Los Angeles. West Hollywood was accommodating to children in the seventies: Laurel Elementary was only four blocks away; the neighborhood was riotous with kids, some with parents burning off their post-hippie years, many, it strikes me now, being raised by defeated-looking widowers or bitter divorcees; almost all Jewish children. It is, or was, an old Jewish neighborhood, populated on the southern side by old Jews, on the northern by first-generation refugees with children my age. My friends were Yaffa and Esther and Riva and Siggy, and there was a mezzuza on our door, which we vague lower-middle-class bohemians of no particular faith never bothered to take down. I used to wonder whether I should be taking classes in Old People's Language or would I just naturally start speaking it when I got old? My mother had to explain to me what Yiddish was and why so many elderly women on the buses in pantyhose that sagged around the ankles had tattoos.

Here is a story that sounds apocryphal but is true, like Willy Wonka's square candies that look round: I was terrified of rock 'n' roll. It wasn't my parents' doing—they played sixties folk (Dylan, the Weavers, the Mamas & the Papas), ancient folk (Theodore Bikel and Burl Ives and Bikel and Cynthia Gooding's *A Young Man and a Maid*, with the sexy LP cover I used to stare at), classical music (Holst's *Planets* and *Pictures at an Exhibition* and *Peter and the Wolf* and the Brandenburg concertos), and weird permutations of all of those (the Swingle Singers, Switched-On Bach). It wasn't the music that was scary, but the images. I lied to my best friend and said I liked Led Zeppelin, even though the thought of all that hair and pants gave me the horrors. I had a particular fascinated fear of one album cover. It was simple and white, with a drawing of a crazed-looking man with wild hair, daunt-ing eyes, and an expression of great seriousness. His face signaled all the dangers of rock—the complete interiority of the musician's existence, the subtle contempt of the audience, the audacity of artistic expression. And that hair! Well, you've seen that drawing of Beethoven, so you know.

I first learned about "punks" through an article in, I think, *Newsweek*. That's just what they are, I thought, gaping disgustedly at thumbnails of Johnny Rotten and Malcolm McLaren. Foul, stump-toothed, ill-kempt, will-ful punks.

Then I bought a Plastic Bertram record, and boy, did it suck.

But I am susceptible to style, and the fashions were kind of cute. The neighborhood burst into bloom around 1978, and it seemed as if West Hollywood was growing up alongside me. Our local movie theater showed only kids' films, which seemed perfectly normal at eight years old. The Santa Monica end of the area began to get very gay just when I was ready to learn a little bit about the world. And then came Let It Rock and Vinyl Fetish and Rene's Records. Poseur, down on Sunset, was the hardest core of punk shop hangouts; I remember frantically calling Pony, the sales clerk, from ballet school and asking him to set aside that last pair of leather pants with a twenty-eight-inch waist for me. Little delis like Izzy's that would give you credit got pushed out for fancy thrift stores and punkabilly shops and places that sold weird Japanese monster toys and metal pins. Never mind the music; I just wanted the clothes.

Fortunately, there was melody to be found in a few corners of the punk world. I liked the first single I ever bought: the Talking Heads' "Take Me to the River," which I didn't know was a cover. And the rockabilly revival, which had all the propulsion of punk and, like, real songs. I was happy to have my mom drive me and some friends out to the Palomino in the Valley to see Ray Campi and his Rockabilly Rebels. An appreciation for vintage made me feel like a very sophisticated fourteen-year-old.

Odds are, any teenager frightened by Beethoven won't be the type to sneak out of the house to go to a club, but that's just what I did. Sort of. Levi & the Rockats were playing at the Whisky, which was all ages, and my parents were out of town. It still felt like sneaking out, though, as I shrugged on a rayon dress from the forties and tried to apply eyeliner like Sue Catwoman wore in all those pictures in a punk photo book called *White Trash*, which I perused greedily—and cheaply, as I never did buy it—every time we were in a bookstore in Westwood Village. I was already in love with the band's heartbreakingly beautiful stand-up bassist, Smutty Smiff, with his night-black hair and fierce tattoos, but the whole band, as *Creem* magazine had proven in a delectable picture spread, was gorgeous. Plus, I had never been to a club before, never heard a band live, never worn my Catwoman eyes in public. It had to be a better experience than my other errant acts of naughtiness like gorging on Three Musketeers bars and listening to Cheap Trick on the headphones.

I realize now how many of my concertgoing habits and attitudes were cemented at that show. We stood right up front, smack in front of Smutty by the eardrum-bursting stage-left speaker. I listened for every song I knew and counted the ones in between, figuring they couldn't play more than a dozen. I am an extremely impatient audience and virtually unable to take in anything I haven't heard before. I dreamed smutty Smutty dreams, and it's still true that everyone is cuter onstage. I wondered if dancing were allowed and if it wouldn't be cool. (So, no dancing, then.) I stuck around for the headlining act because you never know.

X came to my attention the way many punk bands did, through the mainstream media. The *Los Angeles Times* was an early adopter of punk and had many fine writers, some musicians themselves, explicating the local scene for besotted underage readers and shocked older ones. There wasn't anyone cute enough for fourteen-year-old me in the band, and the female singer, Exene, looked as if she had been hit in the face with a shovel. I kind of admired her decision to play to her strengths rather than pretty up, but what they were doing in the image-first arena of rock at all seemed mysterious and subtle.

Well, X came on stage and played "Johnny Hit and Run Paulene," and I felt like I'd been the one hit with the shovel. Nothing had ever come at me that fast. Whatever this was, it wasn't about getting laid. (After all, Exene and John Doe were married, which seemed awfully . . . efficient for punk rockers.) It was about intelligence—those three-minute barn burners of unnatural structural elegance—and the man-woman thing, and taking a poetic hand to the observations of a keen journalistic eye, and it was mostly about my city.

Very few directors, musicians, or novelists get L.A. right. Even if what they report is *a* truth—the grunge, the glamour, the sunsets, the cars, the filth, the isolation, the light—it isn't *the* truth. X burrowed below the city's symptoms and into its causes. To call them the quintessential L.A. band is a compliment, although it wasn't then. Punk had two respectable bastions in the late seventies: London and New York, and X cared for neither of them. They played as if country music had never happened, and they were inventing honky-tonk, with its troubles and hard times and vicious impulses and loneliness and raucous youth, out of their specific experience because it was the only honest way to talk about life in Los Angeles.

And just because the upside down glamour of punk cherished ugliness didn't mean the music couldn't be beautiful, even as it peppered you with buckshot. The slight atonality of the harmonies, if anything, tightened the bond between John Doe and Exene, made them work harder to find each other, put some grit and friction in their partnership. For the first time, I saw a form of rock 'n' roll that wasn't about sex or style; it was about making art out of garbage, literature out of impulse, entertainment out of rage, beauty out of truth. It was about being a grown-up. And if you don't think there's any sex or style in that, you still have some living to do.

I have never since felt that a show ended too early; I would have stood next to that pounding speaker forever if X had kept playing. In the eighties, I saw the Ramones every time they dragged their aging asses to the Palace on their annual pay-the-rent tour, and it was fine. It was fun. I swanned around the balcony chatting with rock critics—having become one myself—and not paying attention to the legends onstage. Being underage when punk broke, I had missed seeing most of my idols and was playing catch-up as they waned, if they were even still together. But I never saw X again.

After that show, the Rockats and their friends repaired to a room above the club. We sat on the bus bench across from the Whisky and watched the girls make silhouettes against the light. My friends sighed over the impossibility of reaching that room, having watched Brian Setzer accompany a pretty blonde in a poodle skirt up the stairs. But the groupies looked like bimbos at a costume party to me. I had wanted to be Gene Vincent or Eddie Cochran, not some frilly girlfriend. Now, I could be Exene. I started to think of a cool punk name to start calling myself, but it seemed all the good ones were taken.

23

The Funk Festival
Los Angeles Coliseum
Los Angeles
May 26, 1979
SUSAN STRAIGHT

EVEN THOUGH IT TOOK place outside on a late May afternoon in the hot sun in 1979, with about sixty-five thousand people dancing in their seats, in the aisles, and on the grassy field of the Los Angeles Coliseum, the Funk Festival was a big old house party where we danced until we sweated, we checked each other out and looked for some love and then fought and scared each other until it was time to go home.

That was how house parties and backyard dances and even our funky dances in the high school gym were back then. Getting a woman, or getting next to the woman you were with, was usually what the men I knew cared about. Everyone was hunting or holding. "Is that *you*, man?" guys would say to each other, nodding toward the woman in question. If it was, they'd evaluate, and if it wasn't, they might move in. Even when we found a club, someone always acted a fool, and we always had to go home. But we went home rubber-limbed from dancing to Parliament Funkadelic, the backs of our necks velvet with sweat that had dried and beaded and then dried again. Our collars were still damp, and the arches of my feet always tingled from doing the Freak and the Worm and even the old Body Language.

Back then, in the late seventies, we were all about the funk. Where did the word come from? I'd heard it all my life, in my hardscrabble neighborhood in Riverside, in my junior high and high school, which were heavily black and Chicano, and from my boyfriend's family. "Man, your room is funky, fool. You better clean that funkhole up." "Y'all built up some funk at practice today. You better hit them showers." "That is one funky-ass brotha, man, and still thinks he can talk enough yang to get a woman."

The Funk Festival posters had been up around the USC campus and all over Los Angeles, on telephone poles and walls and fences, for a while. I was a college freshman, eighteen years old, and even though it was ten to twenty dollars a ticket, we were going to go.

On my dorm floor, I had been blasting Parliament Funkadelic since my arrival in September, scaring the girls from private schools, and causing a lot of stares with my posters of Chaka Khan and Kool & the Gang. There was nothing the private school girls could do but glare, because they were terrified of my friends, with whom I played the card game called Tonk or danced the Freak in the hallways. Huge, dark-skinned USC linebackers, the girls down the hall from Detroit and Chicago, or my broke, far-away boyfriend, a six-feet-four-inch power forward who played at a college in central California but came to visit when we could scrape up Greyhound money.

The boyfriend couldn't come for the Funk Festival, though, so my girl-friend from across the hall, the only one who understood Parliament Funkadelic—though she was a white girl from Bakersfield—went with me. (She is godmother to my three daughters now, and still understands the funk.)

Since I figured Susan and I would possibly be the only white girls in the entire Coliseum, we didn't want to look any more wrong than possible. I wore a halter dress, and she bought what was really cool, what our friends from Detroit and Chicago were wearing: cowboy style. Danskin bodysuit, tight-as-paint Sergio Valente or Gloria Vanderbilt jeans, and a white straw hat with feathers slanting from the hatband. As we streamed across Exposition Boulevard with hundreds of people, plenty of USC football players and others with us, white straw hats bobbed amid the huge naturals, nascent cornrows, and blown-back wings of straightened hair.

I had crossed Exposition and walked this way for football games, when the stadium parking lot was filled with wealthy white alumni having tail-gate parties, wearing Lacoste shirts and Top-Siders. This foreign world made me feel like I was in France or England on some football Saturdays. Game days were a sea of cardinal and gold, with Traveller, the white mascot horse, and his Trojan rider prowling the track.

Now, when we found seats in the closest third of the stadium to the stage, I looked out to see the bowl filling with naturals the size of tumble-weeds, mirror sunglasses like George Clinton wore, and cowboy hats bobbing. The never-ending fashion show began as people walked the track to check each other out. Guys were funky fly, with silky shirts unbuttoned to the navel. Older men wore gangster hats and strange polyester suits and platforms.

And out on the grass, amid the thousands of bodies jostling for position or checking each other out, amid the faint cloud of weed smoke already hanging like a thin veil over the end zone, we saw some youngbloods with Crip shoes. Black cloth Chinese style slippers. Pendletons ironed and hanging loose over the waistband of pressed khakis. My USC friends didn't know, but I'd seen that wardrobe before, in Riverside. I'd already seen too many fights, and heard people talk about guys who liked to "L.A. Stomp" someone.

Instead, I focused on the woman standing in front of me. She wore a halter dress like mine. She swayed slowly to the warm-up music on the speakers, McFadden and Whitehead's "Ain't No Stopping Us Now"—our anthem of the moment. She smiled and nodded until her natural parted in the breeze like seaweed, and she sang the words over and over. Her skin was butterscotch, her Afro was tinted reddish, delicate and transparent as a cloud. On her right shoulder was a dark tick-tack-toe game, as if someone had drawn precisely with a marker and ruler. The large mesh mark was a burn scar, I realized. She had been shoved into a heating vent and held there. Sometime. One day.

Then everyone rose with her because the bands were coming onstage, and the sea of people rippled.

George Clinton had created a whole world for black people in the seventies and early eighties, a complete language and melody, a sly and smirking response to what we really knew: a lot of us were desperate, too many of us were high and most of us were broke. The economy was tanking, because the recession everyone talked about in 1981 had already hit us. I had friends dead from drug overdoses or violence, friends dropping out of college because they couldn't eat, friends sleeping in cars and on couches. My boyfriend sometimes ate one meal a day, as a college ballplayer. He called me collect, from a payphone, and once had to drop it, clanging on the glass, because someone was shooting nearby. Back then, even talking on the phone was a luxury. We didn't have money for bills, bus rides, or clothes. I was on a full scholarship to USC, and when I went home one weekend to raid my Sparkletts bottle full of change to help my boyfriend pay for a bus ride, my brother had taken the money.

But everyone here had scraped up the ten or twenty dollars to get funked up. We wanted to hear George Clinton make fun of the world, and now the first bass lines hit our breastbones hard, even way up in the stands.

People all the way across from the end zone, on the other side of the stadium, were filling those seats, and they must not have seen much. But from where we were, down there on the end zone stage were women dressed in white tights, white platform boots, and white fur tails wrapped around their waists: Parlet, George Clinton's first emissaries of the funk. They sang and strutted, warming up the crowd, dancing until plenty of people on the grass danced, too. Every few feet was an individual show, with women doing the Freak, the Cowboy, and men Pop-Locking when they could.

For the whole concert—until the crazy bad stuff started—the grass was like a huge club, a combination of *Soul Train* line and house party and gym floor. In the stands, we spent most of our time standing, dancing in front of our uncomfortable seats, feeling the sun on our heads as we moved and thinking how strange it was to be dancing in the daylight.

But the shadows were moving in on part of the stadium, and the bands got funkier, and the smoke got heavier, and the stage got hotter: Con Funk Shun, then the Bar Kays who tore it up with "Your Love," which made the woman in front of me raise her stiff hands as if in church. Rick James and the Stone City Band added to the marijuana smoke, singing "Mary Jane." They were joined by the Brides of Funkenstein. Then came the last warm-up, Bootsy's Rubber Band. Bootsy, with his knee-high glitter boots, his star sunglasses, and his roller coaster–whispery voice, did his Bootzilla thing.

But we were waiting for the deep funk. Dr. Funkenstein. Serious funk. We would tear the roof off the sucker, even though there was only the last of the swimming-hot blue sky above us.

My future brother-in-law looked and sounded like Bootsy. I closed my eyes, I remember, and thought about going home in a week or so, when my freshman year was over, trying to get a job, riding in Penguin's Dodge Dart with seven other people while we moved in unison to Cameo or Funkadelic, dancing so hard that the car would leap and hop at the stoplight without hydraulics. Back to dancing in packed living rooms, if we could still find them, hoping no one would fight or call the cops. Dancing in fields behind someone's house, with the music coming from car speakers and open windows, and hoping no one would pull up from the wrong neighborhood.

As the sun set, before me was a huge dark den in someone's mansion, and we were once more on our feet because the Mothership was landing. The air purpled and white smoke rose from the stage. Then a huge skull appeared requesting a joint.

George Clinton came out of the Mothership. He was Dr. Funkenstein returned to earth to bring the funk. The members of Funkadelic (by this time there were twenty or thirty musicians and dancers and singers on stage, in various incarnations and costumes, including Bootsy, the Brides, Parlet, and other characters) brought what must have been a twenty-foot joint to the skull, paraded it around for a time, and Clinton lit it up.

The skull smoked in peace. The eyeholes were quiet. The stage and grassy area in front of it were wreathed in dry ice and smoke and funk.

"Cosmic Slop," and then a long, long version of "Standing on the Verge of Getting It On," with solos that lasted forever. Starchild, another incarnation of Clinton, was subdued, and the guitars screeched for a time, while the dancing slowed with confusion. Then came that familiar bass line thumping *boom boom boom*—"(Not Just) Knee Deep."

Fights started in the end zone. Someone shot a gun—we could hear the *pop pop pop* like baby firecrackers. A wave of people ran from the shooter. We ducked behind the seats. Purses disappeared, people screamed, police and security rushed like ink to the disturbance, and it would either melt away or people would be dragged off, and all the while, everyone was trying to get closer to the stage.

The band pleaded for peace. Then they just kept playing.

We came out from under our seats and danced, warily, but as the music heated up, the fights died down for awhile. A few more times, people started fights as diversionary tactics, and little gangsters would run over and steal what was left unattended.

But all over the grass, people were doing the Freak. The woman with the tick-tack-toe scar was in the aisle, possessed as if the concrete pathway led to an altar, writhing and working thigh-deep.

By the time Funkadelic's set was nearly over and George Clinton and the others were transforming themselves into Parliament, the stage was darkened even more. We could see glints of silver and green. Under the stadium lights, the eerie embers of cigarettes and joints throbbed and sparked in the crowd on the grass, which had grown even bigger because everyone knew this was the last act. With the cave of the stage noisy but black, and all of us waiting, more fights broke out in the end zone, and I felt the urgency I always felt toward the end of the party, when my friends had had too much sinsemillia and sloe gin, when the guys from another neighborhood had figured out where we were, when somebody busted his best friend's jaw on a car trunk after losing at craps.

The Parliament set was a cartoon replica of Atlantis with fake seaweed and the glittering costumes of Mr. Wiggles, his ladies Giggles and Squirm, and Rumpofsteelskin, along with others. But Sir Nose D'Voidoffunk, his proboscis pointy and sharp as a white man's, his nasal declarations of hatred for rhythm, screamed at us all, "I am Sir Nose! I don't swim. I don't dance. I don't even sweat!"

A huge bird swung out into the air over the stage, cawing and croaking and screaming like a diabolical version of some prehistoric pterodactyl, and we all shouted back because that sound was at the beginning of "Aqua Boogie (A Psychoalphadiscobetabioaquadoloop)," the song we needed now.

Sir Nose was hit with the Bop Gun, and he had to dance.

The whole world turned watery and rhythmic, and we moved as if we weren't tired and frightened and waiting to duck under our seats at the sound of gunfire.

> *Aqua boogie, baby*
> *Never learned to swim*
> *Underwater boogie, baby*
> *Can't catch the rhythm of the stroke*
> *Why should I hold my breath*
> *Feelin' that I might choke?*

The bass lines and organ beat against our bones where we all stood and shook and moved with the chorus.

> *With the rhythm it takes to dance to what we have to live through*
> *You can dance underwater and not get wet*

I used that chant as the epilogue to my first book, eleven years later. Parliament Funkadelic had broken up shortly after putting out their final albums in 1980 and '81. Some of the band members died from drug use or illness, and Rick James died recently. I still live in Riverside, in the same place I always have, and when I drive my old van down the same streets lined with pepper trees or eucalyptus, missing my friends who have died or left, missing the funk of eight bodies in the car singing and moving to "Flash Light," I turn on the CD and sit, sometimes, at the curb. The branches move, the van rocks a little, and I close my eyes.

24

Black Flag
Hong Kong Café
Los Angeles
September 2, 1979
JOHN ALBERT

1979. THE SUBURBS OF LOS ANGELES. A landscape of glaring sunlight filtered through brown, hazy smog. The streets are nearly always empty—a meandering maze of unending sameness lined with manicured lawns and identical box-like houses. The majority of kids at my high school are tanned with feathered hair. They wear casual beachwear, though we are thirty miles from the ocean. The good kids listen to the somnambulistic sounds of Jackson Browne and the Eagles and campaign against nuclear power. The bad kids listen to Van Halen and what's left of Led Zeppelin and worship all things weed. I'm fifteen and despise it all (except the drugs). I have cut my hair short and can't stop smashing windows.

I am not alone. A small, disgruntled cadre of us have embraced punk rock. We no longer even go to school, instead spending our days at the un-supervised homes of friends, getting wasted, and listening to records. I have been in trouble since grade school—mainly vandalism, shoplifting, and drugs. Recently the school board has sent a letter home informing my parents that I am to be expelled for chronic truancy. My father has stopped talking to me, and my mom wears the same shell-shocked expression as Ellen Burstyn playing the mother in *The Exorcist*. They consult a psychiatrist; I am given medication. I crush up a month's supply of the pills and snort them with my friends. That night I stay awake grinding my teeth, listening to the dissonant new album by Public Image Ltd., and jerking off. As a diplomatic concession, I agree to attend a group for troubled adolescents in nearby Orange County. I befriend the other patients, and we are soon getting stoned in a nearby vacant lot before therapy sessions. I manage to finger a blonde-haired surfer girl in the restroom. Months later, I see her at an Orange County punk festival. Her hair is blue, and she is wearing a swastika armband.

I love punk rock but know it is a fantasy. We are not in England. My family is not poor. It is not raining. I can relate to the rebellion and anger of the music, and sometimes try to imagine I am in London, but it's difficult. The sun is too bright and there is silence all around. Each night, I sit on the curb outside my parents' house and listen to the sound of cars passing in the distance. There is a growing panic inside me. I can't shake the thought that somewhere else there is something exciting and profound happening—and I am missing it all.

There is definitely something happening in nearby Hollywood. We hear about it every Sunday night on the radio. For two hours each week, an elfin little man named Rodney Bingenheimer plays the latest punk records and raves about all the cool shows happening in town. My friends and I occasionally make it into the city, usually to see bigger English bands like the Clash and the Damned. But none of us drive yet, and our parents are no longer an option since we are all technically grounded forever. The only way is to find someone older and convince them to take us—which is difficult since we despise nearly everyone. There is a well-meaning student from the nearby Claremont Colleges who has driven us a few times. She has a punk radio show on the college station, but when she invites us to be on her show, we lock her out of the room, spray paint the walls, steal records, and yell obscenities over the airwaves. She remains bitter.

My friend Roger and I are trying desperately to start a band, which we plan on calling Christian Death. So far it is just the two of us huddled in my parents' musty garage plucking away on a cheap bass and guitar. Roger goes by the name Xerox Clone, though he will later call himself Rozz Williams and amass a worldwide following before hanging himself. But in 1979, he is still just a pimply faced punk rocker in engineer boots and studded wristbands. He tells me there's a punk show he wants to see the following Sunday at a club called the Hong Kong Café in Chinatown. My initial thought is that going out on a Sunday just means a further escalation in the war with my parents. Then I think that things can't possibly get any worse—so why not? We need a ride. The next day, a few of us are sitting around when someone suggests we call Carol. Everyone sort of fidgets and then exhales in fatalistic resignation.

Carol works at a local record store and fancies herself punk. She is significantly older, in her mid-twenties, and is considered by us to be new wave and a total skank. Several months later when the Ramones play the Garrison Theater on the campus of the Claremont Colleges, Carol confiscates her store's promotional tickets and sits front row in a short skirt. When the band takes the stage, Carol promptly lifts her legs in the air and flashes her beaver. Even from my position towards the back, I can make out expressions of horror on Joey and Dee Dee's faces. Nevertheless, Carol is our only candidate. So Roger, who even as a teenager possesses a subtle and powerful charisma, calls her, and she agrees.

Sunday night, I exit my room wearing a tattered black suit and thick eyeliner and announce that I am simply "going out." As I start for the door, my mom suddenly blocks my path and tells me, "No." My dad walks out of the bathroom and pins me with a steely stare, jaw clenching and face reddening.

"You're not going anywhere, goddammit," he says, seething with controlled rage, disappointment, and concern.

The three of us heatedly debate the topic. As if following some internal prime directive, my adolescent fury starts to build. Decades later, after extensive therapy both court motivated and elective, I can now explain the intricate forces that compelled me towards such destructive behavior. But for purposes of this story none of that really matters. What *is* important is that it was not a choice. It wasn't done for effect or as a rebellious pose. If I could have been happy and well-adjusted, I would have been in a heartbeat. But standing there in my parents' kitchen with everyone shouting, I lose control, flail around, and kick out a small window. Then, I am out the door and gone.

As I walk through the darkness to meet up with my friends, I don't feel good. Deep down, I can sense my life heading somewhere unpleasant and dark. I feel lost and actually a bit scared. But I also know if I can get some alcohol in me things will feel significantly better, at least until the morning.

I wait at the designated street corner studying every approaching headlight. Being a punk in the seventies is a perilous endeavor. Besides traumatized parents and overly suspicious police, there is the constant possibility that grown men in pickup trucks will arbitrarily pull over and attack. Earlier that year, a group of middle-aged tree trimmers attacked my friends in a local park. In a stunning upset, my young pals beat the rednecks until the men tearfully apologized and ran away. But on this night, I feel vulnerable and sincerely glad to hear my friends' catcalls as they pull up in Carol's dented-up little Toyota.

Carol is dressed as a slutty punk schoolgirl. Roger rides shotgun with his hair freshly dyed black. In the backseat is my childhood friend Peter, an "x" carved into his forehead, and Dee—who is even further marginalized as a black punk rocker. Dee is undeniably tough, though. A few years later, he will reunite with his pimp father, rob some banks, and die trying to escape from jail. But on this night, packed into the little car speeding towards the city, the world seems filled with promise. The vodka and orange juice Carol has purchased doesn't hurt, either.

A half hour later we are pulling off the freeway and cutting through the neon-lit streets of Chinatown. We park, pile out into a narrow alleyway smelling of Chinese food and bum urine, and finish what remains of the vodka. The nearby Hong Kong Café is actually a converted Chinese banquet hall upstairs from a little bar. By the time we bound up the stairs, the four of us are brimming with drunken, youthful bravado. Carol, meanwhile, ducks into the downstairs bar for a few more drinks.

The punk rock scene in Los Angeles consists mainly of drugged-out art school types and ex-glam rock fans who have cut their hair upon hearing the Sex Pistols. Actual kids like us are still somewhat of a rarity, though the five members of Red Cross—the first band up—are even younger than we are. I have heard them on Rodney's radio show. Their guitar player is an awkward-looking kid named Greg Hetson who will go on to form the Circle Jerks. The two of us will also play together in the band Bad Religion for a stint. I remember him on this night because some drunk bounces an empty beer can off his head as he plays and he never even glances up. As Red Cross finish, Carol reemerges from the downstairs bar looking significantly more inebriated and trailed by an equally drunk and quite smitten Chinese man.

None of us have heard of the next band, and as they set up their equipment, they certainly don't look very punk. No spiky hair, bondage pants or leather jackets, they seem more like guys who would live in their parents' garage and smoke a lot of weed. Eventually, their singer strolls on to the stage. He is a small, nondescript guy wearing an oversized army jacket and holding a can of Budweiser. When he leans forward and speaks into the mic, it is with a distinctively SoCal drawl—just like every fucked-up kid I have ever known.

"Heeey man, we're Black Flag . . ."

They start playing, and it's as if someone has jammed a syringe into my neck and injected the purest crystal methedrine. One minute we're milling about checking out the Hollywood girls, next there's this blistering wall of sound blasting from the small stage. Everyone is just stunned. It is punk rock, but not like before. This is faster and angrier. Over the next few years, Black Flag will alter the American musical landscape. But what's important this particular night is that it's music made specifically for us. Keith Morris isn't up there singing about political injustice or class oppression; he's screaming about the exact kind of pain and frustration we are feeling.

I'm about to have a nervous breakdown
My head really hurts

And within seconds everyone is careening around the dance floor. Slam dancing (initially called "The Huntington Beach Strut" and later "moshing") hasn't been invented yet, but we're not exactly pogo-ing, either. We're really just—going off. Everything after that is kind of a blur. Some guys attack a smaller guy and Dee jumps in and starts swinging. I soon have a black eye, but not from that particular melee. In my excitement, I turn and joyously hurl Carol across a nearby table. She promptly circles back and unleashes a solid haymaker into the side of my face.

After the show, we stand bruised and elated outside the club in a little tourist square. The riotous music has somehow given our confused lives a fleeting sense of purpose. Carol, on the other hand, is so drunk she can hardly walk. Her Chinese suitor has at last given up and fallen asleep on a bench beside a koi pond. By the time we reach the car, Carol is unconscious. Thankfully, the transmission is automatic. Roger bravely volunteers to drive. We pile in and nervously watch as the fifteen-year-old future "King of Goth" tentatively merges the car onto the eastbound freeway and back towards the suburbs.

A half hour later I am standing outside my parents' house. All the lights are off. There is a note taped to the back door. It reads simply, "Go away." I try the door. It is locked. I trudge into the front yard and start calling my older brother's name while tossing pebbles at his bedroom window. I am more than a little startled when he sheepishly pokes his head out of the shrub next to me.

"What do you want?"

It turns out he and his friends had taken some unexpectedly potent LSD and gone to see the new movie *Alien*. It was not the laugh fest they had anticipated, and he has been huddled in the bush for hours.

The next morning, my family convenes at the breakfast table. It is an understandably tense affair. My parents don't mention my black eye or the window I have broken the night before. In fact, they don't say a word. We all just eat in silence—except for my brother, who stares at his food and coos softly like a pigeon. I quickly leave for school, but a few blocks away decide not to go. There doesn't really seem any point. Instead, I meet my friends at an abandoned baseball dugout where we drink beer and recount the previous night's adventure. Weeks later, I come across Black Flag's first three-song EP at the local record store—and steal it.

25

Horslips
The Whitla Hall
Belfast, Ireland
April 1980
PAUL MULDOON

THERE WAS A DISTINCTLY APOCALYPTIC feel to that concert, one of three played by Horslips in the Whitla Hall, Belfast, on the nights of April 29, April 30, and May 1, 1980. I can't remember which show I saw, though it was either the first or second. Nor indeed can I remember how often I must have heard Horslips in the Whitla Hall before 1980. It was a venue they'd often played in their more than ten years together as the preeminent Irish folk-rock band, before their break up in 1981.

Named after Sir William Whitla, a former pro–vice chancellor of Queen's University, the Whitla Hall was more often used for, and more suited to, large lectures such as the one given there by F. R. Leavis in the early 1970s, when I'd been a student at Queen's. The Leavis lecture was inaudible to anyone beyond the first row or two, and unintelligible to even those who heard him. No one had the nerve to ask the great man to speak up. In the case of Horslips, F. R. Leavis had given way to frayed Levis and the decibel level was such that the concert might well have been heard in Bradbury Place or Shaftsbury Square or a mile away in Belfast's bombed-out city centre. No one would have had the nerve to ask Horslips to turn it down.

They'd begun a lot more gently, so gently in fact that my mother was, from the start, one of their greatest fans. She'd turned me on to them one weekend I spent home from Queen's, probably in 1970. Horslips had a regular spot on a weekly RTE television show, *Fonn*. There they played Irish traditional music on fiddle, flute, *bodhran*, concertina, and acoustic guitar. My mother had hitherto shown interest only in the likes of Tom Jones and Engelbert Humperdinck. Now she was besotted with Horslips.

It's hard to disentangle all the reasons why Horslips had a place in her heart. There was the music, of course, though it was music with which we were, in some sense, overly familiar. We'd heard it beaten to death by *ceilidhe* bands at guest teas in parish halls in Dungannon and Eglish, heard it given mouth-to-mouth resuscitation by the Dubliners in Portadown and Benburb Priory, heard it going under again even as it was being saved from itself by the somnambulistic Ciaran Mac Mathuna on RTE's Sunday morning radio show *Mo Cheol Thu*. Even I, under the influence of Luke Kelly and Barney McKenna of the Dubliners, had tried to learn to play the G and tenor banjos. Come to think of it, the Dubliners and Horslips had something in common that transcended music: hair. Between them, they had more hair than you'd find on a barber's floor on a Saturday afternoon. There was something Horslips had in spades, though, that the Dubliners couldn't quite manage. That something was sex appeal.

And it was sex appeal with a dangerous aspect, one neatly embodied in the name of one of the founding members of Horslips, Declan Sinnott. The idea of sinning or *not* sinning was somehow in the air, particularly since the band's name itself seemed, in one intellection, to be a pun on "whores' lips." The name also seemed akin to the flower names—cowslips and oxlips—but, again, in a perverse way. In years to come, we would hear that Horslips was in fact a play on the phrase "the four horsemen of the Apocalypse," transmogrified to become "the four poxmen of the Horsl(yp)s(e)," which is partly why I used the word "apocalyptic" earlier on. We knew, if largely from Shakespeare, that the pox was one of the wages of sin. One way or another, Horslips was a far cry from the conventional Irish band name. Joe Dolan and the Drifters? Big Tom and the Mighty Mainliners? Drifters? Mainliners? I think not, unless you were talking hoboes on heroin.

In addition to their generalized, free-floating sex appeal, a notion my mother would scarcely have brooked, Horslips had a more local, specific connection. Barry Devlin, the bass player, hailed from nearby Ardboe, and had attended my grammar school, St. Patrick's College, Armagh. Even I could see he was, in the American sense as well as the Irish one, cute. One of his sisters had been a classmate of my sister in Donaghmore Convent. Another had gone out with a friend of mine at Queen's. Another worked for *Vogue*. Yet another was married to Seamus Heaney, my tutor at Queen's and one of my main men, then as now. There was, therefore, a sense that Barry Devlin was one of our own, a sense mere drones often have of great dynastic families.

A similar familiarity attended the drummer, Eamon Carr, whose name I knew from his having shared a party line, as it were, with Peter Fallon in a poetry performance and publication outfit going under the name *Tara Telephone*. The name itself deftly connected the Major Old Heap with the Major New Hip (the telephone was still something of a novelty, as evidenced by our own low phone number—Moy 328). *Tara Telephone* was partly Ireland's answer to the Liverpool Poets, partly an answer to a question no one had ever thought to ask, even in an era of matching shirts and ties. These shirts and ties, mostly of a Paisley design, were *de rigeur* for my brother and myself when we went, with our sister, to dance the night away in the Boat Club in Portadown in the early 1970s. It seems astonishing now to think that we were out at night at all in that era, particularly when the word Paisley conjured up a whole other version of Pandemonium, when the Civil Rights Movement had been hijacked by the IRA, when tit-for-tat killings were the order of the day.

The combination of old and new implicit in *Tara Telephone*, in the very name, was key to the early success of Horslips. Another founding member of the group, the flute-and-concertina-player Jim Lockhart, had studied classical music at Trinity College, Dublin, and was well grounded in the methods of Sean O'Riada and O'Riada's vicars on earth, the Chieftains. When I tried to play T. Rex's "Get It On" on my tenor banjo I could see that there was something missing. That something, apart from my profound lack of musicality, was electricity. Like another founding member of Horslips, Charles O'Connor, who had not the slightest hesitation about the electrification of his fiddle or mandolin, Lockhart knew that their electrified, and electrifying, take on Irish traditional music would make seeing Horslips live a particularly strong selling point.

On the subject of selling themselves, Horslips had been masterful. It may have been that Leopold Bloom was the literary embodiment of the newfangled Irish advertising man, but several members of Horslips—Devlin, Carr, and O'Connor—were *literally* advertising men who specialized in graphic design and understood packaging as an art form. Before Horslips, packaging in Ireland had meant the brown paper bag around six bottles of Bass and a half-pound of mincemeat—which is just what Horslips made of all that. The album art, like the albums themselves, was high concept. That had been true of the first LP, *Happy to Meet, Sorry to Part* (1972), which came in an approximation of an accordion case. It had been true of *The Tain* (1973), with its cover image of a somewhat anachronistic mailed fist argent on a field sable that owed something to Louis le Broquy's illustrations for Thomas Kinsella's *The Tain*, to be sure, but also something to the regalia of early-onset punk. It was also true of *Dancehall Sweethearts*, which gave us a still hairy, fur-flaunting Horslips reflected in a smoked-glass tabletop, suggesting the shotgun wedding of Terence Conran and Conan the Barbarian.

Dancehall Sweethearts had come out in 1974, the year of my own shotgun wedding. This was a shotgun wedding not in the conventional sense but in the sense that it took place in May, during the Ulster Workers Council strike, a strike masterminded by Ian Paisley. The wedding happened only because the wedding party was willing and able to negotiate a series of roadblocks manned by armed men. The country was at a standstill, a standstill in which hairy men look into a stagnant pool.

In that same year, as it happened, I worked with Horslips on the music for an hour-long radio drama entitled *The Great Debate*. This was a joint production between RTE and the BBC, for whom I then worked as a producer. *The Great Debate* was a souped-up version of *Agallamh na Senorach*, the fifteenth-century Gaelic text in which a hairy Saint Patrick and an equally hairy Oisin, son of Finn MacCool, square off to discuss the great changes—for better and worse—that Christianity has brought to Ireland. I was thrilled when Horslips agreed to provide some "theme music." So I recorded the speech tracks, in which Saint Patrick and Oisin were played by Patrick Magee and Norman Rodway, respectively, in Portland Place, then brought the tracks the following day to the BBC music studios in Maida Vale.

The demeanor of Horslips during those recordings was quite striking. They were delighted to be in John Peel's home studio, the studio in which the Beatles and the Who had recorded their "live" sessions, but they were also wonderfully diligent in the way they went about what was still a relatively laborious business of multi-tracking on lumbering eight-inch reels. We recorded a good twenty minutes of music in a single day, including "Oisin's Tune," a version of which would later be included on their 1977 album *Tracks from the Vaults*.

1976, meanwhile, had seen the release of Horslips' masterpiece, *The Book of Invasions: A Celtic Symphony*. Like *The Tain*, this was another concept album, this time based on themes from *Lebor Gabhla Eireann*, the eleventh-century pseudo-history of Ireland. It seemed that here Horslips had found the perfect balance between rock and reels. Little did I know that they were in trouble, perhaps even "Trouble with a Capital T":

High on a mountain stands a boat,
But are they gods or real folk?
We can't see the fire but we smell the smoke.
Who'll be the plough? Who'll be the yoke?
Night after night I don't believe.
We are the ones you won't deceive.
Not a thing will you achieve
'Cos we belong and we won't leave.
Trouble, trouble,
I try to chase trouble but it's chasing me,
Trouble, trouble,
Trouble with a capital T.

The capital T in the song refers to the *Tuatha De Danann*, the people of the goddess Danu, who supposedly burned their boats as they came ashore in Ireland so as to rule out any possibility of turning back. (Hence the boat and smoke imagery in the song.) The *Tuatha De Danann* would defeat the Fir Bolg and Fomorians at the first and second battles of Moytura, respectively, before being themselves supplanted by the Milesians and forced underground to become fairy folk. We recognize the sawn-off stump of their name in that of De Danann, the traditional band founded in 1974 which, with Clannad, founded in 1970, had dominated Irish "real folk."

The trouble in which Horslips found themselves was whether or not to take the same *bodhran*-lined boreen taken by Clannad and De Danann, a lane down which so much of their fan base had followed, or the rocky road from Dublin that seemed more likely to run into Route 66. Sinnott had long since been replaced by another electric guitar virtuoso, Johnny Fean, a devotee of Hendrix and Clapton. It was Fean who, paradoxically, was more inclined, with Carr and O'Connor, to stick to the traditional "backwater" material represented on *The Unfortunate Cup of Tea* (1975) and *Drive the Cold Winter Away* (1975), while Devlin and Lockhart pushed along the "mainstream" with albums such as *Aliens* (1977) and *The Man Who Built America* (1978). By the time *Short Stories, Tall Tales* had come out, in 1979, Messrs. Fean, Carr and O'Connor seemed to have regained the upper hand. Or was it the other way round? Who was the plough? Who the yoke? It wasn't at all clear.

Something might be made ever so slightly clearer the following year, when Horslips would play their final concert in the Ulster Hall. For the moment, the Whitla Hall was itself in darkness. There was a howling that came close to Pandemonium in its strictest sense. Any moment there'd be a great disclosure. Some revelation was at hand. We'd see if Horslips were indeed "gods or real folk." Yes . . . one by one they came on stage, each with a following spot. Just as we'd expected . . . gods.

26

Public Image Ltd.
The Ritz
New York City
May 15, 1981
LUC SANTE

ON FRIDAY, MAY 15, 1981, Public Image Ltd. were booked for a show at the Ritz, a nightclub on East 10th Street, New York City. It was very much a last-minute thing. Bow Wow Wow, who were a big noise just then and had never played in the United States before, had been scheduled in that slot, but abruptly pulled out on Wednesday the thirteenth, apparently because the fourteen-year-old lead singer, Annabella Lu Win, was at odds with her mother. The cancellation could have been disastrous for the club; securing the services of PiL as a fill-in was a major coup—the booking would have been important even under ordinary circumstances. There was no time for publicity of the traditional sort, but within those forty-eight hours word got out to every scenemaker, ligger, and barfly in the metropolitan area, and to everyone who had emotionally identified with the Sex Pistols and had been distressed when they bypassed New York on their final tour.

This would not be PiL's first New York appearance (although it was perhaps their tenth public performance anywhere). Thirteen months earlier, in April 1980, they had played the Palladium, a former opera house that just a few years later would be entirely reconfigured to become, fleetingly, the nightclub incarnation of the eighties bubble. In 1980, though, the theater retained its traditional layout of orchestra, balcony, and proscenium stage, and PiL surprised everybody by turning in a traditional performance—all the crowd-pleasers from their eponymous first album as well as their second, the redoubtable *Metal Box*—and by being, of all things, charming. At least, John Lydon was charming. Keith Levene, the guitarist doubling on synthesizer (playing the keys, sometimes, with the peghead of his guitar); the formidable bassist Jah Wobble; and whoever sat in the drummer's chair that night, all were in top form but failed to acknowledge the audience. Lydon, however, invited members of the crowd up to dance and sing—

even pulling out a notebook so that prospective vocalists could get the words right. A friend of mine who danced onstage was presented by Lydon with a Sex Pistols bandanna. Good feeling reigned. The show seemed to exemplify the democratic ideal of post-punk, Lydon's openness apparently a product of the same impulse that led Scritti Politti to list the exact costs of their first single's production and manufacture on its sleeve. It was a performance people carried away with them (when I saw Jah Wobble play in Paris, in 2005, at one point an unmistakably American voice shouted out, "Palladium 1980!"). A night or two later, the band played again, an unannounced show at a small heavy-metal club on the Bowery called Great Gildersleeves that was reportedly even better and considerably wilder.

By May 1981, though, disarray was ascendant. Wobble had quit, there seemed to be no one occupying the revolving drummer's seat, and the latest vinyl product, *Flowers of Romance*, was a peculiar thing indeed. Fans—me, for one—earnestly tried to convince themselves to like it. It was very, um, Eastern, wasn't it, and kinda Irish, and lo-fi in a way that could be construed as defiant. It featured droning fiddle, "tribal" drumming on what might have been cardboard boxes (samples and imitations of Burundi drumming were all over the post-punk soundtrack that season), and Lydon keening away like a second-line muezzin. The parts didn't necessarily cohere, though, and the record felt as if it had been thrown together from odds and ends, down to the jacket design, a Polaroid of non-musician member Jeanette Lee with a rose between her teeth. Lydon had so far done a good job in his role as his micro-generation's Messenger, even managing the rare feat of returning for a second act. Public Image may not have been as instantly world-historical as the Pistols, but it had it all over them musically, and featured lyrics that eschewed the anthemic for suggestion and ellipsis: "Careering," "Poptones." Now, however, Lydon and company appeared to have mislaid their compass, perhaps under the sway of drugs—we didn't know a thing about their habits, of course, but in all major cities 1981 was a banner year for heroin. Still, we very much wanted to think that exciting new horizons lay ahead.

My friends and I secured tickets, which sold out rapidly at twelve dollars (the previous year's Palladium show had cost $7.50). As we approached the club, in the rain, we passed queues and clumps of those who had not been quick enough to get their hands on the ducats but continued to hope. Punk, as a fluid catchall covering a broad and contradictory terrain of music and behavior, had been dominant in lower Manhattan since the days of the Mercer Arts Center in the early 1970s, but the punk fashion template as developed in London and propagated in Los Angeles took a long time to penetrate the metropolitan area. One minute, it seemed, Sid Vicious, a unique and unmistakable figure, was everywhere—running into the methadone clinic on Lafayette Street, hanging out ostentatiously in the vestibule of Irving Plaza, lying senseless and drooling on a banquette at Max's—and the next he was dead, in his place suddenly appearing a thousand micro-Sids with meticulously spiked hair, dog collars, safety pins, bondage pants, and Perfecto jackets. Not many wore all those things at once—the norm was shlubs, dressed by their mothers, who wore Anarchy T-shirts under their tan windbreakers or had stuck a pin through their cheek on the bus in from Syosset. They thronged 10th Street expecting to see their inspiration, Johnny Rotten, although he himself had been spat upon enough times and had reverted to his birth name as a sign that he was no longer engaged in the punk business. Or was he?

Although we knew enough not to arrive at clubs before midnight, the doors had opened at ten and the place was packed to the walls. The Ritz, once and now again known as Webster Hall, had been a ballroom for many decades, hosting among other things the "rackets" of the original racketeers around 1910 and the art student balls of the 1920s. We shunned it in those days; only an event of this magnitude could draw us there. Whereas a smaller club such as Tier 3 seemed familial, could almost persuade you it was non-profit, and even one as large as Hurrah at least gave the impression of respecting its clients, the Ritz was a processing unit. Its bouncers reeked of anabolic steroids; its bar gave all the value of a strip joint's; its crowd-management techniques had been copied from the Department of Immigration and Naturalization. It represented the point at which the new-wave skinny tie turned into the corporate gold cravat. But it had the size, and so even terribly idealistic bands played there if they were sufficiently popular. PiL was at best ambiguously idealistic and could probably have filled the Ritz four times over. The band—or "corporation," as its members liked to style it—happened to choose that venue for a multimedia experiment better suited to a converted loft on the art fringe. No one in the crowd suspected that quite yet, though, in the interminable trickle of time between our entrance and the lights going down at around 1:20 a.m.

Shortly before that happened, someone behind the scrim that covered the stage picked out the bass part to "Public Image," then someone on drums joined in. Once they got the riff up and running, they stopped. Then they began again. Then they stopped again. After the lights went off, the scrim, contrary to expectations, did not rise like a curtain; it was not, in fact, a scrim but a screen. A projector went into action, showing a painful video by a local group of twinks called Shox Lumania, all primary-colored leggings and gravity-defying asymmetrical haircuts. This was followed by another video, a feeble skit starring Keith Levene. We couldn't make out a word of it (bad sound quality was the curse of video in that Model T era), but it might have been useful if we had: It was a reiterated warning that what followed would not be a concert, and urged the crowd to prepare for disappointment. Then their new record was slapped on a turntable as the four—Lydon, Levene, Jeanette Lee, and a sixty-year-old drummer named Sammy, recruited that day in a city park—appeared in silhouette behind the screen, that tableau interspersed with video images of backstage hi-jinks.

I tape recorded the show, as it happens. I didn't often smuggle a tape recorder into clubs. Before the advent of the Walkman Pro, the enterprise of taping meant lugging around an object not quite as large as a toaster oven—those were also the days before bag searches and metal detectors, but it was still an annoying encumbrance in the close confines of clubs—and the toylike microphone made sound quality a gamble. But I thought the event that night deserved to be preserved for posterity. I switched on the microphone when I heard the opening notes of "Flowers of Romance," then quickly switched it off when I realized I was hearing the record. I switched it back on, after a clip of Lydon and Levene on a TV talk show, to catch a squall of electronic bleeps and blurps. This was accompanied by a collective "Whoooh" from the crowd, who thought something was about to occur, while the band members continued capering, dancing, mugging for the camera. Lydon and Levene launched into "Four Enclosed Walls," a song from the record, played live this time, but broke it off after a few min-utes. When the desultory audiovisuals resumed, the crowd was becoming markedly more restive. One observer noted that the storm of beer bottles—as distinct from the odd bottle here and there—began at 1:45, twenty-five minutes into the show.

At this point, my tape degenerates into what sounds like an insult comic baiting a drunken crowd that is apparently tied to its seats. The exchange is not edifying; it has all the wit of a drunk at the zoo working up the lions from the safe side of the bars. Lydon's lines reprise, among other things, his patter at the Sex Pistols' final performance, at Winterland in San Francisco, just three years earlier: "So glad you're enjoying the show. Aren't you getting your money's worth? Isn't this what rock 'n' roll is all about, maaan? . . . You're not throwing enough bottles . . . It's obvious you're all into peace and love. I can see you're having fun out there." Levene, on the other hand, is plainly enraged: "If you destroy that fucking screen we will destroy you. We have the power to destroy you, all of you . . . Silly fucking audience." To all of which the crowd retorts, monotonously, "Fuck you fuck you fuck you fuck you," along with a constant stream of thuds from objects hitting the screen. Eventually, as Lydon sings "New York, New York," the crowd breaks through the cordon sanitaire of bouncers, lights and equipment slide off the stage, the screen is whisked up by remote control, and the band flees with its instruments while bouncers bust heads and mayhem triumphs.

I left feeling murderous. I would, at that point, have happily watched the crowd destroy the band—or the band destroy the crowd. They richly deserved one another, I thought. My animus against the crowd was, frankly, snobbery. They were followers. They were consumers of the most wretchedly suburban sort. They wore the dog collars and safety pins that you would have to have worn, if at all, in the very first month of their becoming punk accoutrements, and then never again. They demanded the odious commodity called rock 'n' roll, which the Sex Pistols had, in fact, very publicly buried—they didn't see the irony! I could almost look into the future and see them a few months hence, booing Grandmaster Flash and the Furious Five, attempting to open for the Clash, off the stage of Bonds International Casino in Times Square.

My beef with PiL was a bit more complicated. In a way, I was just like the rest of the crowd: I had wanted to hear "Poptones" and "Swan Lake," and I felt cheated. I could be open to experiments, risky performance games, the undermining of expectations, but PiL's show, if not an outright expression of contempt, was at best a perfectly stupid approach to the band-audience conundrum. Lydon, speaking before the show occurred, was quoted in the *SoHo Weekly News*: "We're making it up on the spot . . . We're not presenting ourselves as superstars; you either enjoy it or you don't. I'm not gonna go out there and scream my brains off like an asshole." At this remove it seems scarcely credible that a man who had spent three years being spat upon could have failed to foresee the consequences of foisting a particularly lazy version of performance art upon a beery audience with its heart set on loud, fast noise, an audience that had been further primed by the example of his own earlier career. Perhaps he was insulated by celebrity. Perhaps he simply didn't realize that what might have hit its target as provocation if served up to a coterie audience at the Mudd Club would have a far different effect upon the yobs at the Ritz. Maybe it was self-satisfied ignorance or a death wish once removed. In any event, he called down a curse. He never again in his career did anything worth remarking upon.

The evening stands in my mind as the final ringing-down of the curtain on the phenomenon of punk. At the heart of the punk project had been the dissolution of the boundary between performer and audience. Four of you would be up there—microphone guitar bass drums—but it hardly mattered which four; you were about to trade places anyway. Soon the mystique of stardom would vanish. Eventually you would exorcise the whole rock 'n' roll mess. You would go on to more interesting things. To a degree, that had already happened in May 1981, but necessarily in a small and rather rarefied way. I thought the Young Marble Giants were living proof. When I saw them at Tier 3 the audience numbered no more than a hundred or so; the atmosphere had the hush and concentration of a superior poetry reading. Visiting African bands, such as King Sunny Adé's, provided another sort of example; when they played there were so many people on stage it scarcely mattered whether you were playing an instrument or not—the pleasure was purely communal.

One night, around the same time, I happened to be walking along near the bottom of Second Avenue when a dozen people from the Brazilian samba school Pé de Boi materialized on a corner with agogos and repiques and started a groove. Within minutes, a crowd had formed. Bystanders started beating a clave beat on beer bottles while others ran home for their congas. It went on for hours, and hundreds of people came and went, nearly everybody playing or at least dancing. It was as if the whole city had spontaneously decided to make music. I felt as if I'd been waiting my whole life for that sort of occasion, which was never to occur again. Punk had nothing to do with it, of course, except that it led me there.

27

The Kinks
Madison Square Garden
New York City
October 3, 1981
THOMAS BELLER

NOT LONG AFTER the night in question, the night of the Kinks, there was another visit to Madison Square Garden, to see the Knicks. Kinks. Knicks. Interesting to put the two words side by side. The two nights, like the meaning of the two words, had nothing in common. But, as with the words, there were some odd overlaps. There was my presence, to start. There was the Garden, radically refitted for each occasion but unmistakably itself. There was the theme of clothing. And there was the police officer. The sight of him at the Knicks game would have turned my face white if it hadn't been painted white already.

It was Halloween. Or maybe it was the night before Halloween. I was dressed up in costume, as were a lot of other kids. Except I wasn't exactly a kid. I was fifteen and tall enough to have made the varsity basketball team—as a project. My friend Steve, the best athlete in the grade, had been the last one cut, which was widely seen as an injustice, but he was a good sport about it, and had invited me to this game.

I don't know why the hell I went in costume. I'd worn the same one for the last few years—a black tuxedo, white shirt, my face painted in whiteface with red lipstick. I usually wore a top hat to go with this, but that night I wore a black fedora; the top hat seemed too formal for the Knicks. I was a theater kid, although that year, literally days later with the start of official practices, my life as a basketball person would begin for real, and for reasons both psychic and logistical, that would be the end of the theater for me.

I saw the cop standing at the doorway to one of the levels glancing at people's tickets to make sure they weren't sneaking into better seats. We had decent seats. This was our level. I flashed my ticket. His eyes went from the ticket to my face. Our eyes didn't meet so much as rake past one another. His face registered an apparently benign smile, colored only by a raised eyebrow. To anyone else it would have seemed a friendly smile.

"Shit, shit, shit!" I muttered. "That was him!"

"Who?"

Steve hadn't been with me at the Kinks concert, and I hadn't told him—or anyone else—about it.

My problem was not that the cop had recognized me. I was sure he had. He knew exactly who I was, I thought. My problem was that, now that he had acknowledged our special bond, I felt I ought to do something. I had expected that I would never see him again, and here he was, a fat, turkey-like figure in his blue police officer's uniform and cap. Confronted with this opportunity, what should I do?

The answer was nothing, other than to proceed to our seats. We got sodas on the way. And at some point during the first quarter, while Michael Ray Richardson ran around trying to get the ball to Bill Cartwright and Marvin Webster, Steve reached into his pocket and produced a joint.

The Kinks at the Garden. Four of us had tickets. They had come via one of our parents, who was some kind of agent at ICM. They were free. We were excited, but there was something a bit casual about our excitement. Was this going to be the all-time greatest musical event of our lives? No. Were we especially psyched for the Kinks? Yes, but only sort of, by which I mean we didn't really see the Kinks for what they were. Their big fat rock songs of the late seventies' records blurred them a little with Mick and the Stones, to begin with, as well as other less accomplished titans of rock radio at that time such as Foreigner (who I had seen twice at the Garden and had bought the T-shirts), Cheap Trick, and Bad Company, whose concert at the Garden the previous spring had made a huge impression on me—compared to the other concerts I had been to, it was an older, tougher crowd. I had watched with amazement as two bad ass–looking dudes rushed down to better seats in the sold-out house, which, before the show, with the house lights on, was fogged with pot smoke. When the two guys made it to the vacant seats, they slapped each other five and then turned their goateed visages towards the stage; one of them wore a red beret.

The Kinks. The Kinks at the Garden! The sheer physical reality of that many people in that place sent us into hyperventilation. But their famous ironies were only available to me in the broadest form, and I hadn't really touched base with the wistful, pastoral innocence that inflects so many of Ray Davies's songs, such as "Celluloid Heroes," "Waterloo Sunset," etc.

The Kinks, for us, were "Low Budget," "Catch Me Now I'm Falling," "Destroyer" and Lo-lo-lo-lo-lo-la.

It was autumn 1981. The school year was less than a month old. It was already a disaster on every level, academic and social. As for the musical moment, I was oblivious. I think I first heard about punk rock about a year later. Our posse of four concertgoers came from the New York City milieu of uptown natives, as opposed to downtown émigrés. Our musical taste leaned heavily towards Zeppelin/Stones/Beatles/Who days on WPLJ. We had all heard about Lennon getting shot from the morning DJ and one of us lived in the Dakota. We were city kids; money was everywhere, sluicing around, untethered from reality. To illustrate:

A kid goes on vacation with a friend to a Caribbean island. The friend's parents are paying for everything. Water skiing. Tennis lessons. All the meals.

After a week, the kid returns, tan, elated. On the occasion of his first night back, his mother has made him a steak. He looks at it and says, "Mom, can we order Chinese for dinner?"

The mother is offended. This is perfectly good steak, she says. The feeling that his values have somehow been distorted by proximity to so much wealth comes over her and sickens her a little. All the happiness she felt that her son was having a good time—such a good time, in fact, that he had told her on the phone that he felt guilty about taking so much from his friend's parents, and she had called them, and they had assured her that they insisted, he was their guest, all of which she related back to him, to put him at ease with his carefree happiness—it all evaporates in as much time as it takes for steam to clear off the mirror after a shower once you open the bathroom door.

The kid knows his mom, he knows her in the spirit of love, and he knows her in the spirit of manipulation, the two motives closely entwined. He is responding to both when he explains to her why he needs Chinese food. The problem, he says, is that he has been eating steak every single night for a week. He is, in fact, totally sick of steak! For days he has been fantasizing about shrimp with chili sauce, maybe shredded beef with scallions, and wonton soup. He's dying of steak! And so the mother wraps up the steak and lets him order Chinese.

A few weeks before the Kinks concert, this same kid goes shopping with his mother. The softness in the summer air has been replaced by something crisper. Also, he has had a week of school during which he had to wear psychic sunglasses to protect himself from the glare of new clothing. So, time for a new jacket.

The mom is a prudent, thrifty shopper. And he is a fifteen-year-old whose needs, both abstract and real, have converged in the autumnal moment for new school clothes. Morris Brothers, the local standby for clothes, is being bypassed in favor of something both more extravagant and thrifty, a huge emporium on the East Side called Alexander's. His anticipation is mixed with guilt on account of his many other visits to Alexander's. He has a scam going at the record department that goes like this: you can pay for the records right there at the record department, or you can take them to the registers on the ground floor. He takes them downstairs. But instead of paying for them, he unwraps the record's plastic covering and approaches the security guard in his blue, pseudo-cop outfit. The kid doesn't avoid this figure. On the contrary, he goes right for him and says, "Excuse me! Excuse me, sir?" as loud as is reasonable, and waves the record in front of the security guard. "This record has a scratch!" he says. "I just bought it and it's scratched!"

The guard is about to refer the kid to the record department, but the kid continues, "And I brought it back to exchange it for one that isn't. I came all the way from home and I forgot my receipt! At home! So I have to go home and get it. All right?"

The kid would have acquired the new Kinks record, *Give the People What They Want*, in just such a manner, except that a few weeks earlier, he had been flagrant and lazy, unwrapping the plastic covering and dropping it on the down escalator, and he hadn't even made it to the guard standing at the door before two plainclothes store detectives grabbed him. He spent a while in a small jail cell in a kind of backstage area. A Hispanic man with a brown three-piece suit and a thin mustache made him produce all his money, which wasn't enough for the records, and made him offer a number of someone who he could call. He gave a number for his friend Adrian. The man in the suit was disgusted, threatening, but kind. The kid apologized at length. The man in the suit let him go.

Now, with his mother, he was vaguely terrified that one of the guards or detectives would recognize him. Perhaps the man in the brown three-piece suit himself! The mood of deceit overlapping with the mood surrounding his mother, which was not and had never been deceit, was discomfiting. He had once been a boat docked firmly to her pier, but the ropes holding him there were going slack, there was room in between him and the pier, and sometimes the ropes were thrown off altogether for unofficial night-time journeys to nearby islands.

They looked at jackets. They tried on this one and that one. She used the word "windbreaker" and engaged the salespeople in discussions on the subject of quality. He modeled and shrugged his shoulders and put his hand in various pockets until they encountered something in deep navy blue that was a bit shiny, with no collar to speak of, and had zippers on the pockets and an alligator on the chest. He did not own anything with an alligator on it and was pretty sure he didn't want to. It was, for one thing, too intentional. It would have "follower" overtones at school. The members of his grade, when considered as one single protoplasmic organism, as opposed to individuals, were highly resistant to anything resembling personal evolution and reinvention. He had already stirred some angry animal consciousness by making varsity in a highly theatrical moment of a list posted to the athletic department's bulletin board. To add to this transgression of the established order by buying something with an alligator on it might seem actionable by the piranha consciousness of the student body. This jacket was asking for it. But he couldn't get over how cool it looked and felt. And the zippers on the pockets! His mother liked it, too.

"You look very nice in navy blue," she said. She had been going on about how nice he looked in navy blue his entire life. It was exhausting, but, for once, he forgave her for this.

On their way downstairs, they passed the record department. Also on this floor was the typewriter department. It was part of his record stealing ritual to make a pit stop here once he had his desired records. There was a practical aspect to this—the lost, empty aisles of typewriters, all perched on shelves with pieces of paper in their carriages so you could try them out, were ideal for unwrapping the plastic coverings. He usually stuffed them behind one of the typewriters. He also took the opportunity to doodle a little on the typewriter keys. He blurted out some meaningless series of letters, sometimes words, and then he would veer into a brief coherent narrative that was like a news report from that very moment on that very floor, a kind of diary entry that sooner or later got around to the business at hand.

la la la bam a lam black betty Frankenstein and when I get home I will be home with the new record I am stealing a record!

And now, with the jacket, he had the weird impulse to leave a little note—*I'm buying a jacket!*—just to keep current.

When he got to school the members of his grade, when considered as one single protoplasmic organism, did not seem to give a flying fuck about his new jacket, which was fine with him. He was still into it, and he wore it to the Kinks concert.

The seats were down on the floor, which had been bisected into a front half and a back half. Ours were in the front half. Halfway through the first song, we and everyone else charged up the center aisle, and so came to be a part of that throng of people standing with their heads craned upwards at the man singing into the microphone, playing his guitar. Under the spotlights, Ray Davies looked remarkably pale. He wore a blazer, a button-down shirt, and a bow tie. His look combined freaky professor with aged, rebellious student. We leapt and jumped and waved our hands and marveled at how much spittle came flying out of his mouth as he sang. "Destroyer," "Give the People What They Want," "Art Lover," "Yo-Yo." They were playing the hell out of that new record, and with good reason. They were making money in America!

At some point, some naked dude ran onto the stage covered only by the Union Jack, one of the many that pocked the Garden's interior. That the entire pantheon of AOR rock Gods—Zeppelin/Stones/Beatles/Who, and also Pink Floyd, and also Bad Company and Queen, and also . . . everyone, really, except the Doors, Jimi, and Janice—was English was hard to grasp because it was so pervasive and stretched to all horizons. It was just there, the English thing. It didn't really register that this might mean the musicians themselves came from and currently lived in an actual far away place called England.

In fairness to us, the conundrum of New York provincialism—that it sort of *is* the center of the world—was in full effect on this matter. After all, John Lennon was living in the same building where one of us lived, and the Stones' most recent album, *Some Girls*, had been a postcard written to us from down the block, with the important revision that while the Puerto Rican girls were just dying to meet Mick, it was their brothers who seemed to be dying to mug us, or to at least remove our Arthur Ashe tennis racquet from the video game area of Tommy's Pizza on Columbus Avenue and replace it with a calling card in the form of a switchblade stuck into the wood.

What would the Kinks have seen looking down from the stage that Saturday night? A bunch of bratty, excited kids rocking out, one of them particularly tall and already trying to do that impossible thing of jumping up and down while at the same time not totally obscuring the views of the two or three rows of people behind him, and also wearing a brand new, shiny, navy blue Lacoste windbreaker.

Then it was over. The house lights came up. There was a gradual dispersal. For a while, people milled around. The naked dude with the Union Jack was actually wearing shorts, I saw. Then it was quick, the place emptied, and the four of us boys were walking amidst the many empty seats whose color scheme was red and orange and yellow and green. We took the longest possible route out. The concert exhausted and energized us, fed us and stoked an appetite that needed appeasing. Basically, we didn't want to leave.

Every entrance to every exit was now manned by a police officer. When we finally trudged towards one of the exits, the police officer there directed us elsewhere, to another, different exit. We headed in that direction. Hefty men in T-shirts were disassembling the stage. Otherwise, the four of us kids and the police now seemed to be the only occupants of the arena. When we came to the exit we had been instructed to leave through, the police officer there said we had to go to yet another exit.

"But we were told we had to come here," said one of us.

"Well, now you're told you have to go over there," said the cop.

But that is fiction. Of that part of the night, I only remember one exact phrase; the buildup to the phrase is amorphous. One of us said something, and the cop said something, and there was a reply, and maybe another go around or maybe not. The cop then grabbed my arm rather roughly and shoved me in the direction in which he wanted us to go. Had it been a push, it would have registered differently. But it was this weird combination of shoving me and also holding onto my arm, as if my insolence was a kind of fruit and that if he shook the tree hard enough, it would simply fall away. It didn't hurt, but I looked down to see his hairy fist clenching the shiny fabric of the sleeve of my new jacket, and this offended me.

"Hey!" I said. "Let go of my jacket!"

I tried to yank my arm free. But he was not a letting-go kind of cop. Now we were in a tug of war in which the item being tugged at was my arm—or more specifically my jacket's sleeve with my arm in it. This was very upsetting. I said let me go, let me the fuck go, fucking let me go. Then I got quiet. Or maybe I didn't curse. Maybe I didn't say a word, and it all happened in silence. I can't recall. I was taller than the cop. I was wearing a white turtleneck. And I wore jeans and my new blue jacket. When I picture it now, I see two figures struggling amidst thousands of empty red, orange, yellow, and green seats, each dressed head to toe in blue, and each wearing a white shirt.

Somewhere in the process of trying to yank my arm away, I had the idea to punch the guy in the face. I am not good at throwing punches. I still vividly remember throwing a punch in the cookies and juice line when I was about eight. Someone had cut the line. It was a soft, almost apologetic gesture to my classmate's chin. Its only effect was to enrage him. It's awful to relay this memory. It suggests that I just wanted to get creamed in the cookies and juice line, and that I was now repeating the gesture towards the same end.

When I look back at those years, especially the years just before, the bad junior high school years, I wish I had thrown punches, been angry, physical in my hostility, let off steam, demarked territory, tried to make a stand. But I never threw a punch through those years. This was a kind of a debut.

My fist reached a face, the softness of a cheek. He flinched. Then his arm became very straight and he shoved me against the low wall behind me. I believe I flailed at him a bit more, screaming over and over, "Get off my jacket!"

All over the Garden the little dots of blue that had been positioned next to the exit tunnels began to converge in my direction. I went slack. I was quiet. My three friends stood off to the side, silent, expectant, poised. The little dots of blue got closer and became visible as men with faces and hands. Like the guy straight-arming me into the wall, they were generally on the roly-poly side. One of them put one of my arms behind my back, while another pushed my head down so I was doubled over at the waist. In this incapacitated position, I was marched forward, down some stairs. I was readying my body to be shoved rudely into one of the seats. I wondered if I would be given a talking to. I wondered if I would be in more trouble than that. I was entering a mode of litigation and contrived penance with which I was familiar.

What comes next provokes in me a kind of sick delight. I want to say to that kid, "You stupid shit! This is not shoplifting and these are not department store rent-a-cops!" I practically want to reach into the memory and smack the kid myself, if only so he would have some frame of reference for what was to come, so I could prepare him a little.

After a few steps, me in this awkward doubled over position, several bodies around me, something like a thunderclap occurred, with the full dimensions of thunder—first, a low rumbling, subwoofer kind of thud, then a scary darkness and, finally, a sharp cracking sound that reverberated through my head and my whole body. I had no idea what happened. I wasn't being seated. I was still moving down the flight of stairs. Then it happened again, and I understood that a knee, someone's knee, had just crashed into the side of my head. Then there was a sharp jabbing to the ribs, a punch in the lower back, but none of this registered with nearly as much metaphysical reality as the continual blows to the head. I could vaguely make out the shrill cries of outrage and fear coming from my three friends. But they were far away—at first, because the thunderclap was still receding from the foreground of my consciousness, and then because they were literally far away. I was still moving. At the bottom of the stairs, I was turned left. I walked some more. My arm hurt. I had forgotten all about my jacket.

Now I was back in some restricted area, and my first thought was that this is where they must keep the elephants when the circus comes to town. The memory of this episode seems so outlandish, I am sure I am embellishing. And yet I do recall the bare light bulb hanging down from a very high ceiling, and also fluorescent lights, and a table, like a kind of picnic bench, where some cops gathered, taking off their jackets, while a couple of other cops stood on either side of me and held my arms out. I am remembering them holding my arms out. It can't be that this happened, because it is too neat. I felt as if I was being crucified. So it can't be that I was actually made to stand with arms outstretched. It is too convenient an image.

But that is what I remember, me being held arms out while the cop I had punched leisurely took off his jacket, which had many gold buttons. He folded it on the bench, and rolled up his sleeves. His hairy, thick forearms were what I focused on; I didn't look at his face. He came up to me and smacked me on the side of the head. He smacked me upside the head for a while, and there was some conversation with the other cops. Cigarettes were smoked. I was not without things to say. What I said, over and over while I was smacked around, was: *This is America! I am a citizen! I have my rights!* I said it all in a grand soliloquy of sobs, total wetness, blubbering civics. My discourse on America and my role in it, and the police's role in it, went into hysterical fever pitch at the sight of the baseball bat. I was just sobbing heavily now in fearful, helpless anger.

They poked me in the side with the bat, until eventually they lost interest. And then they all sat around smoking while I stood there sniffling and then silent. Finally, I asked when I could go home. I'd like to report that someone told me to shut up, but I don't remember what they said. The amazing thing about it all was that before the torture scene commenced, my jacket was removed. I can't imagine it was neatly folded on a chair, but in the end I was allowed to pick it up, and it was completely fine. I was lead through the strange bowels of the Garden, following the path of the elephants. Eventually, I was pointed in the direction of a road that twisted circularly down. I followed the road, and after a while I found myself on the street. My friend Peter was there. I never found out how he knew to wait for me there. I was so grateful he was there. He put his arm around my shoulders and told me the other guys were waiting in front, and we started walking. I broke out into sobs, and he made some friendly comforting noises and kept his arm around my shoulders. He was incredibly cool-headed and decent about the whole thing. By the time we met up with the others, I had calmed down. We all agreed that what happened was totally fucked up. And that none of us would tell our parents about it.

While my face swelled a bit, there were no bruises, and I later was told that the beating I got was a kind of "police special" whose purpose was to leave no marks. That's why they kept hitting me in the side of the head and poking my ribs. No one at school noticed and, more importantly, neither did my mother. How that happened I have no idea. She was very attentive. I must have gone into a deep Sunday hibernation in my room, is my only guess. The whole thing receded pretty quickly.

A couple of weeks later, I went to the Knicks game with Steve in my Halloween costume, and saw the same cop who I had punched and who had then beat the crap out of me. After the initial sickening adrenalin rush subsided, and we took our seats, we got around to taking a very surreptitious hit of Steve's joint. It seemed absurdly audacious, but that was what Steve was like then, and me, too, I suppose. I exhaled a plume of smoke into the Garden's basketball ether, and sat back, feeling comforted by our stillness in our seats amidst the big open space of the Garden with the men on the bright floor down there exerting themselves. I tipped the fedora lower over my brow, going undercover. In the next few minutes I was filled with good feeling and comfort. At a certain point, I lifted my head up towards the Garden's rafters. I remember this moment with a peculiar clarity. The memory of it sits beside the memory of Ray Davies's pale, spotlit face all clenched up, his bow tie so tight it's as if a hand is strangling him as he belts a high note into the microphone, spittle flying. Just then, sitting at the Garden, I felt like an alien, the rush of the drug filling my upturned head. But I also felt very much at home.

28

Rush

Cumberland County Civic Center
Portland, Maine
December 4, 1985
HEIDI JULAVITS

THIS IS A STORY ABOUT a memorable concert that took place in Portland, Maine, and about which I remember very little. Chances are this concert occurred in 1985 during a cold month, February or March or April or even May. For certain I attended this concert with my high school boyfriend. For certain the band we saw was Rush. For certain the Cumberland County Civic Center, a poured-concrete octagon as lifelessly gray as the ocean that seized around the toothpicky piers a few blocks to the south, was less than a quarter full. For certain the people who did tromp through the cold and the quiet dark to sit in the loud dark and listen to Rush play atop what was usually a hockey rink were torso-nodding males scattered at suspicious intervals from one another so that the effect was very much like being intensely alone with lots of other intensely alone people who, the empty seats confirmed, were either losers or mullet-headed aesthetes with rarified musical tastes.

We were there, at this Rush concert, my boyfriend and I, because my boyfriend was a mullet-headed aesthete and possibly, in addition, a loser. He was a sophisticated, all-purpose thief who specialized in radar detectors and Vuarnet sunglasses; who liked to get high and drive recklessly around town in his Volkswagen Dasher wearing tanning-bed glasses; who played guitar in a band with other guys who specialized in backstabbing and stealing from one another and other displays of nasty loyalty. He listened to Ronnie James Dio and Yngwie Malmsteen. Rush he admired because he claimed they were, "geniuses," and because of the drummer, whose name, if I had to bet no more than ten dollars on it, was Neil Something. Rush was a great band, yes, but Neil Something was a stratospherically gifted drummer who, if memory isn't supplying ghoulishness to a situation that otherwise failed to interest me at all, had lost an arm. Or maybe he was blind. At

157

any rate, Neil Something's stratospheric greatness was made all the more miraculous by the fact that, with only 50 percent of the arm power or zero sight, he drummed better than any other drummer.

Then again, Neil Something may have had both his arms and two adequately working eyeballs. Neil Something may have just been a very good drummer and that, to me, was hardly reason to single him out.

I do not remember what we did that night before the concert, but chances are my boyfriend forged a check from his parents and we ordered food from Montana Burger, the Daniel Boone–style log fort replica built across from the Civic Center, and around whose pointed roof curled a twenty-foot-long plaster lizard. (When Montana Burger folded and the Daniel Boone fort was razed, the lizard was relocated to a wall-less parking garage—seven horizontal pads supported by see-through vertical girders—and hung from the underside of the roof, where it spun like a prehistoric weathervane in the heavier winds.) My boyfriend was the son of two Irish doctors who had immigrated to America in the sixties. Some combination of his Irish parents and his only son-ness (he had six sisters) meant he possessed the teenaged equivalent of diplomatic immunity, and I, a guilty-minded good grading do-gooder, was his passive and unlikely accessory. I ate the food he purchased with money stolen from his parents. I waited in the car while he shook down the country club parking lot's Audis and Volvos for fuzz busters. I hung out at L.L. Bean while he exploited their absurdly lenient return policy, returning clothes his parents had bought him ten years earlier. (The kindly Bean associate flipped through catalogues from the mid-seventies, located prices, and gave my boyfriend a full cash refund for his old, long-outgrown flannels.) My boyfriend was his own kind of genius—a criminal genius, or just a misguided teen zealot who would someday acquire a conscience—and he would be a spectacular success or a spectacular failure, world famous or incarcerated. Either outcome or sequence of outcomes (world fame then incarceration, incarceration then world fame) was equally likely, and for this reason he attracted many followers like myself, scared and timid people who, if we didn't watch out, were guaranteed to "succeed" in only the most dismally unremarkable ways.

Which makes us all sound like your basic bratty, upper-middle-class kids. Which we were, and yet—not. Yes, there were country clubs and preppy purveyors of outdoor clothing and French designer sunglasses, even if illegally obtained. But Portland was still a grubby, foggy, industrial port city with lots of vinyl-sided apartment houses and a pervasive old bilge stink. During the month of spring and two months of summer, Portland could be a dazzling place. But during winter, the endless nine-month winter, a contagiously sinister mood twanged through the streets.

I lived in a neighborhood of oversized Victorians on the brink of disre-pair—the rich neighborhood, by Portland standards. And yet, our back-yard shared a boundary with a long-defunct nineteenth-century cemetery that had become a haven for molesters and drunks. My friends and I squir-reled away, in boxes, hidden under porches, the rain-sodden pornographic novels found in the cemetery, where we often played after school because of the very perfect climbing tree whose pitch oozed from the knots in translucent, gummy mounds. Flashings by strange men were a regular childhood occurrence and often the first signs that winter was receding. Two standouts: a Freddie Mercury look-alike who drove a camo-green de-livery truck and somehow managed, *while driving*, to pitch his pelvis to window height so he could harshly joggle his penis at me; and an elderly man whose raincoat slyly parted as he passed me to reveal a woman's bra and garters slapping like loose rigging over his bony frame.

And then there were the actual crimes. Just after we moved into our house, a woman appeared on our back porch in the middle of the night, stabbed around the neck and face. Her attacker, she told my father, had worn a nylon stocking over his face. The police arrived, but the attacker had disappeared. The next morning when my mother fetched the paper, she found, on the bottom step of our back porch, a bloody nylon stocking. While living in this house, a man walked in one night, swiped our car keys off the kitchen counter, and stole our car as we slept upstairs. While living in this house, my mother received a phone call from a man who an-nounced he was going to kill himself. She tried to convince him otherwise, but failed. He threw himself out a motel window. We heard about his death the next morning on the radio.

And then there were, as my boyfriend so kindly referred to them, the Cretins. Portland, despite the inclement weather, those endless winters, was also, in the mid-eighties, a haven for the recently deinstitutionalized. Schizophrenics, the mentally disabled, the all-around physically and psy-chically unsound, populated the streets in such numbers that a person might start to doubt their own claims to health and sanity. Old women wearing winter coats and wool stockings in the dead of August sternly be-rated the parking meters. Men with oddly shaped heads, humping gaits, crossed eyes, and/or slurred speech congregated in a bleak slab-concrete park or at the downtown Burger King. This was where I first saw my future best friend, a blonde pixie in a cranberry beret, sharing her fries with a scraggly entourage of homeless people. My future best friend was the straight-A daughter of a doctor. At sixteen, she had moved into an SRO called the Lafayette with a boy she'd met at a Dead concert, a boy who sold frozen peas door-to-door to make rent, a boy on oodles of head meds who threatened, more than once, to kill her with a knife. This girl came from an averagely lovely family, and yet she was a practical runaway, living on her own with a pea-selling madman, eating fast food with former mental patients, and making money working as a telemarketer at a Howard Johnson's. What I'm trying to say is, the boundaries in Portland were extremely fluid. The lines between wealthy neighborhood and flasher haunt, playground and pornographic bookshop, mentally stable and mentally sound, good girl and bad girl, loser and rarified aesthete—these lines were so crisscrossed that they signified nothing. There were no boundaries to exceed or respect because there were no boundaries, and this gave a person, namely a teenager, a sense of opportunity so intense it felt like a heedless charge toward self-obliteration. And so, that night, listening to Rush play in a concrete bunker to a bunch of mullet-headed losers who, by Portland standards, constituted something of a brain bank, I had the sense, which was possibly just a consequence of being seventeen, that we had all been abandoned by scientists in a radically defunded biosphere.

So the concert. Beforehand, as I said, chances were we went to Montana Burger; most definitely we were high. My boyfriend also cherished Rush because of their lyrics—which I'm guessing he found poetic, or at least more poetic than even the most heartfelt stabs at sensitivity by Ronnie James Dio—and because the songs ambled along in some way he considered intricate and unusual for your basic rock band. (I believe this involved something called a time signature.) I remember the lead singer of Rush had a face-obscuring shingle of hair; his voice, as was its habit, over-enunciated the song lyrics in a dorky way that was pure galaxies from the chest-mumbling, syllable-swallowing cool of most rock stars.

During the two years we dated, I came to better appreciate my boyfriend's enthusiasm for Rush, but I wouldn't go so far as to say that I enjoyed the concert given I dreaded, and still dread, concerts so intensely that the eventual experience must be transportive in the extreme to overcome my expectations of misery. Of claustrophobia. Of being trapped and bored. Because you cannot read a book at a concert, because you are stuck in the dark, because the noise obliterates the possibility of conversation (a reason to never attend a concert with someone you don't know well—i.e., someone with whom a shared silence, even one filled with noise, will produce intense social anxiety), I've often felt that concerts were a hell equivalent to suffering from insomnia in a room with other sleeping people whom you cannot disturb by switching on a light. Yes, the Rush concert was more captivating than most because there was a discernible language component. Still, I couldn't now recapture the content of these songs or even a single chorus (not that Rush songs had a chorus). Really, all I can remember is the lead singer's delivery, which I would describe as insistent and earnest and even a bit scoldy.

Not that Rush's lead singer is to blame for being unmemorable. I was not and am not a person to whom music registers in its specifics. I recall music through the people who introduced me to it, and the weather that was happening at the time, and the place where the listening occurred, and how it felt to be in the world for me then. When I do listen to songs it is obsessively and repetitively, then I abandon these songs so thoroughly I forget the band that performed them, the album on which they appeared. You could mention this band to me and I would profess total ignorance. In fact, I have an aversion to listening too frequently to music after it's been imprinted by a certain time and place, for fear that the memories I associate with the hearing of it will be spoiled by the now-life of this new person who is listening.

So. This concert I don't remember. It ended. My boyfriend probably drove me home. The lead singer and his one-armed, blind Wunderkind drummer most likely retired to Portland's Holiday Inn whose windows overlooked a log fort partially obscured by a giant lizard, the streets empty save for an emphatically gesticulating, lone pedestrian, and they thought to themselves, "What a freak show of a city this is. Get me the hell out of here." Or maybe not. Maybe playing to Portland's Loserly Finest was just another in a long string of marginal nights for geniuses like them. Maybe the lead singer of Rush was just another misguided zealot in our echo chamber of a city; or maybe for him, like me, this was just another night in his life whose contours he might recall but whose specifics he would forget. Moving on was implicit for him, as it was for me. He'd jump into his tour bus. I would go to college, live in Asia and San Francisco, and finally end up in New York. I would become a boundary respecter for a time, a tenacious grasper at non-fluidity, an unremarkable success.

Not so, my boyfriend. He'd move to L.A. and continue his life of quasi-crime. He'd discover while driving around the L.A. freeway that he could call the phone number listed on the backs of dump trucks and claim that a rock had tumbled from the truck and smashed his windshield, and he could collect an easy $500. He made $12,000 before he was caught. At this time, he was dating a non-English-speaking Swedish model who turned out not to be Swedish, who turned out, in fact, be a fluent speaker of English from Wisconsin. He changed his name to escape creditors and—not one, it turned out, for incarceration—got bailed out by his parents. I started seeing him around New York, where he frequently appeared, and I would struggle to remember to call him by this new name. He'd phone me, and we'd meet. Last time I saw him was on the Bowery, a decade ago. He was wearing a baseball cap as he religiously did, to hide his receding hair-line. I hurried past him before he could notice me. He hadn't proven to be spectacular in the realms of either success or failure; he was just a misfit with another name. Outside of our defunded biosphere—our small, small pond—he appeared falsely brash and freakishly unready for the world.

Rush, I am told, no longer exists, or if they do, they do so invisibly. Even when I saw them, in 1985, the crowds were waning. There were new geniuses to adore, and since then those geniuses have been replaced by yet newer geniuses, because there can never be too many geniuses at once. Where do the old geniuses go? Maybe they move to Portland. Maybe the scoldy lead singer of Rush and his now toothless (and armless and blind) drummer recalled with fondness their night in Portland, packed their knapsacks, and took their rightful place among the Cretins (who, we always suspected, were old geniuses in their way).

But I doubt it. These days, Portland is like a pleasant suburb, and no place for old geniuses. The cemetery has been scrubbed of vagrants, and snappy-looking people walk their breeded dogs between the righted tombstones and de-graffitied mausoleums. The parks have been beautified, the coffee shops fancified, the sidewalk benches filled by art students and pretty moms, the Burger King swapped for a bistro. The lizard is gone, replaced by higher-tech forms of wind detection. Only the Cretins remain, but this city is no longer theirs. They bounce nervously at intersections waiting for lights to change, en route to nowhere. This new place has vanished the old—this pretty, average, suburban place.

I heard my boyfriend has returned to Portland after a failed marriage and the sudden death of his mother. Maybe he's married again. Maybe he has a proper job and is a proper dad. I don't know if that would depress me more than to think he's drifting around Portland like the Cretins, another displaced person. But even I am a displaced person when I visit Portland—me, a proper mom, a divorcée, a person who no longer judges failures and successes by their degree of spectacle. Despite circa-1985 Portland's evident drawbacks, I cannot help, when faced with its chipper replacement, but yearn for that vanished city, reflect sentimentally on my time there, and wish that all this sweet bettering of things didn't equal erasure.

29

The Pogues
Metro
Boston
July 2, 1986
ROBERT POLITO

EARLIER THAT EVENING, in one of those flukes that promises more than the moment can deliver, we ran into the Pogues, at least some of them, across the street at Fenway Park. The Red Sox were playing the Toronto Blue Jays. With nothing to do until the show started, we purchased cheap bleacher seats and climbed the stairs behind center field. Suddenly, up ahead, loomed a quartet attired like us, despite the season, in dark wool duds: Spider, Cait, and (I'm almost certain) James, alongside a dour manager/driver/minder type.

We clattered into the row back of them, and as Kevin and Maureen, Kristine and I introduced ourselves, the Pogues were visibly tensed, wary at their detection. But this turned out to be their first baseball game, and they had lots of questions.

It was 1986, the year the Red Sox would capture the American League East, and then, one out away from winning the World Series against the Mets—their only World Series since 1918—witness history vaporize as Bill Buckner flubbed a Mookie Wilson ground ball. I saw that World Series game on TV over the telephone with Kristine, she in her apartment in New York while I was back in Cambridge, and you could hear the exultation across Manhattan, even down the phone line from Riverside Drive.

That lay months ahead, but this too was an important game. Roger Clemens was undefeated in his first fourteen outings and going after the American League record for consecutive wins at the start of a season.

I wish I could disclose that the Pogues acted scandalously. But particularly after Clemens gave up the tying run in the eighth inning, and reliever Bob Stanley then yielded two more runs, the Sox fans around us held a monopoly on drunk and vile, slopping beers, roaring curses at the Blue Jays bullpen, and ultimately pissing against the concrete pillars under the stands. Throughout, the Pogues drank Cokes.

What I mostly remember is realizing how difficult baseball is to explain. As we sat behind the Pogues, fielding their confusions, baseball didn't appear so much the harmonious, disciplined contest you might observe in, say, John Updike's iconic recap of a Red Sox game, as it did a lawless inventory of exceptions and irregularities. Three strikes and you're out, of course, unless that third strike is really a foul ball, and thus doesn't count, because only the first two foul balls count as strikes, so a batter can hit as many fouls after that as he wants, unless, of course, someone catches the foul ball, because that's an out, and . . .

The Pogues appeared more fascinated by "The Wave" that periodically surged through Fenway, as from one section to the next in a circle around the park fans stood up, raised their arms, and then sat back down, everyone cheering for themselves once they were done.

Kevin and I assumed it cooler if we didn't ask Cait about Elvis Costello, not even when Spider joked about her being on long distance all night again. But in our Elvis iridescent suits, and my geeky glasses, she must have believed we were lunatics.

Except for Elvis I might never have taken in the Pogues. By the time the band landed at Metro—a music and dance club on Lansdowne Street, opposite Fenway Park—they'd released two albums, *Red Roses for Me* (1984) and *Rum, Sodomy, and the Lash* (1985), along with a crucial EP, *Poguetry in Motion* (1986). Their name was a bowdlerization of Pogue Mahone or *póg mo thóin*, Gaelic for "kiss my arse." The Pogues had performed down the street at Spit the previous March, an early St. Patrick's donnybrook conspicuously attended by JFK Jr. and Joe Kennedy, Robert's son, then running for Congress.

Much of this hoopla, specifically the band's vaunted Irishness among Irish American Bostonians, proved a distraction to my listening, and I resisted when Kevin and Maureen played *Red Roses for Me*. But in 1986, I was still obsessed with Elvis Costello—though, granted, not as obsessed as I was in 1977, 1978, 1979, and 1980, when I'd stay up all night drinking and playing *My Aim Is True, This Year's Model, Armed Forces*, and *Get Happy!!*, confident I would glimpse my own past and future autobiography. Elvis, of course, produced *Rum, Sodomy, and the Lash*, and moreover recently he had fallen in love with the Pogues' bassist, Cait O'Riordan. To this day I believe that *Rum, Sodomy, and the Lash*, maybe even more than Tom Waits's inexhaustible *Rain Dogs*, offers the most transportative—fierce, melancholy, beautiful, and enduring—music from 1985. So, by the night the Pogues climbed on stage at Metro, July 2, 1986, a Wednesday, and for many the blast-off of a long Independence Day holiday weekend, I knew their recordings, as well as their various prior and sideline incarnations—singer Shane MacGowan's Nipple Erectors; guitarist Philip Chevron's Radiators From Space and his cabaret tracks with Agnes Bernelle; O'Riordan's Pride of the Cross.

The Pogues were only three or four songs into their set when Kevin reeled back to where we said we'd all hook up, behind the soundboard. Our friend positioned himself at the edge of every club stage, even for hardcore shows. He luxuriated in the small defensive actions necessary to sustain his patch of concrete amid the shoving and tumbling fans. Slam dancing— at least in Boston during the mid-1980s—manifested a gymnastic decorum, a tough, improvised tenderness of silent directives and solicitudes. The slamming looked wilder the farther outside of the fracas you stood, and I rarely saw anyone get hurt.

Not tonight. Out of Southie via Harvard, Kevin was what my grand-mother tagged "Black Irish," smart, ornery, and as homely as a scare poster for Father Damien's Hawaiian Islands leper colony, his face pimpled, scarred, and swollen. This summer evening, with the Pogues just a few songs along, playing "Transmetropolitan," as I recall, or maybe "Billy's Boys," Kevin's face now also was spilling blood. Around us, couples per-formed frisky jigs and shouted lyrics. But right in front of the Pogues a mostly male assembly—hundreds of Boston boys, their raised arms rip-pling to the beat—hurled themselves at the stage again and again until the crush closest to the band toppled over and the rest of the crowd rebounded backward toward the center of the room.

The sway of the Pogues throng at Metro that night was more furious— and intricate—than any slam dancing I've experienced since. Dylan once remarked that he brought rock 'n' roll attitude to folk music. A shorthand account of the Pogues might observe that they played traditional music with punk attitude. The slamming boys managed to refract both strains in the sound at once, the spasm of a body swilling poison and its antidote si-multaneously. There was a traditional lilt, a silvery cadence pulsing through the upcast arms and bobbing heads, and something like the snap of a whip. Kevin felt that whip across his cheek when he fell, and the audience ground his face against a band monitor.

"I'll meet you here when it's over," Kevin said, after Maureen, his girlfriend, swabbed the blood with a drink napkin, and Kristine and I tried to talk him into staying with us. The Pogues started another song, "The Old Main Drag," their first slow tune so far. Our friend lunged back into the mob.

Kevin's family home overlooked the route of the annual South Boston St. Patrick's Day parade, but I grew up the child of what was locally judged a "mixed marriage," Irish and Italian. Still, my Irish side dominated. We occupied the first floor of a classic brown three-decker in Dorchester purchased by my late grandfather James Lonergan (originally of the County Waterford), and that endured in my grandmother's name, Brigid Lonergan née Connelly (originally of the County Cork), although my father now handled the maintenance and supervised the tenants. Our neighbors bore Irish names, as did my parents' friends. Inside our Dorchester flat, Irish tended to mean Catholic (my Aunt Mary was a nun), Friday and Saturday night booze-ups (my uncle John and his card-playing cronies), and a solemn, singalong pining after a forsaken auld sod that invariably wound up with someone screaming or crying. Outside our house, Irish was the Kennedys (the nuns at my school predicted sainthood for the "martyred" president), mothers taunting "Mayor Black" at Kevin White, and their children tossing rocks at school buses. There was a sinister undertow to Irish: early on, my mother signaled that she thought many priests were "damaged," as she put it, even as she inadvertently sent my brother to a school run by Father Paul Shanley, Boston's notorious "Street Priest." But I fell into zanier confusions, too. One St. Patrick's Day in Park Street Station on the way to the parade with my grandmother, I saw a subway florist spraying white carnations green, and surmised for years that flowers got their colors that way.

For me, Irish American around Boston radiated a delusive sentimentality always about to tumble into havoc. When I really heard *Rum, Sodomy, and the Lash*, I was struck by the stylish way the Pogues flipped that sentimentality/havoc continuum inside out, the way someone in a schoolyard fight would flip an opponent's jacket over his head, the better to confuse and divert him. Those early Pogues albums divided between traditional covers and Shane MacGowan originals. For their reworking (sometimes rewriting) of Irish, Scottish, even American folk tunes and in MacGowan's own scruffy, elegant songs, fury, injury, menace, and anguish are the passions that seize you instantly; only later can you catch the romantic undertone. "Transmetropolitan," for instance, the opening cut on *Red Roses for Me*, transacts a sort of jaunty Paddy *A Clockwork Orange*:

> From Brixton's lovely boulevards
> To Hammersmith's sightly shores
> We'll scare the Camden Palace poofs
> And worry all the whores
> There's lechers up in Whitehall
> And queers in the GLC
> And when we've done those bastards in
> We'll storm the BBC

In "The Old Main Drag," from *Rum, Sodomy, and the Lash*, an aging hustler recounts his trade around Piccadilly Circus:

> In the cold winter nights the old town it was chill
> But there were boys in the cafes who'd give you cheap pills
> If you didn't have the money you'd cajole or you'd beg
> There was always lots of tuinol on the old main drag
> One evening as I was lying down around Leicester Square
> I was picked up by the coppers and kicked in the balls
> Between the metal doors at Vine Street I was beaten and mauled
> And they ruined my looks for the old main drag

"A Pair of Brown Eyes" tracks the wanderings of an Irish infantryman decades after the First World War:

> One summer evening drunk to hell
> I stood there nearly lifeless
> An old man in the corner sang
> Where the water lilies grow
> And on the jukebox Johnny sang
> About a thing called love
> And it's how are you kid, and what's your name
> And how would you bloody know?

In blood and death 'neath a screaming sky
I lay down on the ground
And the arms and legs of other men
Were scattered all around

The mayhem so insistently at the gist of MacGowan's lyrics might only measure the distance between Irish and the phenomenon Maureen Dezell in her book *Irish America: Coming Into Clover* dubs "Eiresatz." But other particulars figure in the distance the Pogues insinuated into the music itself. One, obviously, is punk—before they ever performed traditional Irish music in public, many of the Pogues served time in London and Dublin punk outfits. "Seeing the Sex Pistols changed my life—it changed loads of people's lives," MacGowan once said.[1] "There was a band that just got up there and made a really horrible noise and didn't give a shit. They were all our age and had dyed hair and wore brothel creepers, and it was just a question of, 'Yeah, Fuck it. I hate everything and they're actually doing it.' I thought they were brilliant, the best group I've ever seen."

Another possibly less obvious detail is that the Pogues aren't entirely Irish, or are Irish in a complex, conscious fashion. Of the eight Pogues who took the stage at Metro, only two—Chevron and Terry Woods—were born in Ireland. O'Riordan was born in Nigeria and raised in London, but all the rest, Spider Stacy, Jem Finer, James Fearnley, and Andrew Ranken, come from England. Indeed, MacGowan was born in Kent, although reared on a farm in Tipperary until he was six, when his family moved to central London. "Even at that age, it was a sharp contrast from the country in Ireland," he said.[2] "I used to know bits of Gaelic because my mother speaks it fluently, but once I hit the city I forgot it. I became immersed in the society of London. On the other hand, because there's an Irish scene in London you never forget the fact that you originally came from Ireland. There are lots of Irish pubs, so there was always Irish music in bars and on jukeboxes. I had an uncle who ran a pub in Dagenham, and I stayed there a lot of the time. Then every summer I would spend my school holidays back in Tipp."

By way of Irishness, then, the Pogues located themselves along a slippery, paradoxical slope. Other than O'Riordan's electric bass and, I sup-

---

[1] Ann Scanlon, *The Pogues: The Lost Decade* (London: Omnibus Press, 1988), 12.
[2] Ibid., 10.

pose, Chevron's rockabilly hollowbody electric guitar, all their instrumentation that night at Metro could be tagged traditional—banjo, mandolin, cittern, concertina, and the lead players were, astonishingly, Fearnley on accordion and Stacy on tin whistle. (Another shorthand account of the Pogues is that they played punk music with traditional instruments.) Their songs invoked Irish writers and traditional Irish and Scottish musicians: the Dubliners, John McCormack, Richard Tauber, Philomena Begley, Ray Lynam and the Hillbillies, Sean O'Casey, Joyce, Yeats, and especially Flann O'Brien and Brendan Behan. But all the angles felt askew. It was O'Riordan, for instance, who sang—gorgeously—the Scottish air, "I'm a Man You Don't Meet Everyday," and revised the lyric so that instead of going hunting with a dog, she shoots him. Their jigs, reels, and sea shanties divulged a cracked, amphetamine edge. For "Streams of Whiskey," MacGowan name-checked Behan, and tilted his death wish into dipso overdrive.

Recasting Irish history as punk—or punk as Irish history—there was nothing smirking, nothing routinely ironic about the Pogues. They sounded contemporary as well as ancestral, of London as much as of Dublin. Like most punks, their songs linked them to outlaws, outcasts, renegades, felons, and marauders, yet often executed jolting twists. Besides reliable associations like the Great Hunger, the IRA, or Jesse James, MacGowan's lyrics conjured Australian convicts, fixated on World War I, notably the Irish recruits who fought at Gallipoli, and the Spanish Civil War, alert to betrayals and venality, by turns realistic and phantasmagoric, mythic and personal. His barbed sociopath anthem, "Boys from the County Hell," sports a jaunty couplet that skids from Irish fascists to Lieutenant Calley: "My daddy was a blue shirt and my mother a madam/And my brother earned his medals at My Lai in Vietnam." His "Sick Bed of Cuchuliann" glances at the IRA Republicans who resisted Franco: "Frank Ryan bought you whiskey in a brothel in Madrid/And you decked some fucking blackshirt who was cursing all the Yids"; and unlike, I'm guessing, at least some among their Boston audience, the song also identifies with blacks and immigrants—"Now you'll sing a song of liberty for blacks and paks and jocks/And they'll take you from this dump you're in and stick you in a box." MacGowan sang out of an Irish diaspora, his strongest work shadowing exiles adrift in London, and later New York.

Skeptical and rollicking, a carnival of Irishness and sardonic about Ireland, the Pogues at Metro that July night in 1986 mounted a fearsome, majestic racket that disputed, even denied every sentiment they celebrated. The only event I ever thought matched it was a St. Patrick's Day program at the Boston Public Library when Seamus Heaney disdained to act the professional Irishman, defiantly reading only his darkest poems from *North*, and refusing to soften the cruxes of Irish politics.

With their thrift store Sunday suits and yeasty cotton shirts, MacGowan and Co. resembled impatient undertakers. On slow numbers—"The Old Main Drag," "I'm a Man You Don't Meet Every Day," Behan's "The Auld Triangle," Ewan MacColl's "Dirty Old Town," and Eric Bogle's "The Band Played Waltzing Matilda"—the Pogues lurched like the capsizing of a boat, mournful and grand. On fast songs—"Sally MacLennane," "Transmetropolitan," and "The Sick Bed of Cuchuliann"—Stacy, Fearnley, and Chevron threw themselves around the stage, while MacGowan sauntered as though oblivious to the frenzy, a bottle of beer or a glass of whiskey in his hand, nearly toothless, yet intoning each convulsive phrase. Whether the boys who stormed the band hooked into all the snags, the counterblasts inside the blast, that didn't—couldn't—matter. For two mighty hours that summer night on Lansdowne Street, the Pogues *were* Boston. And as MacGowan sang, "We'll go where spirits take us/To heaven or to hell/And kick up bloody murder in the town we love so well."

I thought of "The Wave" as I watched the surging arms and bouncing heads at Metro. The same gesture, if revved up, likely many of the same fans . . .

As the Pogues finished their set, Kevin returned to our safe house by the club soundboard. Now his other cheek was cut open, and he wanted to go. But the Boston audience called the band back for four encores. You could style those last four songs a frolic—or a riot.

When the Pogues finally quit the stage, Cait O'Riordan lingered at a microphone. The only words I could make out were "love you" and "Red Sox."

30

The Beastie Boys
The Capital Centre
Landover, Maryland
April 5, 1987
MARC NESBITT

WHEN I WAS FIFTEEN, I had a wispy mistake of a moustache—for two reasons. One, all the sap-filled R&B songs we listened to in those days, all the slow jams and quiet storms, were sung by slight, light-skinned guys with their adolescent Mexican moustaches. And two, Vandy, my pseudo-girlfriend at the time, told me to grow one, giving the reason that'll make a fifteen-year-old do anything: *it'll make you look older.* She didn't order me to do it or threaten she'd end whatever stunted form of relationship we claimed to have; she just said it, like people say, "You should lighten up" or "You should really check out the Smithsonian." But sure enough, and very slowly, a moustache arrived. Point being, I was a self-conscious social dipshit as a high school sophomore, and, with the exception of Vandy, girls avoided me as if allergic.

So I still have no idea how, exactly, I managed to go to the *Licensed To Ill* tour in 1987 with my friend EW and four seniors. I've been told there were other people there, and we didn't actually travel with the upperclassmen. But they were dancing right next to us at the show, so as far as I was concerned, at the time, they may as well have carried us in on their backs.

The only explanation was EW, my best friend since we were five, who was far funnier and charming at fifteen than I'd even attempt to imitate until my twenties; was loved by upperclassmen all; and had two older siblings who'd also gone to our high school, making him something of a legacy student. He was a tiny, blond kid built like a twelve-year-old and stuck with braces longer than any human I've ever known. Eventually, he'd go away to college, lift weights every day, and return the next summer, braceless, looking like a superhero stepping out of a phone booth, muscularly inflated to twice his size. Somehow, he'd convinced one of the seniors to bring us.

The senior guys were an attackman named BC and a middie everybody referred to as "The Move"—our word then for the coolest shit imaginable. Usage: three popular black girls who ran track had a clique called Curvation, whose members may or may not have rapped, danced, or sang in their spare time, but definitely covered lockers and desks all over the high school with their slogan: "CURVATION IS THE MOVE."

How a tall, freckled white kid with a high, preppy Opie fade ever got that pseudonym is beyond me, but we were underclassmen and respected all nicknames as fact. If everybody called a guy "Ten Gallon Matt," then as far as we were concerned, he'd *actually* drank ten gallons of Jack Daniels last Preakness. We were walking among legends, sitting across the cafeteria from "Pecos Bill," "Paul Bunyan" over by the salad bar.

I only remember one of the two senior girls—a field hockey player with a long, stolid, Easter Island face. Though I have no recollection of the other girl, I'm sure there was some facial or otherwise physical attribute I worshipped. Or maybe her name was endearing, or, at fifteen, I somehow found sexy her chain-smoking–forty-two-year-old-Long-Island-woman voice.

For a kid whose previous—and only—two concerts had been Sha Na Na and Hall & Oates, this was going to be my Hendrix at Monterey. Though I certainly didn't know enough at the time to make that comparison. All I knew for sure was it'd be better than Sha Na Na and Hall & Oates *combined*.

Once we found our seats, it was a good hour and a half before anything happened, at which point a number of enormous black men began setting up instruments all over the stage, including an inordinate amount of percussion. In fact, it was just one enormous percussion section, with a synthesizer. Rumors began circling around that Junkyard Band was opening. Besides Chuck Brown, the godfather of go-go—who with a full band and a dexterous horn section sounded like an exceptional ghetto wedding band playing a reception at Howard University—Junkyard Band was legendary, the most popular go-go band of the time, with "The Word" and "Sardines" in heavy rotation on all the black DC radio stations. For me this was the equivalent of telling me Michael Jordan was coming to my birthday party. I dismissed it immediately and thought less of the person who'd told me.

Go-go can and has been defined as "a subgenre of funk music developed in and around Washington, DC, in the mid- and late 1970s—defined by continuous, complex, heavy rhythm arrangements focused through two motifs performed on multiple congas, tumbadoras, and rototoms, inter-spersed with timbale and cowbell parts, driven by heavy-footed drum-ming, and punctuated by crowd call-and-response. A swing rhythm is of-ten implied (if not explicitly stated)."[1] To me, it's the hardest parts of hip hop, calypso, and salsa music all combined and filtered through the worst sections of what was then the murder capital of America. It's also one of those endemic musical phenomena, like zydeco, with one main difference being go-go is primarily hated anywhere outside of DC and Northern Virginia. You can put on a zydeco record at a party and some people will love it. Play go-go outside of DC and you'll never see people move as quickly to change the music.

By far the two most successfully mainstream go-go songs, and therefore the only two most people have heard of, are Brown's "Bustin' Loose" and E.U.'s "Da' Butt." "Bustin' Loose" held No. 1 on the Billboard R&B charts for two months in 1979, prompting a movie two years later of the same name starring Richard Pryor. "Da' Butt" was featured prominently in Spike Lee's *School Daze*, and Salt-N-Pepa did a go-go-lite single called "My Mic Sounds Nice." Beyond that, the mass audience has never shown an inter-est.

But to those of us who grew up in the area, it was the aural nectar of the funk gods. And for suburban kids, Junkyard unannounced at the Cap Centre was about the only chance we had of seeing it live. Shows mostly only took place in South East, the most terrifying section of DC, referred to in songs as "Souf Eass," a place name that when uttered inspired in us the same awe as the word "Normandy" or "Danang." The kind of place where you'd be shot through the forehead or shanked in the liver within five sec-onds of stepping out of your vehicle.

So when the lights went down and the PA announcer said, "Ladies and Gentlemen . . . JUNK . . . YAAAAAAAAARD!" people's heads turned in-side out in the loudest spontaneous scream-cheer I've ever taken part in. EW and I were hopping up and down like little girls, and even the seniors went giddy.

Junkyard played "Sardines," "The Word," and a number of other clas-sics, without pause, instrumentally transitioning from one song to the next, for an hour and a half. The crowd in turn sweat heavily, bent over, and gen-

[1]"Go-go," *Wikipedia*, August 30, 2006.

erated nearly nineteen thousand variations on the Wop and Happy Feet for the entirety.

When it was over, I fell into my seat, dazed and smiling, with a feeling as close as I'd ever come to something like post-sex bliss. Everyone had similar expressions on their faces, and no one could stop talking about what they'd just seen.

And then Public Enemy took the stage.

Yo! Bumrush the Show had either just come out, or was about to, and almost no one in the entire arena had ever heard of Public Enemy, let alone actually knew any of their songs.

First, the S1Ws marched out in lockstep, the Security of the First World: two enormous black guys in full Black Panther henchmen all-black uniform—boots, cargo pants, turtleneck, beret—each holding replica Uzis and wearing the largest gold dookie chains I'd ever seen. They assumed posts at either corner of the stage, simultaneously slapping their weapons into position. Some people yelled vaguely, some clapped, but most of us just stood there with our faces pulled together, as if a performance art piece had just broken out.

After an awkward pause, the heavy bass began plodding, so deep as to rattle the ribs and make your blood vibrate. From out between the two enormous speaker towers, Flavor Flav made his entrance, dancing in weird spastic steps like a marionette monkey while screaming rhyming jibberish that was supposed to rile the crowd, inform them of how in effect Public Enemy was, and issue bizarre threats to unnamed entities who wished to defeat them—all at the same time. In further contrast to the at-attention S1Ws, he was decked out entirely in white—from top hat to sneakers, jeans to button-down shirt, suspenders to sunglasses—even his leather gloves were white.

He was the first "hype man" I'd ever seen. A staple of all hip hop shows, the hype man pumps up the crowd, screams things like "Yeah!" and "What!" over or between the emcee's lyrics, and tends to add emphasis on the last word of every line. In groups with two or more emcees, they'll often all serve as one another's hype men, a tactic Run DMC and the Beastie Boys both employed heavily.

But Flavor Flav remains the first and best example of the hype man I ever saw. Problem was, nobody knew what the hell he was saying as he strutted around like a cokehead walking out of a bar bathroom. So all intended "hype" wasn't happening, and people went back to the same confused murmuring from before the music began.

At that point, Chuck D came out in his trademark black satin athletic jacket and black baseball cap and began rapping over stripped down, belligerent beats, stalking around the stage in a way that, in the hat and jacket, made him seem like an incensed baseball manager tearing an umpire to pieces. He never had a chance. As great as everyone would come to realize he was, Chuck D on that night had walked squarely into the artist purgatory known as *Ahead of Their Time*.

To the crowd, these people just seemed furious, and one of them was clearly insane. While we were heavily go-go friendly, everyone had really come to see three crazy white kids act like assholes and throw beer at each other. And so it was that, around the beginning of the third song, one of the most influential rap groups in history got booed off the stage.

Chuck D walked off, disgustedly back to the dugout. Flavor Flav strutted backwards and gave everyone both middle fingers. The S1Ws marched off in perfect unison, good soldiers to the end. Everyone old enough in the crowd went to buy beer.

When the Beastie Boys did finally come out, they performed every song off *Licensed To Ill*, as well as their earlier single "She's On It," all of which lasted about forty-five minutes. There was no encore because they were out of songs. In retrospect, they were raw for an arena show but had the hits and obnoxiousness to pull it off. They'd carted out the girls in cages and their enormous inflatable penis prop, and jumped around in their signature outfits so everyone could tell them apart: Mike D with the pork pie hat and sunglasses, Adrock with the T-shirt and baseball cap, MCA unshaven in a leather jacket. They danced in exaggerated, almost desperate parodies of emcees, an irony I wouldn't catch onto until years afterward, and a perfect example of which was their rocking long thin chains with ripped-off hood ornaments for medallions.

It was a fashion trend suburban kids turned into an epidemic, Mercedes owners getting the brunt. My friends and I all did it and wore them to homecoming thinking we were the height of hilarity, before the school staff confiscated every last one. By far the most impressive medallion, and the best example of the spirit of the Beasties at the time, was worn by "The Grouper": a hubcap-sized Volkswagen bus logo I'd helped him rip off. After we'd pried it free, we threw it back and forth like a Frisbee across the parking lot until one of the studs ripped a chunk out of my thumb.

31

Redd Kross
The Town Pump
Vancouver, British Columbia, Canada
May 1987
CARL NEWMAN

I WAS AT A POINT in my young life where I could spend hours and hours in a record store, flipping through the vinyl, shooting the shit with the jaded clerks, captivated as someone told me about the time they hung out with Lux Interior. If you were forty-two, lived with your parents, but had the Seeds' *A Web of Sound* on cassette, there was still one guy left in town who thought you were the coolest. All I cared about was the "cool" music. For a while there, music seemed like one of the best reasons to be alive.

I went to ANY show, even if it was just a band name that sounded cool (or what passed for cool in my mind). If I'd read about a band anywhere, I was there. I was just bored and young. That's why I went to see Redd Kross having only heard one song that didn't even blow my mind that much—their cover of the Rolling Stones' "Citadel" that was on *Enigma Variations, Vol. 1*. Redd Kross, however, changed me.

When I was growing up, I thought of rock concerts as ten thousand people hanging out in the smoky haze of the Pacific Coliseum, waiting to see KISS or maybe ZZ Top. I was just getting used to the fact that there were great bands that played to almost nobody in small clubs. It seemed unfair, and it didn't make sense. Eventually, I came to appreciate amazing bands that were a secret between a few friends and myself. I went even if no one would go with me. Like the time I went to see the band Christmas at the Town Pump and there was literally nobody there. Maybe the other audience members were hiding in the catacombs of the club. I don't know. It unnerved me so much that I had to leave. I couldn't face a band on my own. Three against one! It was too much to ask.

Anyway, in May 1987, I was still new to the concept of the struggling artist, aside from what I knew about painters only becoming popular after they die. So, initially, these small shows felt very surreal. Not quite right.

Redd Kross bridged the gap for me. They were playing to almost no-body at the aforementioned Pump, but they rocked it like they were play-ing fucking Live Aid. They remembered what rock 'n' roll meant to them: the Beatles, the Stones, Bowie, Led Zep et al. . . . They took the seventies that they grew up in, basically, and they channeled it. They made me re-member. There was an unspoken understanding there. Rock 'n' roll was/is kind of cheesy, but there is a beauty to that cheesiness. Punk rock was supposed to have killed off the bloated bullshit that rock had become, but it threw out the baby with the bathwater. Redd Kross knew that em-bracing the good in seventies pop music was actually, in its way, punk. Not only punk, it was the right thing to do. What's more, they didn't give a shit if it was cool, but must have known it became cool the moment that they touched it.

It was what I'd call the "classic Redd Kross" lineup that night: the brothers, Jeff McDonald on guitar and Steve McDonald on the bass; Robert Hecker on lead guitar; Roy McDonald (no relation) on the drums. They had just released *Neurotica* the month before. This was a short West Coast tour. They had perfected the persona that first showed up on their mini-LP of covers, *Teen Babes of Monsanto*: the arena-ready glam rockers who sounded only vaguely like the trash-punks that made *Born Innocent*. You could recognize the voice, but barely. I would find out all of this his-tory later. That night, I was new to it all.

Like I said, they made you remember: that, honestly, the Partridge Family had their moments; that Linda Blair was cool in her chipmunk-cheeked bad girl way; that Mackenzie Phillips was an addict while she was on *One Day at a Time*; that Charles Manson wrote songs, and a few of them were good. Essentially, everything that was fucked up or cool about the late sixties up through the eighties, redirected through the minds of some Hawthorne hipster brothers. They celebrated our lost trash culture, the culture that is part of our collective consciousness as children of the seventies. All that trash was necessary. It was Judas be-traying Jesus, fulfilling his destiny. It was pop culture going to its logical extreme before swinging back in protest, and it deserved to be remem-bered, since every point in the arc of the pendulum was equally impor-tant. Jonathan Richman said it best: we couldn't let our youth go to waste.

Yes, I'm overanalyzing. Ultimately, Redd Kross just wanted to rock. Yet, we all have our reasons for rocking. Maybe I misread theirs, but maybe that's the point of writing this. We experience music and can't help but misread it, then we write about it or we make our own. These bad translations become part of a new subculture, which might one day grow up and become "real" culture. What I saw in Redd Kross was an adoration of rock music that I'd never seen before in a band, and it translated perfectly to my life. I truly felt like I understood. It was a rock 'n' roll love letter that was usually communicated through the drunken ramblings of record collectors, but these guys weren't geeks. They were clearly getting laid. They took all the music that they loved and ground it up, and what came out the other side was Redd Kross. *THIS is what we love about music, and THIS is what we're going to do onstage.* There was so much history in their show, but it was rock history filtered through the minds of Sid and Marty Krofft, then through the L.A. punk scene, then through the Paisley Underground, then through . . . shit, I don't know. There was a ton of stuff in there.

Their opener, "Neurotica," ripped off almost note for note the beginning of "Sgt. Pepper's Lonely Hearts Club Band," though I didn't notice at the time, and it worked regardless of your knowledge of the reference. They covered the Beatles' "This Boy." It was the first time I'd encountered an onstage tradition that I've come back to many times in my rock 'n' roll life: playing a cover because you're either bored, drunk, or don't give a shit anymore. They did it with such love, though. They obviously felt so much reverence towards the song.

There was other weirdness. In the middle of one of their own songs, they began taking turns doing this nursery rhyme–like breakdown that went something like this:

"My name is (Your Name Here), I like to boogie, and when I boogie, I really do my thing." ("He do his thing!" another one of them sometimes called back.)

After that they would each do a little solo that would be a lick taken from some classic rocker—the guitarline from "Rebel Rebel" or something like that. It's all a reference, I'm sure, to something I still haven't figured out yet. Jeff's verse went something like, "My name is Asshole, I got a pocket, and when I boogie," etc. (That's what *I* heard.) And then for his solo he played the bongos over the band playing the intro to "For Your Love." I don't know what the hell was up with that.

Later they played Toni Basil's "Mickey," with each chorus dedicated to a different rock 'n' roll Mick:

"Oh Mickey, you're so fine, you're so fine, you blow my mind, Mick Ronson! Mick Ronson!"

Next would be Mick Taylor and Mick Fleetwood, etc. . . . . Yes, I know it sounds kind of stupid, but I was young. They were young. It was joyous and fun. They made you remember.

And the clothes! They all had the coolest seventies clothes I'd ever seen. Flares so perfectly flared. Suede and fringes, dangling, spinning, and swirling. Beatles boots pointing ever forward, onwards, inwards. All stars and stripes and shit. American in the best way.

Not only that, there was the hair! The long, flowing, beautiful hair that I could only covet! An old girlfriend once said of seeing them: "I didn't want to fuck Redd Kross, I wanted to BE Redd Kross." Yeah, I wanted to be them, as well.

I started dressing like them after that. At the very least, I tried. I scoured the Value Villages for striped flares, any kind of flares, and loud shirts with big collars. My best friend Warren, who was at the show with me, had the ability to grow long, flowing hair. Not me. With my dense, curly helmet of doll hair, there was no way I could have proper long locks. But I tried. I grew my hair out the best I could, but it went out instead of down. So I had the tacky vintage clothes but also this lion's mane that didn't really connect me with any seventies movement that I could remember. I just looked like maladjusted "I don't care what the fuck I look like" guy. You know the kind. Head's too big for his body. One small step above hobo. There was no thematic center. After a while I pulled my hair back into a ponytail and became "I don't care what the fuck I look like" ponytail guy, which is much worse now that I think of it. What else was I going to do? I didn't want an afro like King Buzzo in the Melvins. It worked for him, but he was King Buzzo. (Things were already brewing in Seattle, just 150 miles away. Green River was breaking up, and Mudhoney was taking form. Soundgarden had made a couple of visits to Vancouver already. The eighties were turning into the nineties, and long hair would soon become very important.)

I didn't know as I watched Redd Kross that I would chase their cool for years. All that time I watched them, I was just so blown away. In the moment. So in the moment that I wanted to chase that moment after it ended, figure out the formula for manufacturing that moment.

After the show, I had to go backstage and meet them. It's not my way to be a hanger-on—I always assumed that no one would want to meet me or talk to me—but they were so damn good, damn them. I would make an exception. With so few in attendance, it was very easy to just walk into the dressing room. Just turn right at the Tetris machine. No backstage pass necessary.

I felt like a freshman walking into a senior party. It was the band and a few other fans in a small, windowless room. They seemed like cocky rock stars onstage, but when I walked up to Steven McDonald and talked to him, I found he was a really nice, soft-spoken guy. He accepted all my fumbling compliments politely. The uneasiness soon went away.

He told me he'd just turned twenty.

"Not a teen babe anymore," he said.

"But you had a record out back in 1980!"

"Yeah," he said. "I was twelve when we put out our first record."

Holy shit! He must have been genetically bred for this. I was nineteen and suddenly feeling like it was too late for my musical dreams. I'd just picked up a guitar for the first time a year before. You should have started at twelve, or earlier, I thought. That's what rock stars do.

Steven signed the back of my newly purchased T-shirt, a mock up of the *Revolver* album cover with their faces replacing the Beatles'. He wrote, "Remember to eat lots of carrots," or something like that. I have red hair, you see. Not insulting, really. I knew I wasn't one of the golden gods, but the golden gods were nice enough to me. Even so, I wasn't too sad when the Sharpie ink started washing out.

Epilogue

I ran into Steven McDonald in an airport a couple of years ago. Denver, I think it was. We were both waiting for a flight to Austin for South by Southwest. I went up and said hi to him, asked him if he was who I thought he was. I couldn't be sure. His hair was short. I don't remember what we talked about. I think I told him that I saw him back in 1987, but nothing more than that. I wanted to tell the guy that he was an inspiration, that I used to dress like an idiot because of him and his brother, that I had both of their *Lovedolls* movies on VHS (even bought the soundtrack), that it's very possible my life would have taken a different path if I hadn't seen him play all those years ago, that I was actually doing pretty well for myself with the music and he shouldn't feel bad about influencing me into wanting to be a musician, that I had a band called the New Pornographers. Ever heard of us? I didn't say anything, except goodbye, have a nice trip, and walked away.

"Hey . . ." he called out.

I turned around.

"Remember to eat lots of carrots."

What a dick.

32

Bon Jovi

Memorial Coliseum
Portland, Oregon
May 8, 1989
JON RAYMOND

WE'VE BEEN LIVING UNDER Reaganism for, what, twenty-six years now? First, we had Reagan himself, that master of stagecraft and stern anticommunism—according to economic advisor Martin Anderson, "the most warmly ruthless man I ever met." Then came George Bush, the colder, less articulate heir, and then soft, huggable Bill Clinton, the rebirth of Reaganism by the other side. And now we've come to George W. Bush, the most inbred variation on the theme thus far, a farce. Over the decades, there have been numerous tweaks on the template, but the basic premises have always been about the same: sixties Liberalism was a failed experiment and a source of national shame; big government must be starved from existence; only through overt self-interest and debt-based consumerism can our social problems be solved. All the messengers have attempted to ape the master's much-vaunted optimism, and all have engaged in the same dysphoric manipulation of image. In this way, Ronald Reagan's imagination has remained the nation's imagination throughout the entirety of my political consciousness.

Jon Bon Jovi is a product of Reaganism, too. He might have stumped for Kerry last time around, but the hair metal moment from whence he sprang was echt-Reagan era. Those boring, hetero mutations of glam rock, those jocks in Lycra with their power chords, took the dirty artifice of seventies glitter and swapped it for studio grease and honeyed, mainstream sentimentality. With his perfect teeth, dimpled chin, and unapologetic careerism, Jon Bon Jovi stood as a poster child for the triumph of corporate hype and airhead apathy over grassroots rock 'n' roll rebellion. After all these years, his blowdried, bubblegum machismo still seems frozen in the eighties, like fingerless gloves or the DeLorean.

I saw Bon Jovi in 1989, my senior year of high school. They were coming through Portland on the *New Jersey* tour, and they were filming a video for

MTV, which meant they needed a packed house for the cameras. The arena did not sell out, though, and so tickets were disbursed to area high schools where some of them found their way into my friends' and my own hands. We were not Bon Jovi fans—we preferred Hüsker Dü and the Replacements back then—but in the spirit of full-bore irony that was the only real response to the ambient evil of the times, we decided to attend.

There were about eight of us that night, two cars' full, and we began the evening's festivities under the Marquam Bridge, the traffic of I–5 humming overhead. We drank our warm beer with purpose, and smoked whatever we had in our possession, and sonically immunized ourselves by listening to *Meat Puppets II*, an album that made Bon Jovi's art wither and die in comparison (and that we had found, I recall with some pride, without any apparatus of authority telling us where to go looking). By the time the sun was going down, we were all well impaired.

The show took place at the Memorial Coliseum, an occult black cube on the eastern bank of the Willamette River. We parked and made our way though the rows of cars, feigning sobriety as we hit the turnstiles, and found our seats in the nosebleed section. To be perfectly honest, I remember almost nothing about the concert itself. I think we arrived during the last song of supporting act Skid Row. Sebastian Bach, that willowy future Broadway star, was likely yowling away, and then I think we waited for a long time between acts. Mostly, I remember that my friend Brad and I decided we wanted to stage dive, which seemed like a properly churlish statement of disrespect in the circumstances. We made a few aborted attempts to get down to the main floor, but every time we began our descent we were accosted by security dudes and sent back to our assigned chairs, thwarted. Instead, we satisfied ourselves with drinking from our smuggled flask of Southern Comfort.

At some point, Bon Jovi must have appeared. Lights must have flashed, smoke must have billowed. This was the period when Jon used a catwalk over the crowd, so perhaps he arrived that way. All I know is that, during the first song, Brad made one more wild bid for the floor and was promptly ejected from the arena by muscle-bound bouncers. Not to be outdone, I made the same vain attempt moments later, and was kicked out as well, led by the bouncers to the parking lot and told to get off the property. Two songs into the big show, and I was done, cast out.

I found Brad sitting on a sidewalk at the edge of the parking lot, reading an issue of *Newsweek*. The streets were empty. It could have been an abandoned stage set, the streetlights illuminating a small patch of concrete. He seemed distressed about something, and I asked him, in that grave teenage manner, what was the matter.

Wordlessly, Brad handed me the magazine. Inside the front spread was an ad for General Dynamics, the defense contractor, and one of our main objects of contempt at the time (we listened to a lot of Jello Biafra lectures back then, and Halliburton wasn't really on the map). I remember the ad vividly. It had no product to sell; rather, it was one of those more general branding efforts, featuring the General Dynamics logo and a short, self-congratulatory text printed over a painting of an Indian war—horses teeming, Anglo cavalry gunning and slashing—the gist being that superior military technology was the only true guarantor of American freedom. The Indian genocide, recast as defense industry propaganda. Great. In an era of ballistic missiles nicknamed the Peacekeeper, this was par for the course, but still, how brazen could the Rightist revisionism become?

I examined the spread, and Brad proceeded to tell me about a conversation he'd had moments before with a man whose daughter was having a CT scan nearby, likely at Providence Hospital about a mile to the north. It was this man who had given him the magazine, having carried it by accident from the waiting room. He was distraught over his daughter's undiagnosed illness; he had no idea if she was going to survive the night. The man had wandered off just moments before, as mysteriously as he'd arrived, but his lingering vibrations infused the night with a jarring kind of weight.

We sat on the curb overlooking the Coliseum's side parking lot, hearing the faint noise of the concert muffled behind multiple walls. It's hard to describe what happened next, what cognitive threads wound or unwound. I can't really defend myself. All I can say is the combination of factors—a girl dying, General Dynamics lying, Bon Jovi rocking, Ronald Reagan passing the torch to the first Bush—carried me to a kind of apotheosis of my adolescence, an orgy of inchoate rage. It began mildly enough, with ripping the pansies from the bark dust lining the sidewalk and hurling them into the night air, the flowers disappearing in the gloom only to reappear moments later, plunging to the ground, the root balls smashing to crumbly bits. They made a satisfying sound, plashing on the concrete, but this only whetted our appetites.

Flannels flapping, we entered the parking lot and walked the aisles of cars, yanking antennae and license plates from the metal bodies. The

antennae were easy, they snapped right off, but the plates took some doing. With much twisting and pulling, though, they came free limned in
sharp crimped metal. We tossed our trophies as soon as we won them, and
when we got tired of the effort we leapt up onto the hood of a Subaru. We
proceeded to jump up and down until the hood was thoroughly de-
formed. From there, we jumped to the next hood. We repeated the process,
hood to hood, roof to roof. For our next trick, we smashed the window of
a BMW and pissed in the backseat.

We did a real number on that parking lot. We considered it our duty to
remind these people—these people who had wasted their freedom on Bon
Jovi—of the absolute dumb luck they enjoyed, the largesse that had blessed
them for no good reason, and the ease with which it all could vanish. That
night, we were the sword of some punk god. As if ketchup were a veg-
etable; as if trees polluted more than cars; as if Nicaragua were only forty-
five minutes from the southern border. The daily mendacity of the Reagan
era had cast an illusion over the land and it necessitated some kind of base-
line rebuttal.

At the end of our fit we smashed a car's fiberglass blower and then, sad
to say, we also vandalized the very car we had driven to the show in, our
friend Paul's Land Rover. Paul, in our minds, had matured of late. He had
stopped smoking weed and eating acid, and he had come to seem like a
sell-out to us for some reason. He planned to major in business at Pomona
the next year, whereas Brad and I, with the money we'd saved tending the
yards of our nouveau riche neighbors, planned to drive around Mexico,
drinking beer with campesinos or something. By whatever ill-conceived
ideology we were packing back then—bits of Dead Kennedys and beat-
nikism and misreadings of Nietzsche, spiked by gushing hormones—the
betrayal seemed utterly reasonable.

We dented Paul's Land Rover pretty good, and then, like the stupid
teenagers we were, we sat on the bumper and waited for everyone to rejoin
us. What were we thinking? I have no idea. Soon enough, the concert
ended and we watched the crowd spill from the arena, all the sweating,
happy fans wearing their freshly purchased Bon Jovi T-shirts and carrying
their Bon Jovi tour programs, sated by the fist-pumping spectacle in which
they had just participated, now returning to their cars to find a horrible,
curdling surprise in wait.

I don't remember what happened when Paul and our friends appeared,
at what point post-concert elation turned to confrontation or regret. I be-

lieve we were quiet about our actions until later in the week, when the secret became too rich to hold onto. Probably we told someone who told someone, and then the word was out. I don't think there was ever any big scene or blow out, but we spread bark dust for Paul's parents that summer to pay for the damage. In the fall, we headed for Mexico.

In retrospect, the whole event is just embarrassing to think about, the absurd high horse we had climbed onto, the insufferable, sanctimonious self-righteousness we displayed. It was an ugly, juvenile episode, no question (and not the only one, either, by far). Even worse, though, is recognizing the shameful pride I continue to take in the memory, the dark glamour I still attribute to my youthful drive toward destruction; it's as if some black seed is polished every time I cast back and remember, and in this way a perpetual teenage identity is maintained.

And what's the pleasure of romanticizing that kind of rebellion anymore, when George W. Bush and his junta have so thoroughly cornered the market on willful, immature, thoughtless destructiveness? What's the point of acting out, when the rowdy, hypocritical policymakers who hold the levers of power so exemplify the self-absorption, false invincibility, and deceit of the teenage years? Watching the path of wreckage lengthen behind the long march of Reaganism, it is abundantly clear that our leaders remain the spoiled, despotic children they always were. If only they had indulged their impulses when the time was right, I sometimes think, when the stakes were low, we might not be in the situation we are today. If only we had lived in a different time, Bon Jovi might not even have sucked.

33

Van Morrison
The Beacon Theatre
New York City
November 30, 1989
ROBERT BURKE WARREN

PREDAWN NEW YORK CITY. November 1989. I am queued up for concert tickets—something I've not done in years and never in Manhattan. There's an unseasonably warm and humid thickness to the air, wet pavement beneath my boots, a blown-out umbrella sprawled on Broadway. Above me, the marquee of the Beacon Theatre reads "Van Morrison—Sixth Show Added!" My newlywed wife Holly George sleeps back in our East Village tenement.

We'd tied the knot the previous May, after a year-and-a-half true romance that involved sharing stages with our respective bands, introducing our cats to one another, and making love in abandoned houses. She'd been amazed that I'd been so willing to take on this early morning adventure. Apparently, a series of Bad Boyfriends had preceded me, and much as I grappled with jealousy, there were times when it was obvious that they'd so lowered the bar that I felt like sending them thank-you notes.

We'd met a few times through mutual friends, but we really got together at a bill our bands shared at a club in East Hampton called the Jag. I played bass in garage rock titans the Fleshtones and Holly played guitar in the Benny Hill/Monks-inspired all-girl punk-polka outfit Das Furlines. The club owners had promised a free barbecue to both bands, but in order to take advantage of this perk, we had to arrive early, making the three-hour trek from New York to arrive around lunchtime. During downtime, I'd been sitting in a corner reading my dog-eared copy of *The Vampire Lestat* by Anne Rice, and this had caught Holly's eye. She was an ardent fan of Rice's *Vampire Chronicles*. So, in the post-barbecue, pre-gig hours, Holly and I talked incessantly about creatures of the night and rock 'n' roll. I vividly recall being deeply smitten, and later mesmerized as she thrashed away at her '59 Fender Jazzmaster (like Tom Verlaine's) in a bustier, black boots, a short black skirt, fishnets, and a huge black sheepskin hat, all five-foot-two of her kickin' ass. As the Fleshtones' van packed up, I leaned over and bit her slender neck. I found out later that her bandmates strenuously advised her not to get her hopes up about me.

Our first real date was a Sunday. Holly invited me to come with her to Sylvia's in Harlem, where we both could enjoy real Southern soul food. Like Holly, I was born a Southerner; I'd left my hometown of Atlanta in 1985, moving to New York to pursue dreams of musical success, but mainly just to be a New Yorker and to face the everyday adventure of getting by on the "Mean Streets." Holly and I bonded in our shared heritage. In her inimitable style, she'd managed to retain a sizable portion of her Southern identity, often wearing cowboy boots and shirts with her punky gear, and never disavowing her deep love for country music, of which I knew almost nothing, save what I'd seen on *Hee Haw*.

I arrived for our date and she asked if I'd like to hear some music. To my delight, an entire exposed-brick wall of her tenement apartment was covered with hundreds of albums crammed into plastic milk crate stacks. I pulled Cheap Trick's *Heaven Tonight* off the shelf (falling deeper in love by the second) and requested she put that on the turntable, whereupon she informed me that she usually played only country on Sundays, but for me she would make an exception.

Being eight-and-a-half years my senior, Holly had moved to New York from Chapel Hill, North Carolina in 1979, in the thick of the flowering punk-new-wave-CBGB's-Max's Kansas City-scene, and she'd masterfully re-invented herself from clog-wearin' hippie chick to foxy club-goin' *New York Rocker*–readin' aficionado of the ragged-but-right underground scene. One of the things that set us apart was that she actually got to see up close and personal many of her musical idols in the many dives that have gone the way of the dodo. I'd seen mine on *The Midnight Special* and *Don Kirshner's Rock Concert*. But even Holly had never seen Van Morrison.

Prior to moving in with her in 1987, I was not a Van fan. I sort of remembered his 1980 appearance on *Saturday Night Live*, when he delivered a jumpy "Wavelength," and I had a dim recollection of his blue jumpsuited turn in *The Last Waltz*, when he belted out "Caravan" and led the Band into an extended rave-up of the song's coda. In those performances he struck me as ill at ease and even shy of the spotlight, not really connecting with the crowd. But he sure was caught in some kind of tempest, and even though he was no glad-handing entertainer, the diminutive Irishman exuded an oddly magnetic presence. I was not sufficiently inspired to seek out his work, however. To poke fun at him, yes, but to look for his LPs, no.

Holly's and my hot-and-heavy courtship served as a crash course for me; as I learned the various ways to make my beloved laugh, cry, and coo, I also found out about music that had flourished in the cracks into which it had slipped, peeking from the shadows like weeds between the paving stones of pop culture. One of my textbooks was a gift from Holly: the Lester Bangs anthology *Psychotic Reactions and Carburetor Dung*. It was through Bangs's eloquent paean to Van Morrison's seminal 1968 album *Astral Weeks* that my curiosity with Morrison truly was piqued. Bangs's writing swept me off my feet like no other music journalist's had, immediately sending me to Holly's formidable LP collection—Gram Parsons, Wanda Jackson, the Carter Family, the Long Ryders, and numerous others—to put on *Astral Weeks*, which did not disappoint. My jaw still drops at its otherworldly beauty, timelessness and grace. Forever will it remind me of when the love of my life was new, exhilarating, and vertigo-inducing.

This late-eighties period also saw Joseph Campbell's *Power of Myth* series debut on PBS, and it had captured us as well, inspiring our developing spiritual lives. The culture was opening up, becoming more inclusive, and looking at old things through a new lens, and Morrison's neatly dovetailed multiple nods to everything from jazz to Celtic to country to blues was a perfect soundtrack. At least, in our apartment it was. His music was our gospel, and Joseph Campbell was our de facto priest. A friend of ours knew a bellhop at the Ritz-Carlton who told a classic story involving both: the bellhop was called to Van Morrison's room, and when he got there, it turned out all Van wanted was for someone to watch *The Power of Myth* on TV with him. Morrison was bouncing excitedly on the edge of the bed, wanting only someone to share his enthusiasm.

As I delved into *St. Dominic's Preview, Moondance, A Sense of Wonder,* and, most chill-inducingly, his live double album magnum opus *It's Too Late to Stop Now*, I became a Morrison devotee. *Irish Heartbeat* came out in 1988, the year I proposed to Holly, and *Avalon Sunset* was released the year we were married—1989.

Both *Irish Heartbeat* and *Avalon Sunset* are hailed by the rock literati as a return to form and a five-night stint at the Beacon Theatre sells out before Holly and I can get it together to get tickets. We are crushed. But a phone call comes to me at my bartending job. It's Holly, breathlessly telling me that Van Morrison has added a sixth show! Tickets go on sale in the morning, at the Beacon box office only!

I've actually brought a copy of James Joyce's *Dubliners* to read while I wait. Rather than leaf through it, however, I hold the opened book in my lap while I doze with my back against the building's granite façade. About a hundred folks have shown up, and as the sun rises through the concrete corridors of upper Broadway, there is much conviviality—people going for coffee, getting bagels for strangers, laughing amongst sleeping bags and lawn chairs. Later, I'm napping back at the apartment—the tickets laid out proudly for Holly to see upon her return from work—and the show sells out.

One thing about seeing a show with Holly—she is an exuberant fan, hooting and bouncing. One of my favorite sensations is her standing in front of me, my hands at her hips, her head bopping just below my chin, her butt bumping against my thighs as we take in a musical event. During the course of the evening she will react with abandon as Van and the band play a favorite tune, often looking at me wordlessly, eyes wide as if to say *Can you believe this?!*, then eyes squeezed shut as she lowers her head and shakes it till her long hair covers her face. It's our first mutual experience of: *They're playing our song!*

Upon arriving, we discover that this last gig of a six-night stint will be videotaped. And to this very day, you can buy *Van Morrison: The Concert*, an edited version of the show we saw. If you pause during a sweeping shot of the orchestra seats (yes, I got great seats for my efforts) you can catch a glimpse of Holly and me.

Georgie Fame and the Blue Flames are Van's warm-up act and his backing band, and Fame's contributions to the musical and visual greatness of the night cannot be overstated. He is a master showman and emcee, connecting to the crowd, delivering ace musicianship on a Hammond B–3 and soulful backup vocals. His toothy grin and bonhomie belie a stately authority over the band, who watch both Van and him for their cues.

Van hits the stage in an ill-fitting suit, the neck of his shirt open, all pent-up energy and purpose. Launching into the strutting R&B of "I Will Be There," he sinks into the music, pacing the stage like a dowser, trying to find the place where the elixir will bubble up. As I mentioned before, it's an odd sort of charisma; experiencing it live, there is a sense of discomfort that tinges my excitement. It's not disappointment, just a sense that he will be waving to us from a distance that we must traverse to meet him halfway.

As the set moves on, it becomes clear that Van's voice is a bit shot. How could it not be? He's been doing this *all week*. And he's no spring chicken, with a comb-over of brownish-red hair pasted to a sweaty, balding head. But it doesn't really matter, because he becomes progressively more animated, picking up a Telecaster and engaging with his band, even cracking quick smiles, which shine all the more brightly because of their rarity. His lack of vocal power is easily obscured under the high beams of his powerful presence and the compelling originality of his phrasing. With the exception of gracious band introductions, there are no shout-outs to the crowd, but in his way, he acknowledges the flow of energy from us to him, and the thrilling reciprocal dynamic of a great show frequently passes from spectator to performer and back again.

The band is not short on chops. In addition to Georgie Fame, the Blue Flames consist of drums, bass, guitar, keys, and a horn section. There's a young buck saxophone player who does an eerie call-and-response bit with Van during "In the Garden," and they all get turns to vamp, even segueing into the tune "Birdland" when Morrison yells, "Weather Report!" in the middle of "Caravan."

Mose Allison comes out for a few tunes around mid-set, and Van takes on a new relaxed assurance as a sideman, proudly showing off one of his own heroes, singing backup, and strumming. Allison—prior to this night unknown to me—exudes a laconic, dry humor in his bearing as well as his songs, which include "Thank God for Self Love" and "Your Mind Is On Vacation." His brief contribution is a palette cleanser, and Van hits his stride soon thereafter. His hit of the day, a cover of "Have I Told You Lately That I Love You," is his seemingly wrong-headed choice for a set-closer, but oddly, it works with surprising power. Then comes a rather abrupt exit, with a quick return for what will be four lengthy encores. As Van hits the stage, Georgie Fame exchanges a hearty laugh with the band, carnival barking, "Van Morrison! Mr. Hospitality!" again and again.

The raucous "Gloria" has Van whacking away at his Tele with abandon, breaking a string, then chanting repeatedly into the microphone, "Don't turn John Lee Hooker away from your door!" Suddenly, an unannounced John Lee Hooker regally strides out. In shades, a jaunty fedora, and a hollow-bodied six string slung over a suit and tie, he looks every bit the archetype of the wizened old black bluesman, back from the crossroads.

The crowd goes nuts. Hooker and company launch into a slithering "Serves Me Right to Suffer," on which Van joins in on vocals, and then a loose-limbed "Boom Boom" that ends with Hooker soloing raw and ragged, then standing somewhat awkwardly upstage, clearly not wanting to leave. Eventually, amongst Morrison's echoing, "John Lee Hooker! John Lee Hooker!" he takes his leave. Van Morrison featuring Georgie Fame and the Blue Flames follow suit.

Again confounding expectations, Van and the band come back out for a haunting, darkly lyrical run through the ancient ballad "She Moved Through the Fair," one of the stronger cuts from *Irish Heartbeat*. The song permeates the Beacon like a fog, its waltz-time modality transporting all to the heath from whence it came. Van repeatedly whispers the closing lines, his possessed rasp assuming the role of a visiting spirit communicating with the fiancée left behind in life, "It will not be long, love/'Till our wedding day." Then Van Morrison briskly walks offstage as Georgie Fame howls in falsetto, and the band members all put down their instruments and exit. Finally, only the drummer remains, beating with mallets on his kit, sending Celtic ghosts, the devil, and Van's Lord and Savior back into the ether. For me, this is the show's high point.

We spill back onto Broadway exhilarated, exhausted, and confounded. It hadn't been like *It's Too Late to Stop Now*, but we hadn't really expected it to be. We'd seen a show that we couldn't encapsulate into a quick and easy definition. It wasn't a rock concert, it wasn't jazz, it wasn't blues, it wasn't a revival. But it was all those things. It was a Van Morrison show. And we've not seen anything like it since.

One of the reasons this concert is special to Holly and me is that it came at a time when we were embarking on what has now turned out to be almost two decades of companionship. It was an intense period: Holly was just achieving some success as a freelance music writer and editor, stepping boldly away from the nine-to-five, and I was fitfully beginning to write my own songs and perform with just an acoustic guitar. We built a covenant between us that we'd ride shotgun for each other as we each navigated the roads of our individual, dicey dreamscapes. And though I didn't consciously realize it then, the songs of the time—Van Morrison's in particular—would serve as touchstones for me, bringing me back to that promise when I lost my way, which I did.

I'm in a bar in the West Village. It's an autumn afternoon, 1995, and I am miserable. My mind is all white noise and dark doubt, the needle of my heart's compass spinning wildly. I don't know why I'm here. I don't know if I should head back to the apartment in which Holly broke her "only-country-on-Sundays" rule. I don't know anything. Then, over the hubbub of the crowd, through the cigarette haze and the smell of beer-soaked floorboards comes the familiar cadence of "Beside You" from *Astral Weeks*. Playing on the jukebox. It delivers me, guiding me as if a hand has been placed at the small of my back, to a payphone, where I call home and leave a message for my wife, telling her I love her.

34

Van Morrison
The Beacon Theatre
New York City
November 30, 1989
HOLLY GEORGE-WARREN

I REMEMBER THE VERY FIRST TIME I heard about a Van Morrison concert. It was a sparkling fall day in 1976 at a party in the pastoral environs of Orange County, North Carolina. What initiated the conversation was Van's voice—"Jackie Wilson Said"—coming out of a pair of stereo speakers standing like stones in a meadow of ankle-deep grass. There were lots of those parties back then, at various farmhouses and cabins nestled in the country outside Chapel Hill. Because of our usual libations—beer, pot, and mushrooms—they all kind of blur together now in a burnished glow. I'd been a Van fan long before that afternoon, thanks to his occasional AM hits, followed by FM's embrace of such albums as *Astral Weeks*. At the party, I must have uttered the wish to see a Van Morrison concert, only to be told by someone standing nearby that all bets were off when it came to his shows. The naysayer had experienced a very disappointing Morrison performance: after a lackluster few songs, Van fled the stage never to return. Hmmmm . . . at the time, it seemed like a new quest to add to my list.

Over the next couple of years, the parties stayed pretty much the same, but the music changed drastically. Instead of Van, singer-songwriters, and country rock, the sounds of Patti Smith, the Sex Pistols, Television, the Ramones, Blondie, and Iggy Pop blurted from speaker cabinets. After seeing the Patti Smith Group at the University of North Carolina's Memorial Hall in January 1977, I vowed to move to New York—and did two years later. Experiencing that incendiary show made me want to live in the city where those songs were hatched. One of the highlights of Smith's shamanistic performance (and of her first album, *Horses*) had been her version of a Van Morrison/Them song, "Gloria"—which was about the only way Van entered my consciousness in those days.

By 1980, I'd followed Patti Smith's example and picked up an electric guitar, learning to play bar chords onstage at Max's and CBGB. Seven years later, I was a veteran of several bands—and a ton of clubs—when my latest combo Das Furlines played a double bill with the Fleshtones, with Robert on bass.

Meeting a guy like Robert—a musician some eight years my junior from the Lower East Side post-punk scene—who could dig Van Morrison as much as I had in the old days, chipped away at my bad-girl cynicism. As square as it sounds, it gave me a new sense of hope about love, and it rekindled old feelings about the transformative power of music. I set aside my Birthday Party albums and started listening to Van again.

The fact that Robert would actually go stand in line at the crack of dawn to buy us tickets to a Van Morrison concert blew my mind. And he scored a pair of fifth-row seats! Could the show ever live up to all those years of anticipation, not to mention my renewed fervor for the man's music? And which way would the pendulum swing on Morrison's notorious love-hate relationship with his audiences? But no matter what happened, I'd be there with Robert, whom I had married after a crazy-head-over-heels twenty-month romance.

Van hit the stage in a tight, skinny-lapelled blue suit. Then forty-four, he'd long ago lost his choirboy looks. Opening with the Stax-Voltish "I Will Be There," he stood glued to the spot, the mike stand gripped in his hand, singing the song in an almost perfunctory fashion. His distinctive voice sounded a bit raspy, but still powerful—especially considering this was his sixth concert in a row. As he launched into "Whenever God Shines His Light," "Cleaning Windows," and "Orangefield," the tightly wound coil inside him gradually loosened. By the time he immersed himself in "When Will I Ever Learn to Live in God," the music had taken hold of him, the years had slipped away. His eyes closed, he swayed as he sang, his distinctive phrasing imbued with emotion.

Van's jazzy backup band sometimes verged on slickness and the vamping went on a bit too long for my taste. But Van got into it, bopping around and listening to the music, sometimes snapping his fingers or clapping his hands. In addition to Georgie Fame, the Blue Flames consisted of saxophonists Richie Buckley and Steve Gregory (who at times switched to flute), drummer Dave Early, bassist Brian Odgers, guitarist Bernie Holland, and Neil Drinkwater on piano and accordion. The first time Van spoke to the audience was halfway through the set: a gruff salute to "one of the great musical heroes of this century," his way of bringing on guest Mose Allison. The composer of "Parchman's Farm" sat down behind the piano, and Van relaxed in sideman mode for a few numbers.

After Allison's departure, Van's intensity grew, as he gave us an emotive Celtic set comprised of "Raglan Road" and "Carrickfergus." Gregory's lilting flute floated ethereally through the lovely melodies. Van was hitting his stride. His energy level increased with a rhapsodic "Summertime in England," fueled by the fervor of a religious revival. Buckley, who was standing *behind* Morrison, did an amazing vocal call-and-response, repeating Van's words with unerring precision, in both the lyrics and the intonation—even his scat singing. Visibly pleased by his pupil, Van was moving on up, getting a little bit higher—as were we. The band members each got a solo turn, then it was over—Van sauntered offstage to the repeated chants of Georgie Fame: "VAN MOR-RI-SON, MIS-TER HOS-PI-TAL-I-TY!!" That was it? It was over too soon.

But wait, Van came prancing back . . . a big smile on his face, probably the biggest one all night. He looked over at Georgie with a certain glance and a nod, as though to say, "I've got a secret, and I can't wait to tell it." Good spirits followed, as he kicked off the encore with his 1970 ode to radio, "Caravan." With Van turning the dial, the Blue Flames played the sonic parts of the classical station; the late-night jazz show; then the R&B of "Wilson Pickett, Solomon Burke, James Brown—turn it up, it's got soul!" A breezy, Tony Bennett–style "Moondance" followed, with Georgie joining in, turning it into a duet. Van was clearly having fun, dipping and bopping, while the song segued into "Fever." Fingers popping, he continued to duet with Fame, his demeanor effusive during the band's vamp. Then he was offstage again.

The *real* show was just beginning. The original concert didn't thrill me as much as the unexpected, seemingly spontaneous encores: Van was starting over, he'd lost the detachment. He was passionate again.

Encore Number Two! The music returned to the Irish sound, the band playing a "Danny Boy" riff, then turning it into the sprightly "Star of the County Down." Van gleefully waved his arms about, even doing his version of an Irish jig. It was hard to believe it was the same man who'd started the show two hours earlier. "In the Garden" was transcendent: he didn't so much sing the song as inhabit it—using powerful dynamics, going from a whisper to belting the chorus. That revival-style fervor was back . . . and as he departed again, Georgie Fame expressed all of our feelings, shouting, "No guru, no teacher, no method—just Van the Man—God bless Van Morrison!!!"

Encore Number Three: Van brought things back down again with his soulful reading of the ballad "Have I Told You Lately That I Love You," written by hillbilly singer Scotty Wiseman and originally a hit for singing cowboy Gene Autry in 1946. (Rod Stewart would score a Top Ten smash with it a few years after Van covered it on his '89 album.) Then "G-L-O-R-I-A," with all its angsty lust, segued into Howlin' Wolf's "Smokestack Lightnin'." WHOA—but that wasn't *it*!

We finally found out why the singer had been so excited, like a kid waiting for Santa. "I'm giving over the last part of the show to John Lee Hooker," he crowed in his Belfast brogue. "Don't turn John Lee away from your door! The King of the Blues!" Whereupon John Lee Hooker strode out wearing a suit and tie, a sheriff's badge pinned to his lapel, and a jaunty fedora pulled down close to his Ray Bans. Hooker and company jammed feverishly on a soul-slicing "Serves Me Right to Suffer," with Van the eager student, echoing John Lee's lyrics (at one point, intoning the words "T.B. Sheets," which Hooker then repeated), slashing at his guitar to Hooker's primal beat. Then the John Lee song that possibly inspired Morrison to form Them in 1964: a swaggering "Boom Boom." Van joyfully joined Hooker on the vocals and lacerated his Tele's strings with that legendary riff. The bluesman finally ended the song with a raggedy solo performed at the lip of the stage, followed by a courtly exit—Morrison and the band on his heels.

Minus Hooker, they returned once more for Encore Number Four. The ghostly "She Moved Through the Fair" had Morrison taking us back to his mother's knee where his musical life began, repeatedly whispering the eerie assurance of a spirit coming back to console a bereft loved one: "It will not be long, love/'Till our wedding day."

Van's music stayed with us long after that concert ended. The following year, we rented a cottage in Woodstock, New York, which turned out be next door to the cabin where Van had written part of *Tupelo Honey*. By then, I had stopped playing in bands and become a music writer and editor. One day, in 1994, I popped into a drugstore in the same building as my office at *Rolling Stone*, and discovered on a sales rack a Van Morrison concert video—*our concert*. It didn't offer much consolation, though, when the next week Robert moved to England for a year to star in a play about Buddy Holly. His acting took him away from me, but music ultimately brought us back together. We now spend our days not far from Woodstock in a century-old house with our son, Jack. I still write about music, among other things, and Robert, now a singer-songwriter, includes the occasional Van Morrison cover among originals at his gigs. And in 2004, under the outstretched branches of a cedar tree in our backyard, we renewed our wedding vows. As Van had showed us fifteen years before, sometimes the encore is the best part.

35

Clarence Carter
Bobby's Hideaway
Waldo, Florida
January 18, 1990
KEVIN CANTY

WE HAD PASSED BY Bobby's Hideaway any number of times, and every time, Peter said that it looked like a good place to get beat up. I thought so, too: a long, windowless, cement-block building painted in rainbows, guitars, and musical notes, six inches from the side of Highway 301 in a town named Waldo in the middle of the swamps of North Florida.

For all I know, Waldo may be a paradise of golf and retirement by now; things change fast in Florida. But then, it was a dumpy, battered-looking town strung out along the highway and the railroad tracks, a few miles down the road from the state prison. We would drive through on our way to the beach or to drop a friend at the Amtrak station, and as we passed we would check out the roadside readerboard to see what was going down, the wet T-shirt contests and line dance lessons, country bands with names like the Dance Hands and Gold Rush. The parking lot, when it was full at all, was mostly pickup trucks, and there always seemed to be a Harley or two outside the door.

It was a surprise, then, to drive past the place one day and see the name CLARENCE CARTER up on their sign.

That Clarence Carter? "Patches"? "Slip Away"? "Making Love (At the Dark End of the Street)"?

I stopped the car—a 1969 Pontiac LeMans—turned around, drove back, parked in the empty gravel lot, and we went in and asked the bartender. Yes, in fact, it was *that* Clarence Carter, playing the day after my birthday, in fact. In the daytime, the bar looked dark and dubious, with the sour smell of spilled beer and leftover Winston smoke; the bartender looked like he might have a felony or two on his résumé; the other clientele, both of them, looked at us like recently landed aliens. Nevertheless, this seemed too good to miss. Reluctantly, the bartender sold us six tickets, and we left wondering what we had let ourselves in for.

Those cars! Those backroads and bars! There have been moments in my life when I could look in the mirror and think *these are the good times*, and this was one of them. I was living on nothing, trying to learn to write, in the South for the first time. I was taking a fiction workshop with Harry Crews, which was like studying with Captain Hook. Nights and weekends, we were hanging around Kate's Fish Camp—a bar that also sold bait and rented rowboats, on the edge of a blackwater lake—or poking around the lakes and swamps, the sand roads and Spanish moss and overhanging oaks of backwoods Florida. The beach was a little more than an hour away, the Gulf the same distance in the other direction. Beer and gas were dirt cheap, and smoking wasn't bad for you. I drove the '69 LeMans. Peter drove a '67 Sport Fury convertible with a cop motor and cop brakes. Bill had a '71 Chrysler New Yorker. And even Jim, the family man, had inherited a Crown Victoria from his father-in-law that would comfortably seat six and go one hundred miles an hour.

In these big plush cars, we went to the Gatornational drag races; we drank our way back from Saint Augustine; we floated down the Ichetucknee River and passed through Cedar Key on our way to Horseshoe Beach, where we saw a man catch a fish and then cook it on an ironing board.

And we drove out to Waldo that January night to see Clarence Carter: Peter and Maria, Lucy and I, Marjorie and Bob and a friend of Marjorie's who was just in town for the weekend, her name long gone, but I do remember that she taught at Harvard. Was Bill there? Wendy? I don't think so, but they might have been. I do remember the way the Harvard girl kept looking around in astonishment, at us in our short sleeves, the windows down as we rode out on a winter night, the warm, damp air that smelled a little like the swamp and a little like the ocean. *This is unbelievable*, she kept saying. And it's true that we had forgotten a little by then, forgotten that there was a world of work and snow and winter and difficulty.

The woman inside the door who took our tickets wore a Mylar wig in pink and black and blue and green tinsel. Behind her, wearing the bored and put-upon look of band girlfriends everywhere, an African-American woman sat behind a table of merchandise: Clarence Carter CDs, singles, autographed pictures, etc., but also a wide range of souvenirs—T-shirts, shot glasses, women's panties—with the slogan on them, "I Be Strokin'."

Aha, I thought. I had been wondering all along what the hell Clarence Carter was doing in a place like this, and now I knew. Clarence had, even by then, a long and strange career, starting off with Atlantic Records and some major soul hits that never quite broke through to the big white market. After a couple of dormant years, he resurfaced with his biggest hit of all, "Patches," a wretchedly sentimental tearjerker of a ballad. Again he couldn't seem to find a follow-up and slowly dropped off the radar, getting dropped by his label and endlessly touring the chitlin' circuit. Then came "Strokin'."

Recorded crudely, released on his own hip pocket record label, dirty, funny and loud, "Strokin'" turned into one of those weird underground hits that don't seem to happen much anymore. It appealed to a lot of very different people while bypassing the mainstream entirely, thanks to lyrics like, "I stroke it to the north/I stroke it to the south/I stroke it everywhere/ I even stroke it with my . . . WOO!" Needless to say, this didn't get anywhere near the radio, but it did get played at truck stops, discos, redneck weddings, and—apparently—country bars. This would explain the very assorted assortment of people in the club that night: truckers, country girls, cowboys, black men in big hats and boots, a couple of working girls, older black couples, backwoods Floridians of every stripe. The one thing they all had in common was that they came to party.

If there was one word I would use to describe the audience that night, that word would be "drunk." We had some serious catching up to do. We found a table overlooking the band and ordered beer and shots over the din of the country disco, which was being blasted out by a demon DJ in a twin sparkly wig to the woman by the door. Or it may have been the same woman. She might have snuck over while we weren't looking. One woman in a Mylar wig looks much like the next. We had smoked a little marijuana on the way over, and all the party lights were on in the bar, which lit it up as dimly as a stoner's aquarium. There was something exotic, too, in the patrons that shouted, drank, and shot pool before us. They didn't look anything like us and we didn't look like them. Everybody seemed friendly enough, though, in an approximate kind of way.

"We might make it out of here, after all," Peter said.

The Harvard girl looked over at him, alarmed.

Peter lit a cigarette and smiled.

Then the band came out and fired up their instruments. They all looked about nineteen, and they announced themselves as being out of Atlanta before they launched into some loud, synth-powered disco. The white half of the crowd left the dance floor immediately; after a sheepish three minutes of getting looked at, the black half of the audience sat down, too. Marjorie's attempt to get our table out dancing, always a long shot, died on the vine. The band launched into another song.

"They suck," Marjorie said.

"They certainly do," I said.

"Safety meeting," Peter said.

"What?" said the Harvard girl.

"Never mind," I told her. "Come along."

We went outside again, and you could see it in her face, the shock of the night air, unreal and damp and warm and full of the breath of the swamp and swamp animals. Birds flew all around us in the dark. We sat leaning on Peter's Sport Fury at the far edge of the parking lot, smoking a joint and passing around a flat pint of bourbon.

"We're a long way from Massachusetts," said the Harvard girl.

And I don't know why, but this was the turning point of the experience, not just the night but my whole time in Florida: the moment where I felt a part of the place, where I felt at home, no longer like a visitor. It's strange how happiness can come so quietly, the way it can surprise you. But just then I didn't want to be anywhere else, in any other company. Even the Harvard girl was perfect, to help us all feel our luck. I was right where I was supposed to be.

Then we heard the band stop and the crowd start to clap, and it was time to go back in.

A vest pocket stage with the band crammed around the edges, the keyboard stand actually sitting on the floor, the drums in one corner, the little spotlight shining down through colored gels in pink and yellow, purple and green. The drummer starts a beat but not a disco beat this time, a mid-tempo, loping soul beat, and one by one the other instruments fall in, bass then organ then rhythm guitar then, loud and strong, the horns, and I know this song: it's "Too Weak to Fight." A grin spreads over my face, involuntarily. This feels like some kind of visitation.

Then a woman leads him out onto the stage, Clarence Carter himself, a huge physical presence in a dapper suit and his trademark blindman shades. He locates himself by touch—here is the microphone, and here is the guitar amp—plugs in his Fender Jazzmaster, steps up to the mic and . . . laughs. This is not an ordinary laugh; it starts down deep where lava comes from and just surfaces through his body, the whole place shakes, and then he starts to sing.

And after that, I don't know what to say. There's something about trying to describe music—and what it does to you—that's like listening to somebody else describe their dreams. You can see how important it was to them but you can't feel it. When music is great—and Clarence Carter was great that night—it lifts you up and out of yourself, whatever part of yourself wants to explain things, leaves you quiet in the quiet parts and loud in the loud parts, moving your body in time to the music and in time to the other bodies all around you. All the adjectives in the world can't make this real to you, but that's what happened. Peter said Clarence Carter actually levitated during "Slip Away," and he might have. I'm not going to tell you he didn't. I do remember, maybe during the twenty-minute, very dirty version of "Making Love (At the Dark End of the Street)," looking across the table at Marjorie and both of us just grinning. This was so much better than it had to be, so much better than we had any right to expect.

And then it's over. Or, actually, it's stopped; and Clarence has left the stage and you're not ready for this to be over and you're back in your own body again, back in a room with a couple of hundred other people who are not ready for it to be over, either, and all of you clapping and whistling and shouting, and he hasn't even played "Strokin'" yet . . . And then he does come out, of course, and sing a ballad—the art of the tease—and only then launch into "Strokin'," and it's exactly the mayhem everybody was hoping for, raunchy and loud and fun.

And then it really is over.

Somewhere—in a box or basement, we would never have thrown them away—somewhere there is a pair of "I Be Strokin'" women's panties signed by Clarence Carter himself. Somewhere, I have a cassette of that fine song, also signed by Clarence, from the steps of the motorhome that served then as his home. Offstage, without the magic, he seemed smaller, quieter, tired and very, very blind. We all lined up to get our merchandise signed, and he had a word for each of us, but he was done. We got our stuff and got it signed, and then we got into our big cars and drove home through the dark of a damp, warm, misty night. This was sixteen years ago. None of the couples that were there that night are still together; none of us live there now, or anywhere near. But once, we were all there together.

36

Nirvana
The Paramount Theatre
Seattle
October 31, 1991
CHARLES R. CROSS

THERE HAS NEVER BEEN—and in all likelihood there never will be—a Seattle Halloween like that of 1991. That fall was, of course, the time when a Seattle-incubated style of loud-yet-melodic guitar rock overtook the world: grunge. Grunge brought madness back to rock, and nowhere was that madness any greater than on the night Nirvana returned to Seattle for the last U.S. date of their *Nevermind* tour. The band had already played a number of wild shows in Seattle the previous year, but none in a venue as large as the Paramount; one drew twelve hundred fans to an abandoned parking garage; another in a tiny club saw them debut "Smells Like Teen Spirit." Seattle was already being identified in the press as their "hometown," though in 1991 Kurt Cobain still officially lived in Olympia, or at least that's where his mail went—he'd been evicted from his apartment that spring for failing to pay the rent and had then spent several weeks living in his 1963 Plymouth Valiant.

The success of *Nevermind* surprised everyone, including the band and their label. It was certified as a gold record on the morning of the Halloween show, but it might have sold even more, at that point, had many stores not sold out of the CD. It sold nowhere better than in Seattle, where the band was so popular one local radio station took to playing "Smells Like Teen Spirit" twice an hour, an unheard-of frequency even in Top 40. And since the Halloween show represented the first time Cobain and Co. would be playing as stars to a crowd that included friends and family, it was a homecoming, and a validating moment in their rise to fame.

Other stars might have spent the time before the concert checking to see how they looked in a mirror, wanting to make a good impression. Kurt Cobain, however, spent the hour before the show buying underwear. He'd been on tour for two months and had run out of clothes, so he took to wearing the same outfit every day. That worked okay for jeans, but socks and underwear were another matter. An hour before showtime, he walked into the Bon Marché with a friend and bought a pair of boxers and some socks. His record had just gone gold, but it would be months before Kurt would see any of that money. To pay for his purchase he used change that he dug out from his pockets and from his shoes. "He was literally dumping his shoe out on the counter in the Bon, and the salesperson was looking at him like he's insane," recalled his friend Carrie Montgomery. Kurt left the department store and walked the nine blocks to the venue carrying his new boxers and socks in a bag. It was not the kind of entrance most ascending superstars would make to their homecoming show.

As Cobain walked towards the venue, what would have struck him first was the size of the crowd assembled, and the number of people outside trying to buy scalped tickets for this sold-out concert. The tour had been booked prior to *Nevermind* coming out, and in almost every city that fall, Nirvana played to overflow crowds. In Seattle, optimistic promoters had booked the show in the three thousand–seat Paramount, the biggest venue the band would play in America that fall, but even this hall had quickly sold out. In truth, by Halloween, Nirvana could have sold fifteen thousand seats anywhere in the Northwest.

There were other distractions backstage: a documentary crew was filming the show, and people with video cameras were everywhere. There were dozens of media types and radio promotion guys, all wanting face time with Kurt, who wanted to be left alone. Though Kurt had consented to allow the filming, he was most concerned with the two friends he'd convinced to serve as go-go dancers and making sure they were treated right. The two dancers were dressed in skintight body suits: the woman's read "Boy" while the man's read "Girl." This mirrored one of Kurt's original concepts behind *Nevermind*—he wanted one side of the album to be titled "Boy" and the reverse to be called "Girl." The "Girl" whom most of the songs on the album were written about—Tobi Vail—also was in the building, since Kurt had asked her band, Bikini Kill, to open up the show. The wisdom of asking your ex to come to your coming-out party was something Kurt hadn't thought through; it is also possible he hoped his kindness would impress Tobi enough to win her back.

When the actual show began, all this backstage drama wasn't obvious to those in the crowd. But, in retrospect, it clearly affected the band's performance, which was shaky from the start. Nirvana began with a little

"Happy Halloween" ditty and then launched into "Jesus Wants Me For a Sunbeam," a cover of a song by the Vaselines. They followed that with a taut one-two punch of "Aneurysm" and "Drain You," and the crowd began going wild. A small throng had been slam dancing at Nirvana shows for a year by then, but now that the band was on MTV every hour, a swarm of kids assumed that slam dancing was required during every song, even the slower ones like "School" and "Floyd the Barber," which followed. It may have represented the first time kids ever danced to "Floyd the Barber," but it was also indicative that—by vaulting up the charts and dominating MTV—whatever Nirvana now did on a Seattle stage would be worshipped.

As for the performance itself, Kurt was clearly having an off night, but that didn't seem to damper anyone's enthusiasm except maybe his own. His voice was a bit hoarse, and there were several moments when he stopped the show to chastise the camera crew to leave his go-go dancers alone. The chaos of the music, the onstage drama, and the crowd's rowdiness gave the impression that the whole evening was just on the brink of being out of control. Had Kurt directed his slam dancing fans to attack the film crew, it would have been a full-on riot. Instead, Cobain directed his frustrations into shouting out the lyrics to his songs. When he began the next number—"Smells Like Teen Spirit"—he sang with a growl, as if he were an angry cur emitting a warning.

At most shows thereafter, "Teen Spirit" would be reserved for a place later in the set, maybe as an encore, or maybe not even played at all on a few occasions (and on one such instance of this omission a crowd in Brazil did riot). By moving the song that made them famous up in the set, Nirvana was subtly giving the crowd notice that they could do whatever they wanted the rest of the show. The weak attempts that security guards had made to stop slam dancing, or to keep kids from jumping off the stage, were abandoned—it was clear by this point that the show belonged to the fans and that no one, not even Cobain, had any control. The Halloween show represented the first chance that many of these Seattle kids had en masse to dance to a song they claimed as their anthem. The crowd went wild: you saw the bottoms of more Converse tennis shoes than you saw heads, as if the entire front of the audience had been inverted.

If Cobain himself was impressed by the wild response of the audience, he didn't show it onstage. Instead, he yelled again at the camera crew and then launched into "About a Girl," one of the only slow songs in the band's catalog. The tempo didn't slow down the dancers—they would have slam danced to silence at this point—but it did seem to deflate some of the energy in the room. It was obvious to me from my seat towards the back that, despite the huge success Cobain was experiencing, he showed no signs of satisfaction. In a later review of the concert, I wrote, "These guys are already rich and famous, but they still represent a pure distillation of what it's like to be unsatisfied in life."

The show did get better three songs later when the band did "Sliver," a tune that in Seattle had been something of a local radio hit. And "Love Buzz," which followed, had always been a crowd favorite with Seattle audiences; in Nirvana's earliest Seattle shows this was their only true crowd pleaser. The dancing reignited in earnest with "Lithium," the track that many had initially thought would be the biggest hit on *Nevermind*.

The Paramount is an old grand dame theater, built originally near the turn of the century as a vaudeville house. In the long history of the hall, no audience had ever thought to use the ornate moldings on the side of the stage as launching pads for jumping into the crowd. But that's exactly what some did at this show. The seating in the hall was bolted down, but if it weren't for those bolts, I have to imagine that chairs would have been thrown like at a Friday night pro wrestling match.

The rest of the show was a bit of a blur for me, and I think for the band: they basically ripped through a half dozen of their fastest songs, and they even played those songs at a faster tempo than usual. By the time they ended the evening with "Endless Nameless," the hidden jam from *Nevermind*, you weren't exactly sure if the crowd was more spent than the band, but you knew a crash was coming. Adrenaline had kept the band going for almost seventy minutes—they weren't capable of playing much longer than that. By the end of the set, even the go-go dancers had slowed down. The set had peaked, as any casual pundit could have predicted, during "Teen Spirit," but that peak had been mountainous. It was not the best Nirvana show I ever saw, but it was certainly one that can't be forgotten if only because the anticipation and build up. In that way, it was like the Super Bowl—never likely to live up to the hype.

Backstage, after the show, friends and family congratulated Kurt as if he had just won the Lombardi Trophy. But while Dave Grohl and Krist Novoselic ran around celebrating and partying, Cobain would have none of it. He thought it was an off show, but he already knew that he was such an icon for a generation that he was not allowed off shows. He sat on a stool in the middle of the room, his hands on his face, looking downtrodden, oblivious of the many people surrounding him, waiting for an audience with him. "The feeling of euphoria disappeared once you got near Kurt," *Seattle Post-Intelligencer* reporter Gene Stout recalled. When Stout leaned down to say hi, Cobain's response was to thrust out a moist, limp hand.

Later, when a photographer asked Kurt if he'd pose with his sister, he yanked her hair at the moment that the photo was taken. "He was all pissed off and being a dick," his sister Kim later recalled. Kurt was most concerned that his ex-girlfriend Tobi felt like she'd gotten a positive reception from the crowd.

An hour later, when Cobain went to leave the venue—still carrying his bag of underwear and socks—he ran into one of his friends back from his hometown of Aberdeen. The friend offered up an observation that couldn't have been more obvious to Kurt, but nonetheless was stated: "You're really famous now, Cobain. You are on television, like, every three hours."

Kurt's only reply had a small amount of truth to it—he was now living in hotel rooms but still had no apartment of his own.

"I don't know about that," he said. "I don't have a TV in the car I live in."

37

The Lounge Lizards
Merkin Concert Hall
New York City
April 12, 1992
RICK MOODY

Some Propositions Concerning the Lounge Lizards

PREFACE: The problem with being an engaged music listener is that it's completely unscientific. Unlike being, e.g., a deranged baseball fan, or a hardcore weather person, or a day trader, or a wine fanatic. Those pursuits have their elective affinities, but they also depend on rigorous templates of factual material. The deployment of these facts becomes an important part of the obsessive lifestyle of the cathected individual. In the case of popular music, however, this absence of statistical abstracts gives rise to annoying compilations of top-ten lists, desert island discs, accounts of various shows. Concerts especially. It's one of those *High Fidelity*–style games, talking about the gigs you've been to. Guys do it a lot. Apparently, going to concerts involves a masculine manipulation of worldly impediments. You have to wait in long lines, you have to exercise Machiavellian crowd control instincts, or you have to exhibit first-rate scalping prowess. ("I just waltzed up to that black dude and got two third-row tickets off him five minutes before the show, only fifteen bucks!") You camp out. You wait until the lights go down, and then you somehow connive your way down to the row where the industry suits repose. In these pages, I attempt to replace the *High Fidelity*–style obsession with a more serious apparatus, one which ideally gives the concert to which I address myself a stately, serious treatment. Please see below.

FIRST PROPOSITION, *that the best concert I ever saw in my life was a gig by the Lounge Lizards, on April 12, 1992, at the Merkin Concert Hall, New York City.* This concert was part of the New Sounds Live concert series, Svengali'd by one John Schaefer, the host of the radio program of the same name, broadcast each night at 11 p.m. on WNYC, public radio affiliate in my fair city. I started listening to the New Sounds radio program when I was in graduate school on the Upper West Side, this being in the mideighties. Soon, I moved to Hoboken, and at that juncture I became passionately addicted to it, would stay up late especially to listen to New Sounds, often recording bits and pieces that interested me, and then searching them out in record stores that specialized in obscurities. I first heard Arvo Paart on New Sounds, first heard Gorecki's third symphony and David Hykes and Lamonte Young and Ingram Marshall and a lot of other stuff. Some of this music has probably been lost to history, alas (viz., A. Leroi's placid and hilarious "Home Sweet Home") especially now that you can no longer listen to archives of the really *old* episodes.

SECOND PROPOSITION, *that a certain period of music by the Lounge Lizards amounted to some of the most transportative music ever recorded.* See, somewhere in the midst of my enchantment with the New Sounds show, in the late eighties, I heard this saxophone solo playing over the airwaves. It was late one night in Hoboken, and I was barely awake. My delusional semi-sleep was a recombinant mixture of hypnagogic voices and New Sounds, and I heard this saxophone playing. Sort of the most beautiful thing I had ever heard in my life. It was what I imagined music could do. I couldn't really fathom how melancholy and enthusiastic it was. Started out with one saxophone, and then there was a second answering horn performing these sort of arpeggio-like runs. Just when I was kind of getting used to the saxophone, a really fractured guitar came in, a downtown-ish guitar, the kind of guitar that would be used to repel gentrifiers on the Lower East Side, then some percussion, then the guitar just broke out into some massive cacophony, like a pallet of submachine guns toppling over onto the floor, drowning out the saxes for an interval. This *was* exactly what I wanted music to do, to ennoble and articulate and unsettle, but in an unpretentious way, in an affecting way. Sort of jazz-like, but too anarchic to be jazz in the *old* sense, without the requisite batch of tri-tones and augmented chords, instead luminous and peaceful and screechy, not ridiculous and embarrassing like some of that supposedly peaceful, gentle music that you sometimes heard on New Sounds. Anyway, the piece ended with this childlike drum section, a rather meditative drum pattern. Then a little more solo sax. I woke, I waited, I stayed awake, just so I could hear John Schaefer announce what the hell it was.

THIRD PROPOSITION, *that the early Lounge Lizards dressed exquisitely.* Well, when John Schaefer announced the band, announced the name of the song (and what a great name: "A Paper Bag and the Sun"), I was a little stunned, because I had heard the Lounge Lizards back in college when their first recording was released. My keenest recollection of that album was that they dressed well on the cover. The cover had them all wearing shirts and ties, as if they were a simulacrum of a genuine jazz band, in which spirit John Lurie, whose band it was, had once described them as "fake jazz." This turned out to be something he ought never have said, as for a time it made it difficult to take them as seriously as they deserved. That first lineup had Arto Lindsay in it, who was a great downtown guitarist, though in my view not as good as Marc Ribot, who later filled the same chair (on, e.g., "A Paper Bag and the Sun"). Originally, they also had Anton Fier on drums, who not long after convened the excellent Golden Palominos, including a configuration with Syd Straw and Jodie Harris that I liked a lot. Still, I just didn't *get* the first Lounge Lizards album, exactly. Seemed like it was a little mannered to me, seemed like it was more about establishing mastery of a genre than about memorable writing. Even the impeccable credentials of producer Teo Macero—the guy who produced Miles's first electric period—was a little too pedigreed. Upon hearing "A Paper Bag and the Sun," however, I was in a fever, convinced that something amazing had happened to the Lounge Lizards, and that I had been wrong to consign them to the file of things given incomplete attention, and so I went in search.

FOURTH PROPOSITION, *that it was also occasionally important to go to the movies.* John Lurie of the Lounge Lizards had appeared in a number of movies in the middle eighties, and I saw these movies, and I thought he was great, a natural actor, but movies just didn't matter to me in the same way that music mattered. I liked Roberto Benigni's rabbit soliloquy in *Down By Law.* I thought Eszter Balint was really pretty in *Stranger Than Paradise.* And I thought John's television program, *Fishing With John,* was one of the best uses ever of the medium. John had an offhanded and relaxed charisma on the screen, whether large or small, but this did not command my more careful interest. It took John Schaefer and New Sounds to do that.

FIFTH PROPOSITION, *that the New Sounds Live concert series, which took place for a half dozen Sundays each year, was almost as good as the radio show.* I think it was in 1991 or 1992 that I started going to the New Sounds concerts, at Merkin Concert Hall, in the Lincoln Center area, and these were often amazing events. Sometime in 1992, e.g., I saw a full-length recital of La Monte Young's *The Melodic Version of The Second Dream of The High-Tension Line Stepdown Transformer from The Four Dreams of China*, scored for brass octet in just intonation. The instruments were situated throughout the hall. Since the piece was scored in this unusual tuning system—unusual at least for Western ears—the players obviously have to listen to each other *really carefully*, so as to avoid slipping back into well-tempered mode. The piece did generate waves of overtones, as advertised, and was mesmerizing and singular and strange. And that was just one show. I was always among rather eccentric-looking types when I was among the other subscribers to the New Sounds Live series. They included homely downtown kids with big glasses, and old hippie guys with unconventional hygiene regimens, people who really thought about music and really cared about it. Music wasn't something that played in the background while they had drinks or tried to pick up somebody. Anyway, in the midst of this regular diet of con-certgoing, I learned that the Lounge Lizards were going to play. And by then I was already deeply in love with *Voice of Chunk,* the 1989 album that had "A Paper Bag and the Sun" on it.

SIXTH PROPOSITION, *that the phrase "the best concert I ever saw in my life" does have something fatuous about it.* And yet, despite my misgivings, it is per-haps worth mentioning that I've been to my share of interesting concerts: a Jones Beach show by Van Morrison where he sang "Sweet Thing" from *Astral Weeks* while lightning was flashing over the stage; Todd Rundgren and Ian Hunter at a John Anderson For President rally in Providence in 1980; Red Krayola at the Knitting Factory, 2005; The dBs, Lupo's, Providence, RI, circa 1982, opening for Tom Verlaine; R.E.M., *Document* tour; Talking Heads, *Remain in Light* tour; George Clinton/P-Funk All Stars, Brooklyn Academy of Music, 2005; Young Fresh Fellows/John Wesley Harding in Albany, 2002. But I'm just not one of these persons who hoards my old ticket stubs, and who speaks reverently of his one hundred Dylan shows, or his two hundred Dead shows. I am glad I never saw the Doors play, and seeing U2 on the tour for the first album is not something I think about often. More often it's the strange stuff that happened at whichever concert I remember. Like this: my very first concert was Frank Zappa and the Mothers of Invention, Halloween 1975 (the series of shows he recorded for *Live in New York*), at the Palladium, to which I took my prep school roommate, Andy, and at which Andy, after getting high with the unknown doper to his left, puked on his shoes during the encore. That I remember. Along with the banner that Zappa had strung across the stage: *Warner Brothers Record Company Sucks.*

SEVENTH PROPOSITION, *that it is the rare band that is actually better live than they are on their recordings.* I saw Guided By Voices once, and they were certainly better live, but that is because their recordings were deliberately low fidelity at that point. Music that is about dancing, as in the case of the B–52's, never came alive for me until I saw it performed. I liked Bow Wow Wow live, and I thought their songs were actually kind of bad. Ditto, from the opposite end of the spectrum, Nine Inch Nails. In the case of the Lounge Lizards, I thought that *Voice of Chunk* was more than well-recorded, and so it didn't occur to me that they could possibly be *better* than the recording. But wait, I guess I'm getting ahead of myself. Let me describe the event! The first half of the New Sounds concert that afternoon, yes, afternoon, 2 p.m., was the Mikel Rouse Broken Consort. Apparently, this portion of the bill was meant to be the Kronos Quartet half (I have since seen them play a couple of times), but they rescheduled. I don't remember much about Mikel Rouse, except that he had synthesizers. I wasn't engrossed. Then there was intermission.

EIGHTH PROPOSITION, *that your memory of the best concert in your life is not to be trusted,* but that doesn't make this memory less important. Your memory is not to be trusted in any case. And yet what I have learned from hoarding my erroneous memories is idealism of a kind. So: there was intermission. Some portion of the Lounge Lizards came out on stage, and then John was meant to go over and talk to John Schaefer at a little interviewing station that Schaefer had at each gig. Schaefer was meant to ask Lurie some polite, diverting, softball questions, as he did with his guests. I was looking forward to this part, because I thought John Lurie was really *cool*, and it was going to be interesting to hear what he had to say. And yet from the second he sat down, the two drummers who had already made their way on stage began playing and Lurie kind of looked at Schaefer, and then he kind of looked at the audience, and threw up his hands, *what am I supposed to do?*, and fled from the chair beside John Schaefer back downstage. Before it was clear what was happening, he had already picked up his horn. Whereupon he began to wail. At about the time of this show, Lurie was also playing some gigs with a much smaller ensemble (this evolved in part because it was easier than mobilizing the numerous Lounge Lizards for national and international tours), called the John Lurie National Orchestra. This ensemble involved the two drummers, Calvin Weston (he can be found on a number of Lurie-related recordings) and Billy Martin, who went on to be in Medeski Martin & Wood. That day, the opening number featured this trio. They just went for it. Of which I write more below. They were as far from the Mikel Rouse Broken Consort as you could get. Meanwhile, it's possible, of course, that the non-conversation I've just described with John Schaefer never happened at all. Before I got a copy of the set list,[1] in order to write this piece, I was sure that the intermission happened in the *middle* of the Lounge Lizards' performance.

NINTH PROPOSITION, *that spontaneity is to be prized highly in the concert setting.* For example, one of the most excellent concerts I ever saw was not a concert at all. It was the regular Sunday service at Al Green's church in Memphis. I went with my friend Darcey, on a break from a literary festival we were attending in Oxford, Misssissippi. I guess Al talked a little bit, but what he mainly did at his service was sing. And how he sang was in a really improvised way, where he would just tease out phrases and ideas until he felt like he was done with them. This process often took a while. It was musical ministry in the best sense of the term and we stayed for two hours or so. The service was still just getting going when we left. That kind of spontaneity, where you just open your mouth and sing, was genuinely inspiring to me. And the opening section of "Lawn For People," the first song that the Lounge Lizards played, trafficked in this very sort of spontaneity. Look, I recognize that Lurie composes a fair amount. He can write the notes on the staffs. He is not a jazz composer the way that Miles was, a purist, where there's just a little phrase, maybe a lead sheet, and once you play the phrase, everybody heads off into the wilderness. But Lurie still manages to invert, subvert, and remodel melody lines on his sax until he feels like he has said what he needs to say. With just the two drummers he was filling Merkin Concert Hall, all the way to the back wall, and he was doing this with this great self-assurance. And the best part was that he

---

[1]"Lawn For People," "Red and Gold Carpet," "Happy Old Yoy," "Uncle Jerry," "Sex with Monster, Volume Two."

hadn't even really got going, because the band came in piece by piece somewhere toward the end of the solo—Mickey Navazio on guitar, Dave Tronzo on slide guitar, Michael Blake on tenor sax, Steve Bernstein on trumpet, and Jane Scarpantoni on cello (or this is my informed guess from this recollective vantage point)—and once they were all playing, it was even louder, and even more ecstatic. And this went on for twenty minutes, this song, before they even broke for a rest.

TENTH PROPOSITION, *that call-and-response is the essence of spontaneity,* and call -and-response connects music back to some ancient impulses, its role in the formation of community, to African music, although I suppose there was call and response in some madrigal singing, too. It is well represented in African music, however, this impulse, in Fela Kuti, in King Sunny Adé, in the music of the pygmies, in almost any African music, and African music has influenced Lurie, at least the way I see it. You can hear West African time signatures, e.g., in the Lounge Lizards and in his pseudonymous Marvin Pontiac recordings. The relationship between the saxophones in the Lounge Lizards, it's all about call-and-response, all about the movement between players, which makes his musical ideas more forceful, legitimizes them. Though I had expected to hear the Lounge Lizards play songs from *Voice of Chunk,* and would have claimed, had I not seen the set list, that they *did* play more than just the one tune from that album, "Uncle Jerry," I didn't care, because the principles were the same in all of these songs (most of which apparently went unreleased, in the long period of Lounge Lizards– related difficulties between *Voice of Chunk* and their last official release, *Queen of All Ears*). The audience was aware that it was hearing something amazing, something greatly celebratory, and so even though it was the *after-noon*, which is a pretty ridiculous time for a concert, there was some palpable energy that was getting fed back and forth, some vibe, and it was apparent in the relationships between the ensemble ("They have to love each other," Lurie said once), in the way ideas got transported from one player to another, and in the communication between ensemble and audience. Lurie, a rather flamboyant, even overpowering character, was nonetheless a *part* of the ensemble. It became very much a *group,* and that was part of the hardcore genius of the later Lounge Lizards, but especially of the Lounge Lizards *live,* that they just hit the groove, like an African drumming ensemble, or an old Dixieland jazz band, and while Lurie wrote the material and the solos, when they came, they weren't egomaniacal or pyrotechnical or overly florid. They were just new ways of thinking about whatever phrase was about to be introduced into the circuit. It was ecstatic, it was confident, it was relaxed, it was never self-satisfied, and while the music of the Lounge Lizards may have been indebted to older jazz forms, the band never *sounded* indebted. They sounded like nothing else on earth, except the Lounge Lizards. *Strange and beautiful,* as Lurie's label name has it.

ELEVENTH PROPOSITION, *that you don't need a big encore and all of that stylized nonsense in order to mount a memorable show.* On April 12, 1992, the Lounge Lizards played only five songs. They scarcely made it over the forty-five-minute mark. And only two of the songs were ever released, one of them long after this particular concert. Who cares? It was an afternoon gig. It was being recorded live for radio broadcast. I assume the Lounge Lizards were encouraged not to go on endlessly, so as to be reasonably edited into the broadcast. Knowing a little about Lurie's life and habits as a young man, he might have been up late the night before. He might not have wanted to do some afternoon gig on the Upper West Side, for the Lincoln Center crowd. Maybe this was nobody's favorite gig, least of all John Lurie's, but it was *mine,* and that's the way it goes. Sometimes the really great gig is the one you had no idea would be so good, and it's not about how many people were in the audience (I saw an outrageously good Wedding Present show in Tucson last week before about twenty-five people), or whether the sound system was good, or whether the band had hangovers or anything else. It just happens sometimes. The Lounge Lizards happened to be flawless the day I saw them. I assume they were just as great other times. (I saw them play on television once, and they were stunning there, too.) But that day I really learned something about music. There was an awful lot of disconsolate music circulating in those days (grunge!), and the only music that attempted to remediate this misery was the jam band baby food of ersatz hippiedom. But the Lounge Lizards operated outside of this opposition. They were joyful, but never in a dim-witted way, or in a way that was somehow approving of the deranged world. *Joyful* because joyful advertises what music can do, and what en-semble playing can do. *Joyful* in a way that makes notions of genre and tax-onomy pointless. *Joyful* where you just pick up the horn and blow.

TWELFTH PROPOSITION, *that all things must pass.* John Lurie has been ill for a few years now. He has trouble playing his horn these days, so much so that the Lounge Lizards are probably on indefinite hiatus. It therefore now seems that the amazing last two albums, *Voice of Chunk* and *Queen of All Ears*, are the endpoints of an astonishing and perennially underrated musical career, a musical career that, at least for me, was an influential thing, a career that has made me a better writer, in a way, because of how it has reminded me to stay loose, to allow talent and inspiration to flourish without getting precious or exercising too much control. That said, I want to append one last morsel of story. A couple of years ago, in the course of speaking in public about how much I love the Lounge Lizards, I got to know Lurie a little bit, and one night we did a reading together, on the Lower East Side. Each reader was meant to try something that he had *never done* in public before. This was hard work for Lurie, because he has done a lot of things in public, and probably reading from his memoir-in-progress *was* the only thing he hadn't. But after he read from his memoir, which was enthusiastically admired by the crowd, he got out his harmonica. Harmonica was among John's first instruments, and he's an extremely good harmonica player, and for a couple of minutes, despite his not-great physical condition, he played one of the most heartrending and beautiful harmonica solos I've ever heard, after which he stumbled out of the room and literally collapsed in the hall. He said to me later that it might have been the last time he ever plays music in public. A respectful silence is probably the only way to greet this news. It's sad, for sure, very sad. Still, by its nature, live music has only its immediate duration. With Lurie and the Lounge Lizards, the music is in the province of memory, now, and that's where it's kept alive. A real shame for those who won't get to see them play. Memory is faulty, full of mistakes, full of longing, but still interacts with music in a flexible way; memory is kind of like music itself, like jazz, it's unpredictable, and memory gives musicians something to work toward, as it also gives writers something to write about.

THIRTEENTH PROPOSITION, *that the artist should have equal time, should perhaps have the opportunity to respond, in his own voice,*[2] to lines written about him by his fans: "I remember that show. It makes me sad what you wrote. What I remember is when Calvin would start in with that groove that was the

---

[2] Lurie responded to my request to append remarks by phone in early March of 2006. He was skeptical, but he gave it a shot.

opening for 'Lawn For People.' I can see him sitting back there playing and just yelling with a rage that was somehow also joy. Billy Martin would come in, playing odd time against Calvin. Then I would play over them. That way, I would really get a chance to play because the rest of the time I was having to lead the whole band. Then the band would come in, one at a time, behind me. Then the main theme came in with Michael Blake on tenor and Dave Tronzo on slide. It was like an anthem to a small, insane country that had just gained its independence, that thing, *ba da doo ba, bo de da*. Tronzo could really nail that line. It was, I think, the only major melody that I ever wrote.

"There was so much love and strength. It was something that, while we were playing, could absolutely not be denied. Of course, in the light of day, in offices in tall buildings all over Manhattan and Los Angeles, by neurotic women in suits with tight lips and short, white men with exceptionally small genitalia, it was denied constantly, without exception. But while we were playing there was a mounting ecstasy and power that could not be stopped. And what you saw was a shortened, forty-five-minute version of the set we normally played for three hours.

"It was macho in a way, but macho like your baby's first steps.

"So it's sad because it was beautiful, sad in a nice way, but also it's sad because of the enormous sense of loss. And also, somehow I feel like I failed. Not that many people, especially in America, ever saw that band. The recordings capture something in moments but not the whole thing. And, from what I can tell, not a ton of people own those recordings anyway, and there were enormous gaps, sometimes five or six years, where I could not afford to bring us into the studio. So as great as the music was, I did fail in a way because it never really got out there.

"If we are playing, no matter how great it is and there is no one there to hear it, then what good is it? How does that do anything for the world? I used to say in interviews, 'I am wiser, stronger, kinder and way more handsome than George Bush. I should have more effect on the world.' But, of course, I didn't.

"I remember that I did talk to John Schaefer for a minute before going on, but it was awkward. Mostly because it is odd to switch gears like that, to go from being interviewed to playing. I remember telling Schaefer that the title of the piece was 'Lawn For People,' and he made an odd face, and I thought he was going to ask me what it meant, but I was rescued because the guys started playing and didn't have to answer. And I remember because it was only one of three or four times we played in the afternoon. I'd just come back from Thailand from shooting *Fishing With John* with Dennis Hopper. I'd written 'Lawn For People' there after the shoot along with another one of the songs we did that day. It was good, and it was new material, and I remember thinking, 'Good, we really got this down.' And then, as excited as I was to listen to the recording, I was equally disappointed to hear the tape. It's not really fair to blame the engineer if the engineer doesn't know the music. The entrances are missed. There's all this chaos going on, but the cello's supposed to be out front. If the cello is not out front, it's just a rumbling mess. But it's not the engineer's fault because he didn't know this.

"I kind of have to agree with you about the early band. We postured really hard because we were shy. At least, I was shy. So in the beginning, we hid behind humor and a sort of sneering, like, 'We are cooler than you.' When we started out we didn't have the courage to be beautiful. But, also, it took years to figure out how to make the music sound like it was suppose to sound. When it was funny and campy, everybody loved it, and then later when it got really good, evolved and became elegant, nobody liked it anymore, except you, I guess. And so now I realize that there were some people out there who were actually feeling what we were doing. I think that because of the early stance of the band and then because I was so known for the movies, that some music types decided that the Lounge Lizards were somehow disingenuous, when nothing could be further from the truth."

38

Katell Keineg
Café Sin-é
New York City
February 1993
MIKE ALBO

I SAW KATELL KEINEG sing my first week in New York City. It was 1993, two days after I decided to leave my post-college politico job in Washington, DC, to come to Manhattan and try to be artsy. My one enormously wealthy friend from college kindly let me stay in her large, two-bedroom apartment on the top floor of a building near Washington Square, which somewhat warped my sense of space because, two weeks later, I would move out of that Old World, Henry Jamesian–area into the closet-sized "second bedroom" of a tiny apartment in the East Village with faulty radiators that made the place smell like wet sandwiches.

My affluent friend raved about Ms. Keineg and said she was playing at Café Sin-é on St. Mark's Place. It was snowing heavily as we walked east. I was so disoriented, and would have been totally lost without my friend. But the walk provided an expansively clean feeling because none of the now-familiar streets held any memories. We got there, and the place was packed. We sat on the floor. I wore a scratchy, vintage seventies ski sweater.

Sin-é, back then, was a tiny, one-room bar with a few tables and wide windows looking out onto the street that still had junkies and drug dealers. The snow was picking up, the start of a major blizzard that would bury the city and disorient me even more. The waitress spazzed around trying to get drinks for everyone. I seriously think Jeff Buckley was in the corner, drinking.

The best thing about Sin-é (I discovered later when I would return again and again to see Keineg sing) was that you could go there armed with just five dollars for one beer and a tip (why does every previous era seem so much cheaper and easier?) and fold yourself in a corner and not feel like you were in the way. Sin-é was the epicenter of a nineties coffeehouse folksy scene where Buckley, David Gray, and many others got their start. It was a warm, comfortable crowd, where people wore secondhand clothes, had frizzy hair, and didn't get too rowdy or cokey, at least until they left.

Ms. Keineg walked up to the mic with her guitar and fresh, wintry face. I thought she was beautiful. She barely wore makeup and radiated. Simple, plain, like someone who would do commercials for butter in another country. I think she was seriously wearing a cowl-neck sweater, fifteen years between its original popularity and its retro revival. She sang a song I have never heard her sing again, called "Most of the Time," a strummy number composed of basic chords. Ms. Keineg closed her eyes, and her clear voice minted the air. She made the snow seem fresher as it sprinkled organically on the other side of the window. She went on to play "Franklin," "Olé, Conquistador" and other songs I have heard again and again because right then I developed a kind of obsession with her that would concern me if I weren't gay.

Between numbers she quoted Rimbaud, sang snippets of traditional Welsh and Breton songs, honored past folksingers by covering Buffy Sainte-Marie's "Qu'appelle Valley, Saskatchewan," and told us she was reading a lot of Artaud. This didn't seem pretentious because she was engaging and smiley and slightly dorky. She would then launch into another song, close her eyes again and make your chest vibrate. At the end of that riveting hour and a half, she sang her ballad "The Gulf of Araby," a mysterious, hugely sad song that I think is about the Protestant/Catholic "Troubles." She truly cried while she sang, tears dribbling down her rosy cheeks. It made everyone's heart hurt, and we all left swearing to never do harm to anyone, ever.

It was either that evening or a couple nights later when I ate some old salsa in my friend's refrigerator, suffered some serious food poisoning, and spent the rest of the night evacuating and vomiting at the same time in her huge bathroom filled with Kiehl's products and expensive potpourri. But I was so thankful to have seen Katell Keineg that night, right when I arrived in the city. Even though I eventually moved into a catbox, had to take a tiring nine-to-five job at a not-for-profit law firm, and had a string of totally weird and unsuccessful trysts with New York City gay guys, I always kept that Katell show in mind. She was unapologetically expressive and filled with promise and poetry like I wanted to be. She was like a wink from the universe that I made the right decision.

I saw her play all the time at Sin-é, Arlene's Grocery, Fez, and other intimate nineties downtown spots. She had a mailing list for a while, and then an e-mail list, but you could never really count on it. She was a difficult one to pin down; you wouldn't know about her shows until the last minute, when you happened to spot her name in *The Village Voice* (this was before the omnipresent Internet made everything easy to find). She had a manager who always seemed to be running around and helping her, but both of them seemed a little overwhelmed and unorganized.

A year or so later, when her first album, *O Seasons O Castles*, came out, she had a party at Sin-é to celebrate the release of the video for the album's first single, "Hestia." There was such a confident feeling among the crowd, all of us assured of Ms. Keineg's ascendant trajectory. Lots of people were there, including a dark-haired man in a blazer who looked like her possible boyfriend. He had his hand on her hip while we all watched the video. He looked swarthy, like an Italian actor in an Antonioni film. I didn't trust him.

Her first album didn't make any ripples in public consciousness, but she did sing backup for Natalie Merchant (on "Carnival") and kept coming into town for shows. Her second album, *Jet*, came out in 1998 and received unanimous raves. I would sleep to it, write to it, put it on and do yoga in my bedroom to it. She performed a series of concerts with a full band. She had cut her hair into a Captain and Tennille–type bowl cut that again seemed squarely between the height of trends and therefore simultaneously nostalgic and ahead of its time. She filled the Mercury Lounge for two nights. Once more we all left knowing she was going to be bigger than Jewel.

It didn't happen. Instead, female singers who wear obscene amounts of lip glop and sing about how sick they are of their own fame became popular. It puzzled me. I watched Katell recede into obscurity while metrosexuality was invented, women started wearing T-shirts that say "Porn Star," and America became a kind of noisy, deadening reality show version of itself. I watched many of the old bars that I hung out in—Cake, Crowbar, the Bar—close down and become pricey wine boîtes or co-ops. I watched gigantic, white SUV limos turn like yachts down St. Mark's, and high-end bakeries for dogs replace bodegas.

Everyone began to look around at each other with these hungry "I want to be FAMOUS" eyes. The air of America became stuffy with a desperate, all-pervading promotional exhaust. Maybe Katell was too complicated, too artsy, and not shameless enough. And shameless, tireless self-promotion seemed to be the only way to make yourself known.

I discovered this as well in my own artistic struggles. You produce work and then immediately feel pressure that you have to publicize it in multi-platforms. "I've got to start a website, tell a million people on MySpace, send gift baskets to seventeen producers, and write a screenplay with a role in it where I play a version of myself but in a fictional, *Curb Your Enthusiasm* kind of way!" There's barely any room to just *be* anymore.

Ms. Keineg often addresses this in her music—defiantly questioning the way money and sales have contorted how we express ourselves, and the very idea of "success" in our culture. Her song "Leonore" is about Leonore Feni, a surrealist painter who was, predictably, not as famous as the male art stars around her, yet never compromised her individuality to achieve success. "Shaking the Disease" from her recent album, *High July*, attacks the rampant consumerism that pervades our lives: "I don't wanna buy it/I don't wanna buy it/Get your food bag out of my face," she sings.

Not long ago there was an article in *The New York Times Magazine* about Ms. Keineg and how she is so underappreciated. She lives in Dublin in a cold apartment with ratty furniture, and travels often making music, and is self-producing her next album. There was a picture of her in a quilted seventies dress, her hair mussy and highlighted, spying up at the camera with caution in her eyes. I was happy to see her finally noticed, but secretly relieved she wasn't all honey-toned, depilated, over-styled, and, well, famous.

I've lived in New York for fourteen years now. Café Sin-é moved to the Lower East Side; I think the former site serves fancy gelato. I guess I have become the artsy person I fantasized about becoming when I was twenty-three, but I also feel like I've been emotionally run over by a tank. Maybe that's a little strong. Anyway, the streets certainly aren't clean of memory anymore. Every block is clammy, full of traffic, crisscrossed with memories—where I was mugged, where I kissed Luke, where I saw my book in a window, where I fought with Gregg.

It's hard to feel "successful" in this atmosphere—especially when you struggle to pay for your crazily expensive health insurance, keep nervous watch over your HSBC account, and then walk outside and observe another bluish-tinted building of $1.5 million luxury apartments going up. It's comforting, though, to think of Katell performing back in 1993, and how little she has changed since then, keeping her voice intact. She refuses to go through the branding firm that is modern fame and inspires all of us expressive people who fall between the cracks. Her self-sufficient, scrappy lifestyle has actually been much more inspirational to me than the typical American multiplatinum success story. She is the voice of the undersung.

I went to hear Katell sing last year, right before *High July* came out. (I had to order it from Amazon and have it delivered because she was dropped by her label and it's not distributed in the United States.) She was still sunny and dorky, still had the Tennille do, and still pulled it out of me. She sang a new song, about a trip with her friends to Coney Island. She reminisced about her career, about how she didn't become "the next big thing," how Julia Roberts won't be playing her in the movie of her life, how she racked up sixty thousand dollars of debt to the music industry, but who cares, because she is with her friends, and it's a beautiful day.

39

Einstürzende Neubauten
Roseland Ballroom
New York City
April 3, 1993
MAGGIE ESTEP

I WAS SITTING IN MY HOVEL on East 5th Street in Manhattan, chain smoking Marlboros and drinking coffee, when my boss's German ex-boyfriend, Hildebrandt, called to invite me to see Einstürzende Neubauten at Roseland later that week.

I grunted noncommittally.

"Is that a yes?" Hildebrandt asked.

"Maybe," I said.

This was 1993. I'd heard of Einstürzende Neubauten but had never gone to see them live. As for the boss's ex-boyfriend, he'd asked for my number a week earlier, as my boss, Julie (a wonderful woman who paid me generously for the computer work I did three days a week at the National Writers' Union), looked on. I didn't think giving Hildebrandt my number had been a violation of the Bond of the Sisterhood since Julie had been right there when I'd given it and, anyway, I had no idea what Hildebrandt wanted from me. Was this a date? Or was he proposing we just pal around and go hear a German band?

"The records are wonderful documents, but to see Neubauten live. Well. That is the pinnacle," Hildebrandt said.

"Uh-huh," I said.

I knew Neubauten were sometimes considered the progenitors of industrial music and that they made instruments out of the sort of heavy machinery one was advised against operating while taking certain medications. I was curious about them, but I am only open to new things when I can find abundant evidence that I'll probably like the new things. The people I had met who liked Neubauten were all crazy (a good thing) and Neubauten was the only band I knew of whose fans often tattooed the band's symbol on their bodies. But the band was German, and I was unconvinced of the

German people's ability to make great music after the eighteenth century.

"You won't be sorry," said Hildebrandt. "They are innovators. Geniuses. Madmen. They will set the stage on fire."

"Fire?"

"Yeah. Well. Maybe. They've done it before."

This rang a bell. My friend Mark Ashwill had broken a leg and been arrested as a result of attending a Neubauten show at the Palladium sometime earlier, and I seemed to remember fire being involved. The band had refused to stop playing and management had lowered some sort of steel curtain to try getting them off the stage. The audience had rioted, my friend Mark instigating much of the rioting.

Hildebrandt's reverential tone, the way he said Neubauten's name softly like that of a deity or a sublime emotion, well, it swayed me a little. Plus, Hildebrandt was cute.

"I guess," I said.

"You won't be sorry."

I grunted again. I wasn't trying to be difficult. It's just that I was dreading an "Is This A Date?" situation. In previous "Is This A Date?" situations, when I'd been pretty sure the guy was taking me on an actual date and had accordingly put on my best panties and ogled the guy like a giant cake with icing, I'd been resoundingly wrong and, at evening's end, as I stood quivering expectantly, the guy had patted me on the back, called me "pal," and said we'd "hang out" again soon. On the other hand, whenever I was sure a guy had zero interest, and I showed up for our rendezvous unbathed and wearing combat boots, the guy turned out to be ravenous for me. The only thing I knew was that I couldn't trust my instincts.

On the appointed evening, I put on clean underwear, black jeans, sexy shoes—a safe "Is This A Date?" uniform.

Hildebrandt was already there when I turned up at Roseland. He was leaning against a wall, hands shoved deep into his pockets. He greeted me with a cheek kiss. He was a fine specimen, yet I didn't feel compelled to rip the clothing from his body. And I was still feeling slightly cranky about seeing a strange band, though I was intrigued by the crowd. There were a lot of them. And every last one of them, from the dyed–black hair Goth kids to the middle-aged office worker types, looked consumed by the kind of passion brought on by dangerous love affairs.

There wasn't any seating at Roseland and being packed in next to strangers makes me homicidal. We hung out at the back of the cavernous room where the crowd wasn't as dense. We talked a little. Hildebrandt was a graphic designer but had no great passion for his work. His passion was playing keyboards and listening to Einstürzende Neubauten. He was very excited to see them, but, more than anything, he seemed thrilled at the possibility of converting me. He kept telling me how much I was going to like the band. I kept telling him not to hold his breath. At some point, I went to the bathroom to freshen my lipstick. I still had no idea if we were on a date and whether or not I *wanted* us to be on a date, but it seemed like a good idea to look attractive. I applied more blood red lipstick.

An hour passed before a loud, electronic pulse started coming from somewhere on the stage. Then, some drumming. The crowd started roaring. But this wasn't the obnoxious drunken shouting of traditional rock concertgoers. No. These people were very serious in their roaring. It was *heartfelt but cool* roaring.

Band members started trickling onto the stage and picking up instruments, each member greeted by louder roaring until finally, the singer, Blixa Bargeld, a tall, handsome man with a dark suit and a forelock of brown hair, appeared. The band launched full force into the first song, and all hell broke loose. The audience didn't start moshing or even dancing violently, but the ecstasy was visible, thousands of pairs of eyes milked over, like the room had received a massive injection of a love drug. The pulsings and drummings became more insistent, and, here and there, a line of melody from a guitar or from Blixa's big, booming voice. This was better than I expected. By the third song, I found myself winding my way forward through the crowd. I didn't really know or care if Hildebrandt was following. I just had to get closer to this *sound*, this perfect, gorgeous sound that went from loud jet engine white noise to something melodic and beautiful. It was schizophrenic. It was perfect. There were even a few songs I recognized. I'd known several Neubauten worshippers who had apparently been playing Neubauten for me when I wasn't looking. "The Interimlovers," a loping, melodic song was familiar, as was the magnificent "Headcleaner," one that brought the house down with its stops and starts and Blixa's percussive screams.

By now, the bass player had shed his shirt, and the main drummer (almost everyone took turns banging on things) hadn't been wearing many clothes to begin with. Blixa was still perfectly suited and coiffed, though. He'd occasionally exhibit passion, striding from one side of the stage to the other, lifting an arm or throwing his head to one side, but mostly, he remained poised, a master of lunacy overseeing the inmates at the asylum.

My heart had started beating faster and, by the time they got to the last song, I was pretty sure I was going to die of love. Not for any one individual in Neubauten, but for their collective greatness. I also felt like a complete idiot for having missed so many good years together. I could even remember what must have been their first New York appearance, back in the very early eighties when I was just a seventeen-year-old snot-nosed punk. The ad in *The Village Voice* said "Einstürzende Neubauten" and, in parentheses, "Collapsing New Buildings." The concert promoters evidently thought a translation of the band's name was required for an audience to be drummed up. I was vaguely offended on the band's behalf, even though I had no idea what they sounded like.

When the Roseland show ended, I stood staring dumbly at the stage for a few minutes before remembering Hildebrandt. I discovered he was standing right next to me. He saw me looking toward him and smiled a knowing smile.

"You like?"

I grinned the biggest grin of my life.

But my passion for Neubauten didn't transfer itself to Hildebrandt as the "Is This A Date?" continued. After the show, we had coffee somewhere downtown. We tried like hell to come up with words to describe what we'd just witnessed, but it was bigger than either of us. Eventually, Hildebrandt walked me home. He didn't make any moves and I didn't, either.

Hildebrandt and I had two more "Is This A Dates?" and then I never saw him again.

For weeks after the show, I asked everyone I knew if they'd heard Neubauten. "Oh yeah, that weird industrial band?" my friend Jenny said.

"No, no, no. They are not weird nor even particularly industrial. They're just brilliant."

I went to my local record shop and bought four different albums hoping to recapture some of the feeling of the concert. It worked, but only slightly. Neubauten proved the antithesis of pianist Glenn Gould's theory that live music was intrusive and music should be enjoyed only on recordings, in the comfort of one's own home. Gould had given up performing very early in his career, citing this as a reason. Obviously, he'd never seen a Neubauten show.

Nearly six years after that first ecstatic experience at Roseland, through a fluke of fate, I got assigned to write a piece about Neubauten for a glossy magazine. I'm a fiction writer, good at making things up, not so good at fact or reality. I was nervous. But there I was, at the Bowery Ballroom just after Christmas 1998, sitting up in the balcony during the band's sound-check, a solicitous publicist asking me if I had everything I needed. I just grinned stupidly.

Perched up in the balcony, I watched the band members drifting in. They were all tall, all wearing crazy fur-trimmed hats and big boots, like they'd just stepped off a sled in Russia. These boys were clearly prepared for any-thing. They were chatting amiably in German and taking turns going onto the stage to gaze at the instruments and machinery that had been laid out for them by some thoughtful roadies and sound people.

The soundcheck was nearly as good as the Roseland show. The boys went from loose and casual to intense and manic as they ran through some of the songs from their recently released record, *Ende Neu*, that was even more melodic and structured than 1993's *Tabula Rasa*. I was so lulled by it all that I was startled when the publicist came over and told me it was time to meet the band.

"Oh," I said. I really didn't want to meet the band. The boys looked scary and my assignment didn't require that I actually meet or speak to them, just that I watch them and write about it.

"Come on," said the publicist, "you have to at least meet Blixa."

"Okay," I shrugged.

Moments later, I was shaking hands with Blixa. He seemed at least ten feet tall as he peered down at me and asked about my assignment.

"I haven't done much magazine writing," I said. "I usually just make things up."

This was apparently a good answer. Blixa beamed and promptly insisted I have dinner with him.

I was terrified—for about five minutes. I discovered that this towering, handsome man had a wicked sense of humor and a keen, sharp mind. Within minutes, we were babbling like old friends. Then, it occurred to me we were having an "Is This A Date?" By the end of dinner, it clearly was, and what ensued was a tumultuous six-month love affair that found me storming out of hotel rooms from Venice to London in the middle of the night. We didn't have the smoothest of liaisons, but there was never a dull moment.

Some part of me mourned the loss of innocence of just being a fan. But there were platinum benefits to my briefly held position as girlfriend. I spent time lounging on a couch in the rehearsal studio as Neubauten worked on their next record, *Silence Is Sexy*. I attended many consecutive shows in many different parts of the world. It was an embarrassment of riches.

Every now and then, I'd think of Hildebrandt and wonder what he'd think if he knew just how far I had come in my appreciation of Neubauten.

40

Beck
The Fillmore Theatre
San Francisco
July 5, 1994
MARC BOJANOWSKI

ON THE NIGHT OF JULY 5, 1994, I borrowed my father's pickup truck and drove sixty-five miles south with two friends of mine to see Beck perform songs from his *Mellow Gold* album at the Fillmore Theatre in San Francisco. I was seventeen years old, and this was my first rock 'n' roll show.

Lucky for me, in 1994 the plaid flannel was considered hip. I didn't drink or smoke, and at the end of each semester I received an embossed piece of paper certifying me as a "scholar athlete." The crew of friends I ran with consisted of two of the fastest Mexicans you'll ever meet, a Libertarian prankster, a mechanically ingenious German, and a long-distance bicycle rider whose diet in those days involved compressed-sawdust bars marketed as protein and electrolyte goop that came in ketchup packets. We spent Friday and Saturday nights soaping the town fountain, cruising sleepy neighborhoods to Creedence in the German's Plymouth Valiant named Charlemagne, or lowering railroad arms on empty intersections while eating burritos. We weren't afterschool TV–special material. At a time when grunge pervaded radio and music television programming, my affiliations were more Reagan youth than rock 'n' roll.

It's not that I disliked grunge. I found it then, and still find it to be sincere, emotional music. Like many teenagers of the day, I memorized Nirvana lyrics and moshed furniture when my parents weren't home. I even made a ceremony out of listening to Pearl Jam's *Ten* through headphones before cross-country races to enrage myself mentally for athletic competition. Thing is, though, I was raised in a stable home with secular, conservative values. I earned slightly better than average grades, held steady after-school jobs, and felt more nervous than rebellious when it came to high school dances. Yet, despite not identifying with, or, rather, not qualifying for the media-suggested prerequisites for grunge appreciation, I aped its style, jargon, and dissatisfied, solipsistic mugging. But I felt like a poseur when I did, because, well, I was one, singing along to all their pretty songs because he knows not what it means.

In March of 1994, Beck's popular single "Loser" was helping to dissipate the rain cloud of grunge. "Loser" is a sincere, thoughtful perspective on life in a post-industrial, media-saturated, and consumer-oriented culture. Cable television plays a pivotal role in the dissemination of this culture. And while I was not unaware of cable television programming, and MTV's role in the killing of the radio star in particular, I did not absorb its content on a daily basis. In the spring of 1994, cable television had yet to stretch out to where I lived with my parents, just beyond the limits of our town. So as "Loser" suffused MTV, I felt frustration at not being able to participate in the dialogue of my peers. I learned this to be the expertise of marketing. I wanted my MTV, too. Instead, I sat at night in front of my stereo with my finger on the record button waiting for "Loser" to play on San Francisco's alt-rock station, cursing the knuckleheaded DJs who repeatedly foiled my act of piracy by stepping on the song's catchy slide guitar intro.

Listening to "Loser" is like sifting through slimy plastic offal. The opening line, "In the time of chimpanzees I was a monkey," is an artful, self-deprecating admission of naïveté that hoodwinked many of the ironic, hyper-self-conscious and self-referential narcissists running about willy-nilly in the nineties music scene. This is not to say that "Loser" cannot be self-conscious to a fun house degree. But its lyrics are also rife with acute observations of the supermarket amalgamations of the time. Beck juxtaposes sincerity and irony to position himself as a media-ripe image of a Gen X slacker, but one who possesses the savvy of a mature eclectic. While the more technologically advanced of our species were going digital, Beck went digital and sifted through the heaps of discarded CD pearls and scratched vinyl to come up with nuggets of platinum. By fusing the anonymity of nascent electronica with the long-standing humility of folk, "Loser" subtly apprised the many clever units of the day, themselves zapped with serious doses of early–information age living, of a landscape beyond the screen, beyond the end of our noses.

Looking back, it's not as if the landscape wasn't already engrossing enough. On April 5, 1994, Kurt Cobain's death preoccupied national media attention. On April 6, the genocide in Rwanda began. Me? I was picking daisies in right field and copying trigonometry homework. However, from that period of time I can distinctly recall an occasion when I heard

"Loser" blaring from two car stereos at opposite ends of my high school parking lot. I stopped to listen. They were out of sync, but not by much. Then, out of the fucking blue, a starling dropped dead onto the pavement in front of me.

Every now and then a song will do this. A skilled musician utilizes the abundant resources available to our omnivorous culture to create stereophonic sounds capable of knocking birds out of the sky. We look around, and the world is different.

After two months of listening to my taped copy of "Loser," my friend Jon—the bicyclist—informed me that Beck was scheduled to play in San Francisco later that summer. I can recall that we were hanging out on this ridge overlooking our hometown. It was a popular make-out spot. We were alone, eating burritos and tossing rocks at beer bottles. It was dusk and the street lights below were coalescing into a mass that resembles—in photographs I've seen that are taken from space—lava flow, but from a hilltop is the network of wood, asphalt, and insulated wires that constitutes our civilization.

"Yeah," I said in my best rock 'n' roll voice, "let's go see Beck."

The day of the show, we picked up our friend Ross at his parents' home tucked away in the hills of Petaluma. Within an hour-and-a-half we dropped in on the Golden Gate entrance to that shining metropolis by the Bay in a red and gold GMC extended cab 4x4, sitting three abreast with the windows down blaring "Loser" on the tape deck. We got lost. One of us leaned out the window and yelled to several smartly dressed, attractive young ladies that we weren't from around there, and would they mind giving us directions, which they did mind, and so didn't. We had trouble finding parking; I had trouble parallel parking the truck once we did. We learned why ticketholders rarely show up when the doors open at seven and the show starts at ten.

The Fillmore Theatre impressed me. I vaguely recall climbing lushly carpeted stairs into the smell of clove cigarette smoke. I knew little then of the building's history as an Italian dance hall, but knew it better from the hazy stories of a back-to-the-land neighbor of ours as a place where Jerry played. The ornate ceiling was high and dimly lit, the balcony seats filled with pale, dark-clad, spectacled, well-informed hipsters of the Science Fiction Bay Area. I was intrigued by a basket of free green apples. Later, the lead singer of the opening band—Geraldine's Fibbers—got struck by one in the forehead during a slow song but never stopped playing, and even dedicated the next song to the "asshole who threw the apple."

This, I remember thinking, must be rock 'n' roll.

When Beck took to the stage, I realized that this was the first time I had ever been a part of a large crowd that was not centered around an athletic event. The scene wasn't like anything I had imagined from when listening to the radio, or on what I'd seen of MTV. How could it be? At some point, a young woman yelled, "I love you Beck," to which he immediately replied, "Thanks, Mom."

I don't remember Beck playing "Loser," although I am certain he did. What I do remember is that, at some point, the lights dimmed even further and the band walked offstage. Beck picked up an acoustic guitar and strapped on a harmonica. He stood in a cone of blue light, breathing in and out of the harmonica, turning his head aside to sing "One Foot in the Grave" into a microphone while stomping his foot and strumming the guitar. The song showcased his ability as a storyteller and poet, in the tradition of Dylan and Guthrie. The lyrics accumulated objects in a whorl of hyperbolic imagery and traditional sound. He transmogrified our landscape into that stuff good artists fascinate, engage, and ultimately encourage us to assist in the making of it something better. The song was funny, but it wasn't all a joke. Where "Loser" embodied my superficial understanding of rock 'n' roll, "One Foot in the Grave" introduced me to the more profound aspects of the American musical tradition. Beck's savvy cool rebuked the self-concerned despondency and sentimentality of the day in a manner that I admired.

On the drive home, our ears were destroyed. We had the windows down and the radio off. We climbed above the cool of the Bay, and then descended into the warm of the grassy hills beyond. That night, I learned firsthand how rock 'n' roll expands horizons, opens doors, and tinkers with the mind. It was late, and the highway was empty. All I could hear was the wind.

41

Joe Maneri
Harvey Pekar's Living Room
Cleveland, Ohio
Summer 1997
HARVEY PEKAR

MOST PEOPLE WHO'VE heard of me at all think of me as a writer of comics. But in 1959, long before I started writing comic book stories, I started contributing articles and reviews to nationally distributed jazz magazines. More than the vast majority of critics, I was interested in the technical aspects of music and dealt little with jazzmen-as-fascinating-personalities. I focused attention on innovation, on people who were expanding the boundaries of the jazz vocabulary. Without innovators, art forms cease to grow. There were and are a lot of original, innovative artists out there who do not receive much attention, and I consider my primary responsibility as a critic to publicize their work. So that meant I had to be constantly on the lookout for new musicians and new schools of music. I loved doing that— discovering people. It's what being a critic's about.

In the mid-seventies, my comic book career started to take off, and I decided that I would spend most of my energy on it rather than on jazz criticism. So, from about 1975 to 1989, I devoted relatively little time to jazz and little money to buying records, while I wrote, published, and tried to sell my comic, *American Splendor*.

In 1989, I found that an old friend of mine, saxophonist-composer Roy Nathanson, was doing some groundbreaking work with a band he co-led, the Jazz Passengers, and then discovered other highly creative musicians including John Zorn and Dave Douglas. What they were doing interested me so much that I began to buy, listen analytically to, and then start writing about new developments in jazz. With my usual lack of humility, I guess I figured no one could explain them as well as I could.

By the mid-nineties, I was contributing articles and reviews to several newspapers and jazz magazines, including *The Boston Herald*. This put me in contact with a Boston publicity firm, Braithwaite and Katz, who sent me an amazing CD by Joe Maneri, a guy teaching at the highly regarded New England Conservatory of Music. Maneri was sixty-eight when I received his disc, but he was still one of the most modern, innovative jazz artists in the world. He played free jazz, incorporating into it a lot of atonality and microtonality. Who was this cat? I got his phone number, gave him a call in Boston, and got him to send me copies of some private tapes he'd made. Not only his music, but his biography was astonishing. Talk about someone who'd conquered some obstacles; this guy had surmounted an Everest of them.

He was born in New York City in 1927, the son of working-class Sicilian parents. Unfortunately, he'd had attention deficit disorder at a time when no one knew what it was or how to cope with it. Because of ADD, he was flunking all of his subjects in school. At fifteen, he decided to drop out and try to make his living as a professional musician. (He'd been playing clarinet for several years.) Somehow he managed to survive and gradually find his way in the New York music scene. He played a variety of gigs, and in 1946 found himself in the band of pianist Ted Harris. Harris was playing straight-ahead jazz in clubs, but had an intense interest in modern classical music, and was studying with Josef Schmid, a disciple of the great Viennese composer Alban Berg. Joe caught the bug from Harris and began studying with him. Their relationship lasted for years, during which time Joe learned thoroughly about atonal and twelve-tone music. (Actually, Schmid started him with Palestrina.)

During the fifties, Maneri's knowledge of classical music grew; he began teaching it, as well as remaining a freelance saxophonist and clarinetist, playing everything from jazz gigs to weddings and bar mitzvahs.

In the mid-fifties, he created a unique soundtrack for a friend's film about the sea, using three instruments: clarinet, tenor sax, and piano. He taped them separately, speeding up the clarinet track to approximate the sounds of sea birds, slowing down the tenor track so he could mimic a foghorn, and letting the piano play at normal speed. Influenced by Schoenberg and Varèse, he then mixed the freely improvised tracks to create a truly unique sonic experience.

For a while, Joe seemed to be placing more emphasis on classical music than jazz. In 1961, three of his compositions were performed at Carnegie Recital Hall and received excellent newspaper reviews. Conductor Erich Leinsdorf read one, and it led him to commission a piano concerto from Joe for the Boston Symphony.

Soon after that, Gunther Schuller, French hornist, conductor, composer, and leader of a movement that aimed to synthesize jazz and classical music into a new "third stream music," heard about Maneri. In February 1963, Schuller used him to play tenor sax in a contemporary classical piece, "Number One for Twelve Performers," written by David Reck and dedicated to free jazz pioneer Ornette Coleman. Schuller conducted, and Joe's improvised playing fit so well into the piece that it seemed written by him. Schuller was impressed and attempted to get Atlantic Records to cut a Maneri LP. (Schuller, who'd become president of the New England Conservatory in 1970, was also to thank for landing Joe his teaching gig.)

The 1963 project wasn't completed, but Joe did make a demo tape for Atlantic featuring him on clarinet and tenor sax, backed by piano, bass, and drums. Here again, Joe employs a free improvisation style. Some of the compositions are influenced by Greek music—Joe played a lot of Greek weddings—and employ odd time signatures. One of the selections is a twelve-tone piece. Without being strongly connected with other jazz musicians, Joe was continuing to develop his own musical genre.

When I heard about this stuff, I asked Joe to send me a cassette. It not only was, but still is far ahead of its time. I got so excited, I called John Zorn, who has connections with Japanese record companies, and played the cassette over the phone for him. He was very impressed, and was able to get all the Atlantic tracks released on *Paniot's Nine*, on the Japanese Avant label, plus a long klezmer selection he cut at a 1981 New England Conservatory concert. (Joe also worked a lot of Jewish weddings.)

Joe continued sending me all these fabulous cassettes that virtually no one knew about, and I was calling him all the time on the phone about them. I really enjoyed talking on the phone to Joe. For one thing, I dug the way he sounded: he still had a heavy Brooklyn accent that was music to my ears. And, in addition to being a very friendly, good-humored guy, he was very intelligent and well-informed. I learned a lot about music in our conversations. His students were crazy about him. He was always accessible to them. I remember talking to one guy, now among the world's greatest tuba players, who studied with Joe. Like Joe, he was from Brooklyn, and didn't feel entirely at ease among some of the more upper-class students at the New England Conservatory. But he recalled how one day Joe had come into the classroom eating a sandwich, and he thought, "If this guy can make it, I can make it."

So anyway, by 1997 or so, Joe and I had built up a very pleasant personal relationship. I was determined to do what I could to publicize and explain his music anytime I got a chance, partly because I considered him one of the greatest musicians of our time, partly because I really liked him and related to him very easily.

One day, Joe called me to tell me he was going to drive to some kind of family affair, maybe a wedding, around Detroit in a few weeks, and would stop off to see me if I'd be around. You bet I would. I even invited a jazz historian friend of mine over to meet him, especially in case he decided to honor us with a spontaneous concert. If he did, I wanted a knowledgeable student of jazz to witness it with me.

Joe and his entourage, including his wife, his Sicilian-born cousin, and his cousin's girlfriend, crossed my threshold in the early afternoon of a summer Sunday. I'll tell you, I was never prouder of any guest I'd ever had in my house. I can't remember specifically much of what we talked about, maybe because I was so exhilarated, but it was all very pleasant. My kid and historian pal really enjoyed his company. After a while, Joe decided to give us a shot of his music. He went back out to his car and got his tenor sax out of the trunk. Before he played, he recited a poem in a language that he'd made up himself. Then he blew this real long tenor sax solo. Man, it was great. He really opened up and played lengthy, idea-rich lines. And everything he improvised made sense; the solo had fine continuity. When he finished, I was awestruck.

We sat around a while longer, talking. Again, I don't recall anything earthshaking being said, but I was thoroughly enjoying myself. Then Joe had to go, so we said our goodbyes.

I called Joe when he got back, and we renewed our series of rather frequent phone calls. I'm really not sure if my writing had anything to do with it, but Joe became better known, and was soon recording for a couple of labels, including ECM, a pretty prestigious outfit. There was a small group of serious young musicians who were very interested in his work, and every now and then he would drive down to New York to play the Knitting Factory. It began to look like maybe he'd be getting his historical due in a few years.

But then times turned worse. Jazz accounted for about 3 percent of all CD sales when I'd gotten to know Joe; now that figure dropped to 2 percent. Joe's morale similarly plummeted as his live gigs and record dates practically stopped.

To this day, I keep in touch with Joe, still looking for places to write about him, like here. I want to keep people listening to his stuff, talking about him. People think if you're great you'll eventually get recognition, even if posthumously, but that's simply not true. Man, there are so many outstanding musicians and even authors—George Ade and Andrei Bely, to name a couple—who have simply gone out of sight without anyone noticing them when they were here or after they'd gone.

I asked Joe how he was feeling the last time I talked to him. He said he was okay, but his wife heard my question and said to Joe, "Tell him how you had that car accident and got twenty-four stitches in your head."

42

The Mekons
The Mercury Lounge
New York City
September 12, 1997
LYDIA MILLET

THE DAY I WENT TO my first Mekons show was a hard day, for it was the day I had to dress up as a giant strawberry. This was for a protest outside an overpriced gourmet food store on Broadway; I was a strawberry holding a sign. I was a strawberry with social convictions who wished to secure protections for strawberry pickers in California.

At the time, I was in my twenties and attending weekly meetings of a workers' party, at which I sat wearing lipstick and platform shoes on folding chairs between large, sad men with industrial burn scars. At these gatherings I felt—not irrationally, since I'd never worked a union day in my life—like a bourgeois pig. I came from a white-collar family; I lived in a co-op in the West Village; by day I wrote grants for a non-profit group, and by night I wrote books. I believed the underdog should rise up, but I wasn't much of an underdog myself. The one time I ever worked on an assembly line was because my mother owned it.

Still, distress and fear at the workings of power were always with me, nagging; so I was flailing around to find a useful outlet for this. This was how, one cold afternoon, I came to be encased in a foam strawberry suit in Soho.

While waddling around in the company of my fellow protesters—with none of whom I ever actually succeeded in having a decent conversation— it occurred to me that if a friend of mine came anywhere near this protest, it would be to enter the very store we were picketing, where a small log of goat cheese could be purchased for the price of an orphan in Botswana. (I myself had eaten that goat cheese. It was tasty.) My friends were mostly writers and artists who viewed activism with ironic detachment; and even though, like me, they were progressive in their politics, they felt no duty to participate. None of them would stoop to donning a strawberry. I was alone among strangers, itchy with awkwardness. I did not want to be holding up my poignant sign with someone else's words on it; I did not want to shout out someone else's slogans, which always seemed reductive and ludicrous no matter how true they might be. I did not want to look like a Fruit of the Loom commercial. I hated my self-consciousness and the instincts that made everything earnest look like cliché: but there they were, insistently surfacing.

The culture of dissent, as I encountered it, had always grated on me this way, whether it was the insularity of labor activists or the hippiedom of environmentalists. Yet a sense of social morality lay over my shoulders like a wet blanket, and sporadically I felt compelled to try to court change, nudging myself into niches where inevitably I then felt out of place. I was a prisoner in my ill-fitting fruit.

Having shucked the fruit suit, I made my way on foot to the nearby club where the Mekons were scheduled to play; the whole way, I struggled to shrug off the lingering sense of being an idiot. I wished I was just going home to hunker down, eat a pizza and watch *Law & Order*. But I had listened to the Mekons for years by then—to their early punk records, their folksy post-punk ballads, their drunken sea shanty agit-pop, their rebel-country foot-stompers—and was curious to see them live; their songs stuck like catechisms.

Besides, the tickets were already bought. Inertia carried me.

At the front of the Mercury Lounge was a bar area that allowed customers to fraternize with performers, if the performers so chose. Waiting for the show to begin, I saw Jon Langford making jolly in a group in the corner; I stood with some friends a bare few feet from Tom Greenhalgh, who looked gaunt and devilishly handsome quaffing what looked like some kind of a gin drink. (Gin and other spirits figure prominently in the Mekons' lexicon.) I wanted to think he was smiling at me and briefly envisioned a life filled with Greenhalgh, booze, music, and prominent cheekbones. I believed I might levitate. But suddenly, Greenhalgh turned away. I thought I saw an expression of distaste cross his face; I smelled something faintly rancid. Then I realized it was the afterscent of the strawberry. It had been worn by many others before me.

A few minutes later, they all took the stage, nasty, British, and not so short. Immediately they were bantering combatively, badgering and mocking each other with funny insults—a sharp, sometimes sexy badinage that secured them at once in my affections. I was smitten.

Each Mekon had charm; each Mekon was articulate and stinging, sarcastic and wise. And in the music and the gentle cast of dim lights and the warmth, from the very first seconds of the first song, I saw what it was to lose my reserve and the shame of my own bad dancing. I forgot the shock it can give onlookers suddenly to behold me, enthusiastic and in the throes of a seemingly private rhythm. I laughed at these hovering opinions and felt how they vanished. Because here was thrill; here was the delight of complete submission. I forgot the constant pressure to be distant from all things, for the world was glowing. What force! I thought. What dust we are, what blood. We stand swirling in the middle of time, the pillars of our separate identities transformed into rivers: we shed our skins and join the chaos of the endlessly redeemable soul.

It was as though I had speed or coke in my system, although in fact I had tepid light beer.

And I knew, standing there in a daze, that though I was far past the years of teen groupiedom, I was as one with all groupies. I understood them. And I wanted not merely to sleep with a Mekon, but, more than that, to be one. The Mekons were far more than me, elevated—and yet I did not begrudge them this; rather I wished to partake of it. They were what I would have hoped for in myself had I been made of rock star stuff, and had I not been the type who suffered white-knuckled fear when forced to sing karaoke. (That the Mekons never actually reached rock star status, despite a devoted following, was nothing short of tragic but did not diminish my admiration.) I saw made flesh in the merry band from Leeds a kind of ultimate social and artistic persona, one that fulfilled all my wishes about myself in the world and answered all my regrets. They stood at the crossroads where the mundane met the divine; they were the culmination of a secret and subversive idea. They were not music alone, though the sublimity of music would surely have been enough.

It was not incidental that they were an overtly socialist band with strong opinions, opinions they did not hesitate to offer up with just enough snarky wit to save them from seeming simplistic or hackneyed. Their politics and their aesthetics seemed to coalesce into a perfect whole; whereas I, ten years later, would still be struggling for the balance that would infuse my work with a political center without reducing it to a dull polemic. Nothing could have been more enviable to me.

And what I felt, listening to their nostalgic dirge to Western civilization that was always also a call to arms—they sang about the fall of Soviet communism, the opium trade, the first men on the moon, the arms race, miners' strikes—was a kind of rapture. I imagine worshippers in an ecstatic faith must feel this, caught up in a frenzy and given over to a vision of paradise or of boundless mercy. Standing in the crowd, where almost everyone seemed transfixed, I was suspended in a sheerly idealistic moment. The actual fell away and the ideal was embraced, not by one of us but by many. An imagination of justice, somehow, was present and felt: within the arc of the songs, a feeling of infinite freedom was loosed on us all.

This, at least, was how I felt—as though my heart was breaking and I welcomed it; as though joy and grief were a hair apart. I felt certain, for once, of not being alone in longing.

When the show ended and I had to go home, I felt no time had passed. I bought tickets for the show the following night, and from then on, until the day when I moved across the country, saw the Mekons whenever they played in New York or New Jersey. I never spoke to any of them, though they were fairly approachable: my awe was such that I would have been struck dumb.

In the weeks and months afterward, I became a defender of the faith. If I played a Mekons album for a friend and it met with indifference, a quick disappointment would lodge itself in my skin like a splinter. I would be forced to dismiss not only the musical tastes of the friend in question, but, in all likelihood, the immortal soul; within me diagnosis and condemnation would occur. Poor spirit, I thought. Poor thing. Too small; too mean; too slight.

For to understand the ascendance of the Mekons was to fathom infinite possibility; to see the goodness of the Mekons was to acknowledge the persistence of luminous particles in the dark.

Eventually, I gave up on the strawberry and lent myself to other, less overt forms of advocacy, finally conceding that, much as I was not cut out to be a sexy socialist rock singer, neither was I cut out to march and wave banners in front of Dean & DeLuca. Whatever anger I had did not express itself in groups but in solitary work. This felt like a cop-out for some time, but it also felt inevitable. Even if, in my dreams, I was someone else entirely, I had to agree to be myself when awake, or life would stretch on far too long.

The Mekons, like all musicians, are lucky. They run little risk of being accused of stridency, of didacticism, of arrogance: for everything is forgiven them in the powerful and euphoric joy that music, unique among the arts, can bring. Their audiences, unlike, for instance, my readers, are primed for abandonment—liquor in their stomachs, blood running thin, floating in a womblike embrace that invites direct political speech in a way that other forms, including literary fiction, do not.

But something I first understood that night has strengthened me in the years between then and now: the certainty that cynicism is finally deeply boring, that all great things are shot full of anger, sadness, and remorse.

The band turned twenty and then twenty-five; they were middle-aged and still, to me, captivating. They made albums that were almost gospel, and I loved them more than ever. "And there's no peace/On this terrible shore," they sang in 2002. "Every day is a battle/How we still love the war." For me, they would never lose their novelty. And years after that first show at the Mercury Lounge, in my own house in the desert far away from anywhere the band ever plays, the Mekons test formerly performed on so many unwitting guests has fallen into disuse in favor of less lofty criteria for the determination of personal mettle—"Does he tolerate my snuffling pug dog?" for instance, or "Does she frown disapprovingly at my food-smeared toddler?"

But I never fell out of love, and I continue to feel a nagging distrust of those who, given the chance, fail to see the singular beauty of my heroes.

43

Prince
The Fargodome
Fargo, North Dakota
December 8, 1997
CHUCK KLOSTERMAN

I LOVED PRINCE when I was thirteen, and that was humiliating. It was among my darkest secrets. Seven hours before the first day of junior high, I laid in bed and listened to my sister's *Purple Rain* cassette, mortified by my own womanliness. "This will destroy me," I privately thought. "People will see right through me. I am a pussy." At the time, the only other artists I loved were Mötley Crüe, Ratt, KISS, and Ozzy. As far as I could tell, these were the only artists any intelligent, heterosexual male could (or would) love. While much of 1985 America may have secretly appreciated "Round and Round," I was a deeply closeted Prince fanatic, unwilling to tell even my friends and family. I listened to the solo on "Let's Go Crazy," and my creeping fears were instantaneously validated: Prince was a better guitar player than Warren DeMartini. It was true, and I could not deny it. When I watch *Before Stonewall*, this is the experience I relate to.

Twelve years later, I had to review a Prince concert for the *Forum* newspaper in Fargo, North Dakota. By then, I had been "out" as a Prince person for seven or eight years. The only problem was that I didn't really care anymore: Prince was working through his preposterous TAFKAP period and was slowly releasing long-awaited records that mostly sucked. Oddly, I found myself lying about Prince *again*, but now the context was reversed: I kept finding myself saying things like, "A bad record by Prince is still better is than 90 percent of the albums that will come out this year, because he is a genius. A bad Prince record is still better than anything by the Crystal Method." Which was true, I suppose, but really only proved that MTV's *Amp* appeared to be inventing a dystopic future.

So ANYWAY, I went to this show cautiously pessimistic. I suspected it might be embarrassing, or devoid of familiar material, or punctuated by Prince walking onto the stage and wordlessly holding up four inexplicable fingers for the duration of the evening. However, my main trepidation involved time: I had to file my review by 11:10 p.m. that night, and that deadline was inflexible. The site of the concert (the Fargodome!) was a ten-minute drive from the *Forum* office, and this was the pre-laptop era. All the radio stations claimed the show would begin at eight, but everybody knew Prince usually played long and never played on time; at his club in Minneapolis, he would (supposedly) begin impromptu rock sets at 3:45 a.m. in the middle of the week. Nonetheless, I would need to exit the Dome parking lot by 10:15—this would give me fifty minutes to write a fifteen-inch, seven hundred–word review (plus or minus five minutes to self-edit the copy before sending it to the Night Desk). If Prince played two hours, I would almost certainly miss the encore; this is a common problem for anyone who has ever covered music for a daily newspaper. I think I saw three encores in eight years.

I arrived at the Dome around 7:30, pleasantly surprised to find I was directly in front of the stage (reviewers are usually relegated to the side of the arena, but not tonight). My friend Ross and I idly chatted about which songs might or might not be performed. (Ross was pulling hard for "Housequake" and "Pussy Control," if I recall correctly). We also snickered about the smallness of the crowd; while more than twenty thousand people had showed up to the Dome for Elton John, there were only 7,114 people in the building for TAFKAP. Prince had implemented a Byzantine anti-scalping policy where he would only announce a show two weeks before the actual date, and then everyone had to purchase vouchers that could only be exchanged for tickets at the door; I believe it was modeled after the method in which citizens of communist Russia were able to attain bread. Prince has been a goofball his entire life, but the middle nineties were truly the apex of his insanity. He was so crazy in 1997 that most people didn't even notice.

So . . . 7,114 of us sat there and waited. And waited. I was not surprised Prince didn't go on at eight, but I grew a little irritated at 8:30. And then—off in the distance, at the rear of the auditorium—there emerged the sound of a bass drum. "Aha!" we collectively thought. "This is it. Prepare for Prince!" The drum grew louder as it moved toward the stage; the beat emanated from (what looked like) a substantial marching band (the kind of band that might perform at halftime during the annual Grambling/ Southern football game). We all searched for rock's purple elf within the melee. Was he leading the pack? No. Was he hidden among their broad shoulders and flamboyant outfits? No. Was he *inside* the bass drum, like the Lucky Charms leprechaun? Nay.

He was not there.

He was not there, because this was actually Larry Graham and Graham Central Station. Now, I have attended many shows where the audience was unfamiliar with the opening act. However, this was the only major concert I've ever attended where every single member of the audience was completely unaware that an opening act was appearing. There had been no publicity about this whatsoever. Everybody—including myself—immediately assumed this had to be Prince's entourage. I mean, I had no fucking idea what Larry Graham looked like; I hadn't seen a picture of him since the seventies. They took the stage and tried to bury us with funk, but we all kept waiting for Prince to come out. "This is rather curious," I thought. "Why is the backing band performing 'Thank You (Falettin Me Be Mice Elf Agin)' in its *totality*?" Twenty minutes passed before we finally concluded that this was, in fact, a group relatively unrelated to Prince. And they were excellent, but they played a long time; their set was over an hour. It was now 9:45, and—for all I knew—Prince wasn't even in Fargo. He was probably sitting inside Biosphere II, talking to a puppet and thinking about Paul's First Letter to the Corinthians.

It now seemed plausible that this concert might not begin before eleven, which would turn my seven hundred–word review into a less-nuanced four-word review: "Prince is a jerk." This was a real problem; there are no journalistic alternatives for covering an event that does exist. Ross found this scenario increasingly comical. But then—at 9:59—a certain kind of existence began; this tiny, capricious freak walked onstage and started making rock music. And it was so goddamn mesmerizing that I remember almost none of it.

In my mind, I initially recall thinking, "Okay, I can maybe watch five songs, and then I have to go write this stupid story." But I have no idea how many songs I experienced, or what most of these songs were, or if any of them were "Housequake" or "Pussy Control." I had a notebook, but I didn't take any notes. There may have been a medley that included "Little Red Corvette," "Raspberry Beret," and "I Could Never Take the Place of Your Man," but that might have actually occurred at a Prince concert I would see in Cleveland three years later. He was just so amazingly good at *everything*. There was a sixty-second span where he played a keyboard, a bass, and a guitar in immediate succession, and I think he played each individual instrument better than anyone ever had played them before, any-where, during any historical period over the past eleven thousand years. *And Prince didn't even care.* He didn't look happy, and he didn't look bored. He didn't even look focused. It seemed completely spontaneous, yet it wouldn't have mattered if he had rehearsed those specific sixty seconds for eight or nine months; the experience would have been exactly the same. And what I learned at this concert—and what I suspect can only be learned through seeing Prince live—is that all the moronic bullshit I made up about Prince's bad records and the Crystal Method was completely true: Prince is a genius. I was completely right. I just didn't know what "being right" meant.

Prior to this concert, what I actually meant when I said, "Prince is a ge-nius," was that, "Prince is considerably more gifted and creative than al-most everyone else who aspires to do the things he does best." By this cri-teria, there are a handful of other musicians who would qualify as geniuses: John Lennon and Paul McCartney, Jimmy Page, Donald Fagan and Walter Becker, Tony Iommi, Ike Turner, Lindsey Buckingham, Kevin Shields, and probably twenty-five other very famous people I can't recall at the moment I'm writing this particular sentence. For anecdotal purposes, this definition of "genius" is usually acceptable. But those artists are not geniuses; they are simply very, very, very good at a vocation they have se-lected. That difference became weirdly lucid whenever Prince did anything onstage, including his attempt to have sexual intercourse with a piano. Eddie Van Halen plays guitar like a genius, but that is something he *figured out* how to do. He *turned himself into a genius,* and that isn't the same thing.

I suppose it's possible that Prince has worked harder at his music than any of his peers; I know almost nothing about his life that hasn't been fic-tionalized for his semi-autobiographical movies. This is not an attempt to discredit his work ethic, or to suggest he's lazy. However, this singular Fargo concert forces me to believe that the degree to which he has (or has-n't) worked on his craft is almost completely irrelevant. Prince doesn't re-ally deserve credit for being a genius because he is not a normal human. His ability to create and perform music is so inherent and instinctual that it cannot really be measured against normal criteria; the only other rock mu-sicians in this class are Jimi Hendrix and (maybe) Bob Dylan. And I only realized this by *seeing* Prince from a distance of twenty-five feet. His tran-scendence is not accurately felt through his songs or his albums, because a lot of those songs and records aren't especially good. Some of them are semi-terrible. But bad Prince records are still valuable because *he made them*. They are like triptychs from Stonehenge.

I do not know what time I exited the show, but it was not even half over. I know I arrived at the *Forum* office at 10:50 and wrote 492 bland words that did not reflect the experience in any meaningful way (and this review does not mention any specific song Prince played). According to my best calculations, I probably saw forty minutes of that concert. Which were thirty-nine more than I needed.

44

Glen Branca, Rudolph Grey, and Wharton Tiers
The Knitting Factory
New York City
1999
THURSTON MOORE

GLEN HAD HIS SPORTS JACKET on, the one he's never taken off since the summer of sam. he got on stage with the other two—they plugged in and you could hear the amps frizzing and buzzing. glen announced to rudolph, "lemme finish this cigarette first"—a filterless pall mall. rudolph had no response as he was finishing off a hot smoke of his own—one of those thin brown numbers. wharton waited. every once in a while glen would turn around to the audience and squint up towards where maybe the balcony was as if thinking that maybe the sound guy up there would hopefully be on the same insane page as he was. rudolph kept his back to the audience— for no reason except he had no desire to get friendly. they both stubbed out their cigs and glen pushed his fingers through his thick dirty gray blond hair. he fumbled through his sports coat pockets—you could hear maybe apartment keys and pens and maybe picks and a slide. he pulled out a bottle of aspirin. "i have to take some aspirin. i almost forgot." he picked up the plastic cup of beer to swallow the pills with. "rudolph, you want some aspirin?"—rudolph had been keeping a black shade watch in glen's very anxious direction the whole time as patient as a kid accustomed to standing in line forever. he registered glen's proffer and quipped, "no, not yet."— glen downed the pills and spent a good thirty seconds trying to negotiate where to place the fucking cup of beer—he couldn't set it on the amp obviously, and if he puts it on the floor it's just gonna get kicked over. wharton sees the problem and gets up from his drumstool in three-quarter squat, "here, glen, give me the cup."—glen hands it over and wharton sets it on the floor somewhere. glen's ready and from the side of his mouth says, "you ready rudolph?"—"yeah, i think so . . ."—they know wharton's ready

251

and doesn't need any realities reinforced. so the amps are turned up and glen pulls out a glass slide and starts to ping out loud electric harmonics from his completely bizarro guitar "thing." rudolph pulls out a metal slide and rolls about the strings on the lower neck of his black guitar. the rhythmic snarl of a musical motor saw. wharton establishes a slowly crescending jungle beat from kick to snare to tom to second tom. this creates a contracting and expanding circle of sound which at times becomes only a forward propulsion with parallel bars of beat madness. the guitarists are quickly realizing their mix is successful—glen is sharp and splattering with the harmonics lined with fuzzed core notes and like a sonic slinky resultant harmonics spin around and in and about. rudolph, instead of moving a to b and onwards decides to make the a to z move with his slide whipping from neck end to bridge bottom. but mostly he hovers about the low neck end drawing dark rain clouds of amp-fried squall. he gets into classic rudolph move where he kneels down on one leg just off of ear-damage reach of the amp. here he slips the slide into his black suitcoat pocket and brings in fingered chords that he hits and strums with improvisatory jolts of meaning.—glen hears rudolph's more facile advancement and decides to move about the double length neck of his double length guitar and crash around for sound and violence never losing control of the concept of glory—even when he doesn't find a transcendent flash it is still exciting as the strings are emitting a raceway of energy and spontaneity. but he does indeed hit the nirvana point in time at times and his body jerks and dances and he starts to rock. rudolph realizes this and bites his lower lip and continues to pan for gold. wharton fully realizes this and adds an ecstatic level to his unchanging idea of rolling no-wave primtivism. rudolph now has his tongue out clenched between teeth and is in full action. he finds an amazing crunged out hardcore mantra of a chord strum and glen swoops and flares around it and begins to rock right into it and under it. it is now a sexual rock 'n' roll animal and gives the piece another five minutes of supreme life. this has to stop before it becomes soiled and they let it transmute into a sizzling drone again with glen's harmonics flicking off the speaker cones. it's a steady state and it ceases and wharton's in a continuous daze and will play his meditation to a stop . . . alone. and then he laughs, sweat steaming off his face and arms. glen reaches over and grabs wharton's head and kisses his face and then exits.

45

Antony and the Johnsons featuring Lou Reed

PS 122
New York City
November 10, 2001
SAMANTHA HUNT

THE SILENCE PERSISTED as the oxygen vanished. Antony was standing in a spotlight while the rest of the small, 125-seat theater was absolutely dark. The Johnsons, Antony's band, flanked him with their bows held rigid, their hands poised above the piano keys, attendant on his exhales. The light held steady on Antony while small motes of dust passing through the air in front of him made the only movement in the room. He was draped in a garment that had no name. Yellow chiffon, yes. But a yellow chiffon what? Wrap? Blossom? Ruffle? Shrug? His blond head was both pistol and stamen to the outfit.

The silence persisted, opening a hole that memory rushed to fill in.

I lived up north for a long time, packed underneath two feet of snow. The dark, the ice, the perfect camouflage of living where it's too cold for most other people to live, was perfect for me because the cold worked an odd physiological protection: my skin became tough so that inside I could remain as tearful, as tender as the mouth of a Venus flytrap.

When I was a girl, I was in a tiny, rough, fishing town where the coast was rocky, the boys were rednecks and the ocean that far north never got warm enough for swimming. It wasn't that kind of ocean. I was a million miles away. A friend of mine lowered the needle on her phonograph, and we listened while the guitarist wanked his way through the intro. It was a really, really long intro. I could tell that something big was about to happen. Why else would the guitarist keep us in such drawn-out suspense? I was staring out the window. My friend was trying on a pair of jeans and asking me how she looked when the song took a turn. There was nothing subtle about it. A simple rock 'n' roll chord progression that sliced my ribcage open and started gnawing on my heart.

"Remember me?" it said. And I did. Though I'd never heard the song before, I remembered it like I'd grown it myself. The music cut me. The guitar riff repeated and repeated, building each time it hit the shore. I played it cool. It was freezing outside. Standing on the corner. Suitcase in my hand.

"Uhm, who's this?" I asked my friend. She turned to look. She tossed me the album cover.

"Me, honey? I'm a rock 'n' roll band."

I loved living up north, but I always felt I was missing something: human contact, things to do on Friday nights, Mexican food, New York City. I'd play "Sweet Jane" over and over, and I'd kick myself for having been born too late. Eventually, after years, I finally kicked myself hard enough that I landed in an East Village sublet where I immediately started kicking myself some more. I was too late. Every day I saw the proof. Coming from the north, my first impression of 1999 New York City was money and cell phones. The pale and sickly looking boys strolling down St. Mark's, boys who I had always adored from afar, had bought and paid for their sunken eyes, their heroin chic. They made me pine for the snow, for the silence, for people who had plenty to say but just never did.

A friend who'd heard Antony sing had warned me, "Don't miss this show." He had once traveled to Buffalo, New York, with Antony, but when I asked him what kind of music it was, he didn't have a good answer. He thought on the question for a moment and told me instead what he and Antony had discussed on their journey. "Decorative cabbages," he said nodding, smiling as if kale were some sort of knowing explanation for a music that defies description.

The silence swelled like the throat of a frog seconds before his ribet, expectant and full and totally endangered as if the room had an edge. The air seemed to be looking for balloons to burst, skins to pierce on an evening already ripe with scars. I haven't even mentioned that Antony had performed his first number dressed as the Elephant Man, his voice rising up through a small hole in his canvas mask, or that Dr. Julia Yasuda, the hermaphrodite math theorist, had already graced the stage as muse while performance artist Johanna Constantine transformed her body into part tree, part deer, part woman.

I could hear Antony breathing and wondered how long a capacity-filled room in impatient New York City could stay still, stay staring. The answer was much longer than I had ever thought possible.

Once, I had eaten lunch at a Buddhist monastery. We were asked to dine in silence. Forty of us—some monks, some not—sat on the floor in two opposing rows, chewing, staring at one another, chewing, staring at one another. A scream waiting in my abdomen flirted with ideas of escape during the meal. Silence when one is all alone is a simple, nice thing, but silence in a room full of people is overwhelming; it is more complicated than sex. It is an opening that's both beautiful and dangerous.

Antony parted his lips only to hold the silence a beat longer. My thoughts were darting through the prehistoric and the present. Time means nothing to silence. He inhaled, and it seemed that he was drawing us all up into his lungs with that breath. He finally started to sing again, returning to the song he'd begun only a few moments earlier, the song that had a gaping hole of quiet right in its very center. We thought we'd lost our hero over the icy precipice, but here he was clawing his way back up, hand over hand. I couldn't believe what I heard.

Gothically, dripping with the dreary, I'd made a life out of falling in love with dead boys. Legions of them. Jeff Buckley. River Phoenix. The Shangri-Las' "Leader of the Pack." James Dean. John Keats. Michael Furey. My father. Damaged goods. Drug addicts. Gay beauties who'd never be able to return my love. Vacuums I could pour my heart out into. My first dead love was a photo torn from a magazine that I'd kept in my wallet as a girl: a snapshot of some kid from Rhode Island who been killed by a drunk driver. I never even knew that boy's name. It didn't matter. He was dead, and I loved him. He stayed with me in my wallet for years.

But I'd come to the concert with a Southerner, a man who talked, a man who never got weepy or took to his bed for four days after a week-long drug binge. This was a first for me. The man was surprisingly non-damaged, and because of this he made me uneasy. How would I ever finish the book I was working on without someone to twist and torture and break my heart every day?

When Antony, a gorgeous sea anemone of a man, opened his mouth and began singing about loving dead boys, it was my song he was singing. I recognized it immediately though, again, I'd never heard it before. The silence broke. I considered grabbing the hand of the very alive man I was sitting beside, but that seemed perhaps too healthy. I wrapped my arms around myself.

I fell in love with you. It was nothing short of angels.

Now you're my one and only. Such beauty was not possible from humans. Anthony was, quite probably, a visitor from outer space. The drums joined in.

> *'Cause all my life I've been so blue*
> *But in that moment you fulfilled me*
> *Now I'll tell all my friends, I fell in love with a dead boy*
> *Now I'll tell my family, I wish you could have met him*
> *Now, write letters to Australia*
> *Now, throw bottles out to sea*
> *I whisper the secret in the ground*
> *No one's gonna take you away from me*
> *I fell in love with a dead boy*
> *Oh such a beautiful boy*
> *I ask him are you a boy or are you a girl?*

That was a good question.

The world had always presented itself to me as a situation of opposites: boys/girls, dead/alive, city/woods, whole/broken, frozen/warm. Each extreme had its pleasures, but I'd always sided with broken dead boys in the cold woods who liked to wear black nail polish on their toes. They were my teammates. Our rallying cry was a breathy "ugghhh." Up to that point, the world had said, *You have to choose one opposite or the other. You can't have both.* And yet here was a performer who held opposites in his hand with ease, with calm beauty. Here he was warm and frozen. Here he was a boy and a girl.

Antony rolled through one gem after the next. I'd gone sub-verbal. The music felt as if swimming in a warm, dark pool where every memory I could conjure of my snowy life so far pointed not back to the cold but to here, to this one moment.

Halfway through the evening, Antony called Lou Reed up to the stage. Both men seemed shy, awed in each other's presence. Lou was nervous, affected by the emotion, or maybe scared to share the stage with such a beauty. Perhaps it was the daring feat before him that made Lou apprehensive. He sang "Candy Says" for the first time ever before a live audience, thirty-two years after the song had been written. The evening went from unforgettable to unnamable. Ant-ny. L-u. I hyphenated them into deities.

When Lou returned to his seat, not more than two or three feet from where I was sitting in the small room, I watched Laurie Anderson put her arm around his shoulder and whisper in his ear, "You did a good job, honey." They were humans? They were humans.

The realization couldn't have hit me much harder.

Even gods and aliens, dead boys and icicles love being loved. At that moment, in that room full of so much odd beauty, Laurie Anderson's "You did a good job, honey" seemed a gesture of pure courage. Melting is the hardest thing.

I turned to look at the alive man next to me. I already knew that he'd try to make me talk to him when the show was over. The thought scared me but, still, I unwrapped my arms. I fished my fingers in between his like a small surprise, an ice cube, into the palm of his very warm hand.

46

David Bowie
The Greek Theatre
Los Angeles
April 22, 2004
JERRY STAHL

SO IF YOU ASKED ME, a seventeen-year-old in the seventies, "What's rock 'n' roll?" I'd have had to say doing drugs and getting paid for it. Pretty much staying high, fucking anything you want, and being so entirely weird around the clock your whole life is a giant fuck you to everybody who is not you.

Rock stars exist to show us who we're not, the dimensions of our own Nothinghood. Even the cheesiest rocker gets more sex in a week than you got in college, even when you were passing out pills at mixers. Which, on one level, has nothing to do with David Bowie live at the Greek in Los Angeles in 2004. But fuck that. Who wants to get off on that floor?

Full disclosure: you are reading the spew of some middle-aged loser who bought the rock 'n' roll ethos but, like millions, lacked the talent to be subsidized to live the dream.

Rock 'n' roll was what the late Hubert Selby referred to as a "sugar tit." But creepazoid quasi-agoraphobic poseurs like myself weren't exactly sucking on it. The heroin helped, but still . . . The glamour of pawning your shoes doesn't last forever. Whatever it was David Bowie did to be David Bowie, you knew he had it delivered.

No, wait! It's kismet. I've got some bullshit television show on as I bang this out, and when I hear "Rebel Rebel" I look up and there's . . . Matthew McConaughey. Turns out it's the trailer for the McConaughey/Sarah Jessica Parker rom-com *Failure to Launch*. And I don't know whether that's profoundly depressing or proof that life's worth living. Or whether there is any greater evidence of spiritual, ethical, and artistic decline than writing with the TV on. I used to write with music. Now it's the secret hell of back-to-back *Matlock* at three in the afternoon, cranking out the snappy patter. What did Syd Barrett do all day anyway?

But enough about you. See, even before the actual Bowie show, I'd already had a couple of semi-freakish, almost mawkishly life-defining Bowie moments. Like—

My first week in Los Angeles. I saw two celebrities. Number One, John Wayne, muttering drunk, lobbing maxi pads into his shopping cart in an all-night market on Cahuenga an hour before dawn. (Party or cancer-related bowel issue? You be the judge!)

Celebrity Two was David Bowie. At Book Soup, on the Strip, around the corner from the legendary Sunset Marquis, where staff reputedly fought to the death for the right to lick Keith Richards's ashtrays after the Stones checked out.

From the back, Bowie was just some trim little redhead with a good haircut in a tight black T, black jeans, and boots. West Hollywood. But the second he walked out—everybody in the store started *Oh My Godding!* and turned to catch him, in profile. Cars honked. He glammed by the window, giving the universe temporary style.

"What'd he buy?" somebody asked the mascaraed clerk, whose name was Marv. But I didn't hear the answer. Even though I hated it, I had gone on a crystal run a few days earlier, and any undue stimuli triggered these weird whiteouts where I couldn't see or hear. After three days up, I experienced bouts of telepathic connection. Which, pathetically, drove me to run out of the door and tail him to the entrance to the hotel, where, responding to a query I'd felt emanate from the back of his carrot shag, I began to explain the title of my concept album, *Your Love (Is a Museum of My Need)*.

Which I apparently shouted—before being set upon by a pair of goateed Asians in black suits who did some elbow work on my throat that left me unable to spit or swallow. Though that could have been the speed. Sometimes you'd forget to do liquids. There wasn't any heroin around.

It means something, crossing paths with your hero at the lip-chewing, babbly, the-radiator-knows-my-mother's-name height of chemical psychosis. And it means even more when—what are the odds?—the shitbat crazy version of oneself gets to meet the Hero again, a decade and change later. And—more unlikely still—speak with him. Chew the fat in the laid-back, unfolding intimacy of a fifteen-minute-a-hack media record company promo-blitz. In this case, to launch *Black Tie, White Noise*, the post–L.A. uprising, post-marriage to Iman album, notable for boasting two guys named Bowie—singer David and avant trumpet player Lester (from the Art Ensemble of Chicago)—on one disc.

This will all add up when we get to the concert. Or not. Or give up and turn the page. Why should a book be any different than a CD, where you know going in that, even if you love the band, half the cuts are going to be crap? And yes, thank you, I am one of those morons who still buys CDs.

I'll make it fast. Bowie Moment Two. Maybe a decade later. I'm a month off heroin, and going in for an operation on my left testicle. (Not to brag.) Maybe cancer. Maybe not. They wouldn't know till they got in there. When you're strung out, you don't notice things like one nut being five times the size of its brother. Get clean and you start catching colds—or jumbo gonads. They offered to freeze my sperm, but the cost of the splooge fridge was twice as much as what I was paying for rent. (Bragging again.)

Anyway, my first post-needle jockey employment, the gig that was going to pay the rent, was a magazine piece on Bowie.

The mini-junket was being held at the Peninsula Hotel in Beverly Hills. Every quarter hour an Armani rodeo clown went into the pen, lassoed a journalist, and led him into the room with the erstwhile Mr. Stardust.

All fairly ho-hum for a professional. But I'd never done it before. And, as mentioned, I was already a two-legged nerve end from the recent kick party—and knowing I had to go from the hotel up the street to Cedars. I had to interview him the day I was going in. Or so it seems in toxic recollection. Then again, I don't remember ever writing the article.

I do—oddly for a man with the mnemonic equivalent of Tyrannosaurus arms—remember my first question. I asked about "Always Crashing in the Same Car." A song you could crawl to and make your doom beautiful.

I was going round and round the hotel garage
Must have been touching close to ninety-four

As open and relaxed as I was wracked, he smiled and stepped out onto the veranda. In Berlin, he was so depressed he wanted to kill himself. So he got his car in the garage and drove around as fast he could, getting up to ninety miles an hour in hopes of hitting a pillar. But he didn't crash the car. He crashed in it. That's what it was like then.

Yes! I thought my heart was going to fly out of my eyes in singing teardrops. *Me and Bowie, just two guys trying to live on the natch . . .* The magnitude of feeling, I imagine, was not unlike what a schizophrenic might feel if, after a lifetime of thinking the television was talking just to him, one day a Sony portable actually began chatting.

Thus choked up and boundary-challenged, I heard myself blurt, "I haven't shot dope in a month."

Real class is always tested in the face of those who haven't got any. And, rather than sneering—or having another set of Asian suit-guys show up to dent my can—David Bowie gave me a hug. A warm gesture—pulled off cool, compassionate, and amused. It was as if I'd shown him the secret handshake. His one blue eye was even bluer in person.

Naturally, I cringe just thinking about this. But the star's response—in my Jell-O-legged post-dope dementia—was as life-affirming as if Jesus had swung down from heaven with a Rapture-pass. More importantly, his kindness shocked all the questions out of my head. ("Is it hard being a god?" "I wouldn't know," in that hipster Bing Crosby baritone).

So, I packed up my purchased-with-cash-that-morning Radio Shack recorder and, mercifully, flew out of the hospitality suite without adding any codas to my dramatic (to me) confession: "And guess what else? My left nut is the size of monkey's fist and I was strung out the first two years of my daughter's life . . ." I know about wanting to drive into hotel parking garage pillars.

Cut to fourteen years after the Peninsula, and that lucky little ex-two-year-old is fifteen, slinking south in the front seat of the car we're both metaphorically crashing in as I try unsuccessfully to sneak into a restricted parking area at the Greek Theatre.

So begins my Third Bowie Moment. Her first—though, as a teenager in postmillennial America, she loves him. The way Kids Today can love their parents' music in a manner unthinkable when, say, Jethro Tull was meaningful. The parking attendants go to her high school. Me screaming at them is mortifying for all involved. When I start waving twenties around like Spiro Agnew—a reference no one reading should rightfully comprehend—I recognize all the signs of a shame spiral. The horror! I remembered outings with my own mother, where, inevitably, the evening ended with her shrieking in front of a restaurant full of strangers, "The boy wishes I was dead . . ." Seconds of shame, a lifetime of clichéd angst.

But here comes Bowie, in more or less the same outfit I'd glimpsed him the first time. Jean jacket, collar up. A cheer from the celebrity audience—that's Johnny Knoxville, waving—and all at once he's launching into—

Hey, I'm old enough to get junk mail from AARP. I can't remember everything. But I'll tell you about the shiver when he launched into "Heroes." I can remember that, because it's a Holy Memory.

Listen: I'm not a guy who dances. I'm not even a guy who tears up at Kodak moments. I think the technical term is "tight-ass." But halfway through "Rebel Rebel"—*your face is a mess*—my sixteen-year-old daughter looked at me, and I knew, the way you know, that she got it. And in that instant I was so filled with love, and gratitude, and all the other emotions whose very utterance would have made me puke as a young failure, only now just make me cringe a little. But what dwarfed all of these was an emotion far less noble. Relief. My own good luck scares me. David Bowie saved my life, inspired me to scrape enough psychic ganglia off the sidewalk to still be here.

So, okay, it's all kind of Hallmark-y. A long way from carburetor dung. You think, rock 'n' roll is about rebellion, about *fuck you*. All true. But *fuck you* at pre–Shalom Rest Home age looks a little different than *fuck you* at fifteen. It's a weirdly uplifting, age-defiant, cosmically amused *fuck you*. But maybe that's the point. After the band peels the paint off "Suffragette City," David Bowie laughs and says, "I feel like I'm fifty again."

47

Kevin Spacey

House Of Blues
Chicago
December 29, 2004
MAX ALLAN COLLINS

THUS FAR, I have only one regret in my life: I never saw Bobby Darin perform live, in concert. The closest I came was Kevin Spacey's 2004 tribute to Darin, performed as part of a breakneck multiple-city tour in support of *Beyond the Sea*, the biographical film the Academy Award–winning actor starred in, directed, and co-produced.

Over more decades than I'd care admit, I've been a fairly regular concert-goer, and have seen some incredible live shows. In the late sixties, before people stood up throughout concerts, I sat comfortably catching the Beach Boys, the Turtles, Buffalo Springfield, Jimi Hendrix, and many others of the day. As a garage band rocker, I even opened with my band the Daybreakers for a number of great acts, including the Young Rascals, the Buckinghams, and the Strawberry Alarm Clock. As an aging garage-band rocker on the oldies circuit, with my later band Crusin', I opened for Peter Noone, the Grass Roots, and a version of the Mamas & the Papas best described by Noone's greenroom comment: "No fucking Mamas, no fucking Papas!"; and also a latter-day version of the Rascals, who had long since lost the "Young." And when we opened for the Turtles twenty years after I'd first seen them, I even got to hang out with Flo and Eddie, who are as hilarious offstage as on.

During the new wave period, I took in incredible performances by Elvis Costello, Blondie, and Lene Lovich, any one of which is worth an article. Just last year I went to a Weezer concert with my college-age son, Nathan, and, loving that band, got there early enough to position myself right up front . . . only to become a guy in his fifties trapped in a mosh pit. I had no idea having college girls hurl their nubile flesh (and bones) at you could be so unpleasant. Great tunes, though.

These were all memorable shows, to be sure. But of all these possibilities, I have chosen a surrogate concert, a tribute to Bobby Darin, rather than following Darin's own vaguely salacious advice at the end of his classic "Artificial Flowers" to "give 'em the real thing." I have my doubts that anyone else in this book will discuss an Elvis impersonator or one of the several little-people KISS tribute bands. Call it a hunch.

But I can't discuss a real Bobby Darin concert, because I never went to one. No doubt some of those reading this piece will wonder why I would ever have wanted to see Darin in the first place, dismissing him as a road show Sinatra, or a rocker who sold out and became a lounge lizard, or a silly fifties artifact who embarrassingly tried to keep up in the late sixties and early seventies with shifts into Dylan-esque rock and even ersatz disco fever. The worst kind of showbiz dilettante.

Don't feel bad if you reacted that way, however wrong you might be (and you are very wrong). Bobby was similarly dissed throughout his own brief performing career—he hit in 1958 and was dead by 1973—and, however loved and popular he was, he was also perhaps the most hated, vilified performer of his day.

It remains a peculiar phenomenon—Fabian and Frankie Avalon and even Paul Anka, Darin's fellow teen idols, are obviously lightweights by comparison. Bobby Rydell, the best of Darin's contemporaries, was his acolyte ("Volare," "That Old Black Magic"). Jerry Lee Lewis condemned all the "Bobbies" who were taking his place on the charts, even credible Buddy Holly follower Bobby Vee. Rock critics for decades now have looked back in scorn at the post-Elvis, pre-Beatles teen idols, as if saying something profound about the era, rooted in historical perspective; truth is, those idols were considered jokes even then. Rydell and Vee, in particular, didn't deserve it, and of course neither does Darin—the performer for whom the others of that group profess the most admiration.

Darin was a sickly kid named Walden Robert Cassotto who listened to Sinatra and Jolson records, went to a New York high school for kids gifted in the arts, and was performing in the Catskills by age sixteen. He was still in his teens when Decca signed him, and four singles followed, notably "Rock Island Line," a cover of the UK Lonnie Donnegan skiffle hit.

Young Darin, who was also songwriting at the Brill Building and writing commercial jingles with Don Kirshner, became the first white artist signed by the great rhythm and blues label, Atlantic Records. This must have been a dream come true for Darin, who was heavily into Ray Charles and Fats Domino, and was playing his own bluesy piano. His 1958 breakthrough, "Splish Splash," the greatest Jerry Lee Lewis record Jerry Lee Lewis never made, topped the charts and remains a pop-culture presence into the twenty-first century.

After a succession of funky rock records ("Queen of the Hop," "Early in the Morning"—the latter covered by Buddy Holly, though Bobby's version charted higher), Darin wanted to reach out to the adult, album-buying audience (45 singles were for kids, 33 1/3 LPs were for grown-ups). Against the advice and wishes of Atlantic honcho Ahmet Ertegun, Darin used his own money to record the classic big band pop album, *That's All*, which includes both "Mack the Knife" and "Beyond the Sea." He was twenty-two years old.

For several years Darin played a shrewd game, alternating single records for the teen market (the sublime "Dream Lover," the ridiculous "Multiplication") and wonderful Sinatra-school albums (*This is Darin*, *Love Swings*, *Oh! Look at Me Now*). His nightclub act was a sensation, and he was the youngest performer to have his own network TV special; he was embraced by George Burns, Bob Hope, Jimmy Durante, and other showbiz royalty of the day. Sammy Davis, Jr., said Darin was the only performer alive who he feared to follow onstage; and Jerry (not Lee) Lewis said Darin alone in the new generation was qualified to join the roster of such show business greats as Frank Sinatra, Bing Crosby, Dean Martin, and, well, Jerry Lewis.

Darin's "adult" albums were praised by *Down Beat* (which dubbed him the only "real competition" Sinatra ever had) and various other trade magazines; but his brash style, both on and offstage ("I want to be a legend by twenty-five!"), drew brickbats from older critics. What is lost to today's rock writers is a key aspect of Darin's success: he brought a strong element of rock and R&B to the Great American Songbook, a cocky, snarly sex appeal that was not exactly found in Vic Damone or Al Martino; back then, he was often described as a "rhythm" singer, and for all the Sinatra comparisons, you can look to Frank's discography for examples of FAS swinging as hard as Darin and you will come up empty. "Mack the Knife," with its insistent bass, continual key changes, and building momentum, is Darin's alone (he even had his own Nelson Riddle, the unfortunately unsung Richard Wess). Sinatra's one imitation of Darin's "Mack," the fairly pathetic "Old MacDonald," speaks volumes on this subject.

I was in grade school when I discovered Bobby Darin. Already I was fascinated with detective and crime stories, and unwittingly prepping for a career in blood-and-thunder latter-day pulp fiction; but I was also the son of a high school music director, an ambitious musician who staged the first high school productions of such Broadway shows as *Oklahoma!* and *Carousel*. At the same time, I already loved rock 'n' roll ("Hound Dog" backed with "Don't Be Cruel" was the first non-kiddie record I ever owned—a 78!) and I had loved "Splish Splash" on the radio the summer before, though didn't really know anything about Bobby Darin.

One Saturday afternoon in 1959, I was plopped down in front of a TV, watching a variety special, some kind of fund-raiser for the Heart Fund. Bobby Darin came on and did "Mack the Knife," which I had never heard before. My mouth dropped open at Darin's performance; it has remained—mentally, at least—in the same stunned position ever since.

This baby-faced young singer in sharkskin was gleefully singing about a serial killer, inserting enthusiastic sounds ("Hut! Ho!") into the casual recital of blood and gore, and clapping and dancing and grabbing the air and snapping his fingers. He was rocking. But it wasn't a rock song . . . how strange . . . how wonderful . . . how exciting . . .

I became obsessed (this state, too, remains intact). I bought "Mack the Knife," and then "Beyond the Sea," and thereafter every single by Darin I could find (including the obscure Decca ones). I bought *That's All* ($3.98) and listened to it till the grooves turned gray. I glommed onto fan magazines and plastered my room with Darin pictures. (I'm sure my father was questioning my sexuality in those years, but if my dad had really been paying attention, he would have noticed I was also buying all of Annette Funicello's albums, and no boy in those days was buying Annette's albums because of the great music).

Now, I've always been motivated by my enthusiasms. I idolized mystery writer Mickey Spillane, and this created my eventual career path. And pretty much everybody in junior high who knew me understood that I was the Bobby Darin guy (just as in high school I would be the Mickey Spillane guy). As early as the sixth grade, I had violent arguments with followers of such anti-Christs as Fabian and Frankie Avalon, usually with girls who were about as interested in Fabe and Frankie's musical gifts as I was in Annette's.

Because of my youth, and location (a small town in Iowa), seeing Darin live was not an option. Years later, my writer pal Ed Gorman made me weep when he reported having seen Bobby Darin on a "Dream Lover" tour at a ballroom in nearby Cedar Rapids. (Between sets, Ed found Bobby sitting on the restroom floor, smoking a cigarette—the can being Iowa's version of a dressing room, at the time. Still is, in many cases.) But even if I'd known about the Darin "personal appearance" back then, Cedar Rapids might as well have been the moon—it was more than sixty miles away! (In high school, I would miss the Beatles, too, because they were on Mars, i.e., Chicago.)

Had I known Darin was going to die so goddamn young, I'd have made it to a concert or Vegas appearance in my college years (I was finishing up grad school when he died). I never lost my love for his music, and even when I got swept up with everybody else by the Beatles and the British invasion, I kept buying Bobby's albums.

Actually, Darin fared better in the Beatles era than his contemporaries, charting with such big records as "You're the Reason I'm Living" and "18 Yellow Roses," plus his hippie-era smash, the Tim Hardin cover, "If I Were a Carpenter." Darin's love for different styles of music often got him labeled as a trend-follower, but the truth is, his earliest Decca records included nascent folk-rock ("Timber") and in the early sixties he did several genuine folk-rock albums, one of which (*Earthy*) predated the Hootenanny craze; Jim/Roger McGuinn of the Byrds was in Darin's backup band. Darin was probably the first mainstream pop artist to cover Dylan, whose praises he loudly sang in interviews as early as 1962.

Still, nobody of Darin's generation really thrived in the Beatles era (though Gerry and the Pacemakers had a hit with songwriter Darin's "I'll Be There," and so did the Searchers with his "When I Get Home"). Ironically, shortly before the Beatles hit, Darin had been signed to what would be their American label, Capitol, to replace Frank Sinatra, who had departed to his own Reprise. Darin did several Sinatra-esque albums for Capitol, but double-crossed the execs by experimenting with country western and folk-rock. Rather than following trends, Darin—the Elvis Costello of his day—followed his musical enthusiasms; with his strong foundation in rock and R&B, Darin was able, in his short lifetime, to create a wide-ranging body of work (including acting—he was an Academy Award nominee for *Captain Newman, M.D.*). If Bobby Darin's recording output alone survived to represent the entire body of twentieth-century pop music, pop music would be well served—no, that's not an absurd assertion: no other single artist could demonstrate as many genres and as well.

Kevin Spacey understands this. Like me, he is a fanatic about Darin, and for a decade tried to mount a biographical film about Bobby (before that, many attempts were made at getting a Darin biopic going, by Dick Clark and Barry Levinson, among others, with such potential stars as Rob Lowe and Johnny Depp mentioned for the lead). Shortly after Spacey really hit the big time with *The Usual Suspects* (1995) and *American Beauty* (1999), he began openly lobbying for his dream Darin project.

In the summer of 2001, when my graphic novel *Road to Perdition* was being transformed into Sam Mendes's fine film, I visited the set in Chicago. Keep in mind, Tom Hanks and Paul Newman and Jennifer Jason Leigh and cinematographer Conrad Hall and producer Richard Zanuck were here and there around me, a pop culture fever dream come true. What was my first priority? Cornering director Sam Mendes for a ten-minute talk. About what he was doing with my story? No, to question him about (a) his extensive use of Bobby Darin songs in his film *American Beauty*, and (b) what he knew about how his friend Spacey's Darin biopic efforts were going . . .

Let's get this out of the way: Spacey's *Beyond the Sea* is considered by many critics a flop, even an embarrassment; and by any reasonable calculation, the movie was certainly a financial disappointment. On the other hand, a strong vocal minority of critics loved the film, which approached Darin's life much as Bob Fosse did his own in *All That Jazz* (1979). The biggest *Beyond the Sea* complaint seemed to be that Spacey was too old for the part—but the film was structured as a fanciful look back by Darin at the end of his life, a film he is making either in heaven or in his own mind at the point of death, a clever conceit on Spacey's part. Another recurring complaint was that Darin himself wasn't worthy of such a project.

The ignorance of the latter is matched only by the unintentional irony of critics lambasting Spacey for his egotistical arrogance, paralleling the kind of stupid critical attacks the confident Darin suffered in his own lifetime. Some of the attacks on Spacey came from the Darin fanbase, resentful that Darin's original tracks would not be used. Spacey felt, rightly I think, that he needed to fully "act" Darin's songs and, as director, wanted to intersperse them thematically within the narrative as well as frequently expand them for production numbers—*Beyond the Sea* is, on one level anyway, a musical.

Spacey's film—in both its execution and the critical response it engendered—strongly reminds me of Anthony Newley's *Can Hieronymus Merkin Ever Forget Mercy Humppe and Find True Happiness?* (1969). Newley, another gifted and much reviled performer/composer (Darin recorded many of his songs), directed and starred in the autobiographical, Felliniesque feature, only to have it (and himself) critically savaged. *Merkin* has all but disappeared, even though the musical represents the best representation we have of the quirkily egotistical yet self-loathing genius performer/songwriter who (with partner Leslie Briccuse) created the Broadway shows *Stop the World—I Want to Get Off* and *The Roar of the Greasepaint—The Smell of the Crowd*, and provided the music for the original *Willy Wonka and the Chocolate Factory* (1971).

I'm not here chiefly to defend Spacey's film, though I admit through my Darin-colored glasses, *Beyond the Sea* pleases me greatly; it's a valentine to my favorite recording artist, and a lovely one. And as for Spacey's age, well, as Ed Gorman has said, "Bobby Darin was born thirty-seven years old." And died thirty-seven, looking fifty. So screw the critics who didn't (and don't) like Bobby Darin, and screw the critics who don't like *Beyond the Sea*. None of them have a particle of the talent of either Darin or Spacey (or Newley, for that matter).

My wife Barb, herself a writer, and my son Nathan, who at the time of Spacey's concert was in his senior year at the University of Iowa, have been subjected to my Bobby Darin obsession beyond anything any reasonable person should be expected to tolerate. And yet Barb has become a Darin fan herself, and my son—if not quite a fan—an admirer of Darin's, in part due to Nate's interest (in his high school years) of such neo-swing bands as the Squirrel Nut Zippers, Big Bad Voodoo Daddy, and the Brian Setzer Orchestra—Setzer being in several senses a vocal admirer of Darin's.

So both Barb and Nate were game to accompany me to Kevin Spacey's Darin tribute concert at the House of Blues in Chicago. We hadn't seen the film yet—it would be out in a week or so—but I wanted to support Spacey's pro-Darin efforts, and somewhere in the back of my brain the notion was bubbling that this might be as close to actually seeing Darin live as I might ever come.

The moment tickets became available, I purchased them directly, calling the House of Blues—open seating, nothing reserved, first come, first served. So we got there early and were able to snag a prime place in line, indoors; it was late December and bitterly cold, and the line extended outdoors and down and around the block, hundreds of Spacey and/or Darin fans of a widely ranging demographic. A few fans of my writing recognized me (I've done lots of signings in the Chicago area), came up to chat and get autographs, and my son was almost impressed.

We were among the first through the door. I'd been wondering from the moment I purchased the tickets if the club-like floor of the funky House of

Blues auditorium meant we'd be standing throughout, as of course is the fashion for modern rock concerts. But since this was not really a rock concert, filling that space with chairs made more sense, and this proved to be the case. Only when we—and the other early attendees—sought out good seats, the House of Blues staff—most of whom had the social skills of a Hell's Angel on crank—herded us rudely away.

Turned out the entire first floor had been sold out to special parties. Again, no reserved seating had been available either directly from the House of Blues or online. But these special parties had reserved them, all right. Darkly pissed, I led my family to the first balcony, most of which had been similarly sold out. The other two balconies were already packed, though we lucked out on two seats in the second. We could almost see the stage, the House of Blues balconies consisting of bars with little tables, perches designed by someone determined to make sure no one would be distracted from their drinking by the visibility of anyone performing on stage.

I was in a black mood. We'd driven four hours, and suffered the vagaries of downtown Chicago traffic (and mortgage-your-house parking), and now were consigned to a dreary, smoky tier of Hell. I bought Barb and Nate drinks to take the edge off, and proceeded down to the first floor, where the special people were, to fulfill another mission.

I'd brought with me a signed copy of *Road to Purgatory*, my novel sequel to my graphic novel *Road to Perdition*—Spacey and I had in common that we'd both been involved in Academy Award–winning Sam Mendes films. Inserted in the book was a brief note thanking the actor for his efforts on Darin's behalf. I had no plans to use whatever limited entree I might have to get back and see Spacey; my only agenda was to thank him, as a crazed Darin fan, for putting our boy back in the spotlight.

For the next thirty or forty minutes, I dealt with House of Blues staff, both security and management. Again and again, I politely explained who I was (I was wearing a *Road to Perdition* production jacket, so if this was a hoax, it was a particularly elaborate and stupid one). I continually emphasized that I wasn't trying to get backstage, just to have my book passed back there.

In fairness, these guys always have their hands full at any concert; they don't need having to deal with people like me. On the other hand, I had already been screwed out of a decent seat, essentially swindled into paying top dollar for a ridiculously bad view.

So I just hung in there—refused to go away. I was given the bum's rush, I was threatened, I was lied to. But I held my ground, standing near a door to the backstage. And finally I got lucky—a gent who turned out to be Spacey's personal assistant came out to ask a security staffer a question, and when I got my shot, I introduced myself, was received warmly and my book was soon in possession of someone who promised to deliver it to Spacey.

Feeling better, now that one small victory had been achieved, I climbed the stairs to the second tier of Hell for my seat with its splendid view of nothing at all. Fifteen minutes passed uneventfully. Spacey, like all artists these days, was running a little late, though a full orchestra had taken the stage, including conductor Roger Kellaway, a legend in his own right, a composer and arranger who had worked with Darin on tour and in the studio. A white-haired, white-bearded gentleman, Kellaway was prepping with the musicians, as well as fanning through music at the piano from which he would do much of his conducting.

Suddenly, a voice roared over the sound system, scaring the bejesus out of everybody: *"Would Max Allan Collins come to the sound booth?"*

Barb and Nate looked at me, wondering if I'd somehow managed to get us kicked out.

Back down the two flights of stairs I went. The sound booth was on the main floor, at the back of the area where the reserved seating was now filled. For a few minutes I waited, and then was approached by Spacey's personal assistant.

"Kevin wants to thank you for the book," he said, and handed me three full-access passes. "And he'd like to meet you and your family afterward."

I offered stunned and suitably profuse thanks.

"Is there anything else we can do for you?"

"Actually, yes. We're stuck up in the second balcony and can't see a thing. Could you find seats for us down here?"

Then, in one of the sweetest moments of my life, the personal assistant called over a House of Blues manager who had earlier treated me rudely and dismissively, and made the guy put three seats right in front of the sound board, providing a direct, unimpaired down-the-aisle view of center stage.

I went up and gathered Barb and Nate, and I have to say, both of them seemed vaguely glad to know me, for once. We settled into our special chairs and I had a stray thought: *after all these years of freelance writing . . . finally a perk . . .*

The audience was an odd mix—I had the strong feeling that a good third of them were Spacey fans who hadn't the slightest idea who Bobby Darin was. Perhaps another third were baby boomers who knew Spacey, obviously, but were more there for Darin. The middle third mixed the two categories in varying degrees.

Spacey came out exuding confidence and brash energy worthy of Darin himself, starting with "Hello Young Lovers," an up-tempo version that Bobby often opened with himself in later years. The chart was unmistakable, and I was soon to gather that these were, indeed, Darin's original charts, solidly, beautifully delivered by Kellaway's big band supplemented by strings.

In a charming, self-deprecating hello speech to the enthusiastic audience, Spacey made clear that he was not "doing" Darin in the sense that he would be pretending to be the artist—there was only one Bobby Darin, and he was not him. But he would share with us some songs associated with Bobby Darin and do his best to do them, and Darin, justice.

What followed was a letter-perfect rendition of Darin's nightclub act from the early seventies, the only period of the artist's career that integrated all phases of the Darin musical catalogue.

In the late sixties and early seventies, Darin—a committed leftist, stunned by his friend Bobby Kennedy's assassination—had abandoned his Vegas approach both in the recording studio and performance venues for a mix of self-composed songs, alternately political and personal, often reverting to his rock and R&B roots. But "Bob Darin" was met with little interest—despite one minor hit, the riveting prison commentary "Long Line Rider"—and, as the heart problems that had dogged him all his life worsened, increasing his need for cash flow, Darin at last came to terms with himself as a pop star. Asked by Dick Cavett at the time, Darin said, "I decided to put on my toup and my tux and give the people what they want." "Bobby Darin" was a character he'd created, Walden Robert Cassotto had come to understand; and he was willing to play it—particularly since in this final incarnation, he was able to bring all the strands together in a whole cloth, from "Mack the Knife" to his anti-war "A Simple Song of Freedom."

Many Darin fans like this phase least. Darin was, secretly, very ill, so as polished as he was, the energy of youth was just not there, even if the charisma still was. The sins of the seventies also encroached, as he often covered tunes in his act that weren't really worthy of him.

Still, Spacey was wise to use the seventies nightclub act as his model. For one thing, Darin's late-in-life television series meant that performances from that era were the most widely available for study; also, Darin was roughly the same age as Spacey when the original performances went down. And the wide mix of material was one the House of Blues audience could relate to—"Can't Take My Eyes Off of You" and "Hi Di Ho," the kind of seventies tunes Darin only did in clubs—widening the nostalgia value. "Sail Away" made the little-known point that Darin was among the first to record Randy Newman material, and even collaborated with him.

Spacey also included Sinatra standards—not major recordings of Darin's but performed by him in nightclubs, such as "Sittin' On Top of the World" and "It Was Just One of Those Things"—which further shored up the connection between the two artists (Darin is often, inaccurately, thought of as a Rat Pack member). Like Darin, Spacey is a gifted mimic, and he reworked from Darin's act a piece of special material about a drunken tourist in Hollywood that allowed Spacey to impersonate, to solid effect, stars from Darin's era (Dean Martin) and from Spacey's own (Christopher Walken).

Weakest was the early rock material—Spacey seemed to have the least interest in this, and essentially threw it away in a medley, his fragment of "Splish Splash" having a mechanical quality, whereas Darin was committed to rock and R&B, delivering it easily and soulfully, often rocking out at the piano. That small flaw aside, the energy and showmanship Spacey brought to the task were thrilling. Despite his claim not to be "doing" Bobby, most of Spacey's patter was straight from Darin's act, delivered with the offhanded naturalness worthy of the fine actor Spacey is. Though his baritone is his own, Spacey used his actor's chops to put enough Darin-esque touches to the delivery that I did, at times, think I was finally experiencing Bobby Darin in concert. My smile split my face, and my eyes were frequently moist, and my son at one point wryly whispered, "Too bad you're not enjoying this."

Afterward, we indeed met Spacey. We were herded with another twenty people or so into yet another balcony, where we waited maybe fifteen minutes. During this lull, I was lucky enough to speak with conductor Kellaway, who was gracious but seemed somewhat shell-shocked from the pressures of touring doing one-night stands.

When Spacey came up the stairs, I moved in with the same relentless determination that took Bobby Darin to the top. For five or maybe even ten minutes, I shamelessly monopolized the star. And we talked of nothing but

Darin, his affection clear, his obsession undoubted—for all the critical carping, *Beyond the Sea* and this concert tour were not about Kevin Spacey, but about Kevin Spacey's love for Bobby Darin.

I wish I could report the exact words we exchanged—a lot of it had to do with how shortchanged Bobby has been over the years, how much he accomplished in so short time, what a good actor Darin was (check out 1962's *Pressure Point*) and how underestimated his contribution has been.

Before I let the other "meet and greeters" have at him, I told Spacey a story that he seemed to enjoy a great deal.

"Maybe fifteen years ago," I said, "I started going to record shows, trying to pick up better copies of Darin albums, since I'd worn so many of them out. At an Iowa City show, I picked up a mint stereo copy of *That's All* from a graying dealer, and as I was giving him his twenty-five bucks, he said, 'I played with Bobby Darin. He was a bastard. A real prick.'

"'Really?' I said. 'Well, you gotta tell me about it.'

"And he did. Seemed he'd been a musician in those days, playing with his own weekend rock band. But artists like Darin and Chuck Berry and others would come through the area and need pickup musicians and would call the local musician's union chapter. And Darin, out pushing 'Splish Splash,' needed a full combo.

"'He rehearsed us all day,' the dealer said. 'I'll never forget it. Worked our asses off. Just made our lives miserable, rode us till our fingers bled.'"

"'Really,' I said.

"'Really. He was a complete bastard. Real son of a bitch . . .' Then the dealer got a strange, dreamy look. ' . . . most talented man I ever met.'"

Kevin Spacey smiled.

48

The White Stripes
House of Blues
Atlantic City, New Jersey
September 28, 2005
ALICE ELLIOTT DARK

THERE WERE RUMORS rippling up and down the line to get in. I remembered this aspect of band-following life, how fun it was to have insider information. My concertgoing days were largely over, but I hadn't completely forgotten what it was like. I'd had the chance to talk about it, too, with my fourteen-year-old son, Asher, who wanted to know how the Dead were live, and Jimi, George Harrison, Brian Wilson, Iggy Pop, as well as all the bands I'd seen when I lived in London for two years in the late seventies: the 2 Tone bands such as the Specials and Madness, and the Police, the Pretenders, Gang of Four, the Clash, on and on. It's almost a reason to have a kid, to be able to tell him about these particular memories that, over time, seem as private as reading a book. I'd had my moments with bands and musicians I loved, and Asher shared them vicariously. Now, we were going together to see the White Stripes.

The venue was the House of Blues in the Showboat Atlantic City. Gone were the days when you had to be a Rat Pack–type to go anywhere near a casino. The billboards along the Atlantic City expressway touted lots of current acts of the sort who'd never been caught dead there when I was a disaffected youth. But the White Stripes were as cool as they came at the moment, and I wasn't young anymore.

The guys in front of us in line were about twenty-five, rough looking in their dirty jeans and ill-kempt hair, but sweet to talk to. Together, we debated the whole Meg White-as-wife-or-sister issue. We agreed that wife was the real truth, but gave Jack the benefit of the doubt for being able to pull off the double hoax of convincing the world that his sister was his ex. They wanted to know when I'd gotten into the Stripes, and I had to admit to my chagrin—I used to pride myself on being in the know—that my conversion was recent, as of the album they were presently touring, *Get Behind Me Satan*. Kindly, they didn't try to one-up me too much.

I passed along some intel I had, that the House of Blues was a small venue that held only a couple thousand people. This was awesome news; it meant that we were all going to see Jack and Meg up close. To celebrate our good fortune, we nodded at each other appreciatively, the cool man's substitute for squealing. I felt like squealing, but Asher would lose all respect for me if I made any noise at all. He knew how to act. He was cool. He was even cool enough to want to go hear music with me—no embarrassment about being with mom. He'd found this concert for us on the Stripes' Web site. All I had to do was pay for the tickets and drive down from North Jersey where we live.

"Is that your kid?" the guys asked me.

I nodded. It was a jarring moment. I'd let go of my regular self as we walked past the gaming room where people in wheelchairs breathed oxygen through tubes in their nostrils. I was a babe compared to them. In line for a concert, it was easy for me to feel I was the same age as the guys I was talking to, and to feel a little buzz passing between us. But the kid thing snapped me back to reality.

"Hey, it's great for you to bring him to hear this," one of the guys said. "My mom took me to a Pearl Jam concert when I was about his age."

I gave a tepid smile, tempted to tell him I'd been going to concerts by myself since I was twelve, just so he'd know how cool I'd been, even if I was old now. But I restrained myself. He could have his Pearl Jam moment. "Thanks," I said.

He smiled at Asher. "Your mom's cool."

Asher nodded. At least I had his respect.

The line moved slowly, and I found out why when we arrived up front. They were checking IDs to see who was of drinking age. They asked me if I was going to drink. No, I wasn't. That was too "casino" for me. Besides, I thought of music as being a dope thing, not a background to a drunk. In London, I saw lots of music in pubs, but the beer consumption always seemed antithetical to the event, more ice hockey than punk. Whatever happened to that good, solid high that literally colored the notes? Long jail sentences, I guess. Too bad.

I'd bought seats so Asher could see, and so I could sit. They were in a balcony that hung over the dance floor. The opening act was nearly done by the time we got settled, and they were cleared away quickly and efficiently and the Stripes' set assembled. Music blared; I didn't recognize it, but it was thumping loud and funny. Loud enough for me to finally squeal a little. A red, white, and black scrim hung behind the horseshoe of instruments on the stage. My friends from the line had bet they were going to have a backup band; how could they not, considering the layering of tracks on the recordings? But I'd heard from a couple of people who'd just seen them in Coney Island that they played alone, just the two of them, though there were enough instruments onstage for ten people: Meg's drum kit, a marimba, scads of guitars, a mandolin, bongo drums, a grand piano, and keyboards.

It was godlike sitting on high, looking down at the set-up as if looking down at the newly formed earth to see what the humans would do. Would they fulfill my expectations or be something else? There is no anticipation like the one that waits for music to begin.

The concert was scheduled to begin at ten, and they arrived onstage a little after. Meg came on first, wearing a tight white T-shirt and red pants. She was skinny and looked older than I expected, and was instantly adorable. She climbed onto her seat but was only there for a second when Jack came running across the stage, grabbed her arm, and pulled her back into the wings. His urgency was alluring and odd, odd, odd. Was this part of the act, or had something happened? In any case, it got everyone's attention. A glimpse, a disappearance. Enticement and romance. I think the whole audience was half in love before they played a note.

Then, they came back out. Meg took her seat again, Jack picked up a guitar, and a great blast of noise filled the hall. Noise! A muddled assault, messy and blurred. I couldn't get it, couldn't pick the sound apart; it was all vibration and overamped. What was he doing? Meg was clear and crisp. I'd heard so many people dis her drumming, but I found it smart and interesting, and obviously there was a lot in it for Jack. But I wanted to hear him, too, and I couldn't.

Then, suddenly, I could. It was like looking up at an angry gray cloud and suddenly seeing snow fall out of it in thick, gorgeous flakes.

Describing the renditions of individual songs can't capture the concert I saw. The extraordinary thing about the concert was the shape of the whole, from where it began to where it ended. It was about a person, not a song: Jack White.

He was thinner than he looked in his pictures, muscular, sexy, very Ponyboy, really, with his pretty black hair that flew around his head as he pranced around the stage. He touched the toes of his boots together often as he swayed his body around the guitar and moved into the music. All great guitarists absorb their instruments, and it is beautiful to see the individual ways they manage this. Jack curled around his, rocked, coddled, shook, and babied it; it was easy to imagine him lying down for a nap with one of his guitars, slinging a loose and loving arm over it as he slept.

His guitars seemed to have an opinion, a way of communicating with him. Several times, he started a song, then stopped and played another. What accounted for the switch? I wish I knew. Did he even have a plan, a predetermined set list? It didn't seem so. There were songs from the latest album, but many more from the past. There was no sense in which he could be said to be promoting his album, except for the fact and timing of the tour.

There also seemed to be no attempt to connect with the audience, or any interest on the part of either him or Meg in the fact that hundreds of people were in the room with them, watching them play. They played for each other only, and the play was bright and deeply engaged. Sister, I decided, as I watched them, even if that was only figuratively true. She was the little sister who he'd taught to drum so he'd have someone to play along with him. Or vice versa. He looked to her, I don't want to presume to know exactly what for, but I saw the look, the lean, the microphone placed at the edge of her drums where they could watch each other. He wandered to that microphone over and over again, drawing energy from her drumming, from her. Watching the two of them was like standing in front of a walled aquarium where beautiful dolphins played and called to each other, oblivious to being spied upon. She played exactly the same as she did on the recording, but he was quite free in his interpretation of his more formal, layered self. It appeared she afforded him that freedom.

When he wasn't standing by Meg, Jack spun around his playhouse of a stage from one instrument to the next in a buoying way so thrilling that I could only dance and laugh. Asher felt the same; his eyes widened each time the opening chords of one of his favorite songs pierced our bodies. The songs came fast, one on top of another, with no verbal introductions, no Springsteenesque canned rap in between. After about an hour and a half, they abruptly walked offstage. It didn't seem like they were ending the concert or waiting to be cheered back for an encore. It was more like they went to get a drink of water, maybe regroup a bit. This vibe was so strong that the crowd waited patiently to see what was going to happen and didn't clamor for more.

They came back out and played several more songs. This was the strongest part of the show. The sound expanded from the quiet and sweet "We Are Going to Be Friends" on through the sing-along "Little Ghost." By then, everyone was up and moving, ready to go nuts when Jack struck up the unforgettable opening notes of "Seven Nation Army" for the second time. How could two people fill a cavernous room with so much sound?

It got even bigger with "The Hardest Button to Button," their best of the night. Little Jacky White, as he called himself, had us all. The only way to describe his power is to ask the reader to remember a moment in your life when you were overwhelmed by a person's genius and felt your mind grow as a result. The dimensions of the music were luscious and extraordinary. Jack and Meg were small and glorious. I had that heady feeling of understanding what they were doing, the sensation imparted by all great artists who have you in their palm. Yet still, their remoteness, their unwillingness to break the barrier at the front of the stage. Still, the feeling that they didn't know the audience was there, or didn't care much. They were like that aloof boy you give up on trying to get to notice you, but you admire all the same. Or even continue to love.

Finally, Jack played "Boll Weevil" on the fiddle, and then Jack and Meg stood together, holding hands, to take a bow. "I thank you, and my sister thanks you," Jack said.

Asher and I walked downstairs and waded through an inch-deep slick of beer that covered the whole floor to the T-shirt stand, but we didn't like any of the designs. Back out through the seedy casino to the car. We drove into the salty night listening to "Seven Nation Army," and my son felt that satiated post-concert feeling, while I was sorry for all the people in the cars around us who hadn't been in the House of Blues that evening, because it had been, for two hours, the center of the universe.

Metric

Slim's
San Francisco
November 3, 2005
DANIEL HANDLER AND ANDREW SEAN GREER

ASG: I JUST WANT TO SAY, bam chicka bam chicka boom boom bam—

DH: Um—

ASG: Sha lang sha lang boom. Metric!

DH: Metric! When I was fourteen someone taught me that the best thing to shout at a show is the name of the band, because that's what they're doing, and that's who they are. Metric!

ASG: Metric!

Metric is Emily Haines on vocals and synthesizer, Jimmy Shaw on guitar, Josh Winstead on bass, and Joules Scott-Key on drums. To Mr. Greer and Mr. Handler, they are Eurythmics for people born too late for Eurythmics. They are electronic in sound and gesture, but never emotionless; Ms. Haines's singing ranges from haunted to pissed off. They are very catchy and make fun of being very catchy. There's no mistaking their politics. They sound bruised and resigned, but ultimately their songs are all about: why freak out, why break down, why not go on anyway? You'll survive it. That is to say: a band for every fourteen-year-old.

Mr. Handler first heard Metric by listening to the singer, Emily Haines, perform on a song called "Going, Going, Gone" by the band Stars. It's a heartbreaking song, or at least it was for Mr. Handler. He kept listening to it whenever he flew, and at the time he was doing a lot of flying to promote a film made from his children's books. "Going, Going, Gone" ends with the lyric, "All I see/All I see/All I see is me, everywhere." When he found himself crying on a late-night airplane to that lyric, looking over promotional materials with his photograph on them, he decided to read up on this singer. He read she was in a band called Metric. He went to a store and bought their first album, *Old World Underground, Where Are You Now?*, liking that the title was also the first lyric on the album, like an Emily Dickinson poem.

Mr. Greer first heard Metric at the show.

Mr. Greer and Mr. Handler went to see Metric in November of 2005 at Slim's in San Francisco. They were older than fourteen at the time, but like fourteen-year-olds, they couldn't stop thinking about the show, and they couldn't stop talking about it, either. While talking about it, they shared a pitcher of margaritas at a Mexican restaurant, and recorded the conversation.

DH: There's something about the way I've been loving Metric that feels like I loved music when I was fourteen, and I wonder if (a) you never love music the way you did as great as when you were fourteen, and (b) how you can get sort of back in touch with that. What was your favorite album when you were fourteen?

ASG: Definitely, definitely Eurythmics. Listening to Annie Lennox was the main young teen experience, you would listen deeply, deeply to get the lyrics.

DH: I never really wondered too much what lyrics meant.

ASG: What about that Eurythmics song we both loved, "Jennifer"? "Underneath the water/Underneath the water"?

DH: I don't know—I always thought she drowned. But what I reacted to in Eurythmics was something bitterly jaded, and yet longing and romantic, and I find that in Metric. Part of the experience of going to the concert was it was raining and I felt old and then they performed "Hustle Rose." In the middle of a cynical song I think is about a hooker, there's this moment of longing. *Why wouldn't I stand in line tonight?* It's worth it—of course it's worth it. It goes without saying I would stand in line for the right moment. That's fourteen.

ASG: But why would we still be moved by the same thing?

DH: The first Metric album was a grower for me. After two weeks I thought, "Oh, it has two or three good songs," and after one month I thought, "Oh, it has six or seven good songs," and after three months I thought, "I really like this album," and by the time the second album came out, I almost gasped when I came across it, unexpectedly, in a music store. I was in New York, on a book tour. I'll never forget hearing it for the first time, because I went back to my hotel room and put it on the hotel room CD player, and the first twenty seconds or so are just an ambient drone. So I turned the volume up, and the guitar came in, and I thought, "Gosh, they went in this totally different direction. It's sort of mellow, sort of resigned . . ." And then BANG! They hit me! I was so happy. I couldn't remember the last time I was surprised like that by a record that didn't seem gratuitous. You could tell they designed it so I would turn it up too loud. You could almost picture a band exhausted from touring, and that they would write this completely resigned, exhausted song, and they were just waiting for you to fall for it. It felt like the way a wonderful plot twist in a novel will make you want to look up and share the moment with other people and you realize you're on the bus and no one else is reading the novel. That moment when you're absolutely drawn in, absolutely knocked out of your socks, you've managed to leave behind a jaded POV, and I was lying alone on the bed of my hotel room.

Mr. Handler bought the tickets. It was his New Year's resolution to go see more live music. It was a New Year's resolution that had brought about some pleasure but a great deal of mortification, mostly due to opening bands. His wife was fed up with the resolution. Mr. Handler's wife is a short woman, and rock shows often find her wedged into the armpits of sweaty clubgoers. She wanted to stay home. So Mr. Handler called Mr. Greer.

Mr. Greer had been coaxed into going to shows before, and had learned that a spouse canceling was usually a very bad sign. It meant that either the marriage was on the rocks or the band playing was such a deep indulgence that not even the spouse was willing to participate; his own spouse had often lured him to Latino pop concerts, the most notable of which was a Ricky Martin concert on Mr. Greer's twenty-ninth birthday. But Mr. Handler's marriage seemed stable, and these Metric people seemed reliably Canadian. He also downloaded both albums from iTunes but listened to them mistakenly on *shuffle* and couldn't distill, until later, which album was which. He had once also done this with the novel *A Very Long Engagement*, which he listened to on CD on a road trip and reported widely and with excitement that it had "a breakthrough structure" until it was pointed out he had been listening to the chapters in random order.

It was raining buckets. Mr. Greer and Mr. Handler met up at a bar to have a drink first. Because of the weather it was likely Manhattans. The bar has two nicknames for locals—Jurassic Park and the Glass Coffin—due to the predominance of older, occasionally predatory gay men in the clientele. Mr. Greer and Mr. Handler were not preyed upon. They took a cab to the show.

Outside, there was a crowd, getting soaked between the bouncers and the rock band bus parked out front. Everyone was younger than Mr. Greer and Mr. Handler. They felt old, particularly when it turned out they did not have to wait in the line, because of Priority Seating. Mr. Handler had purchased the only tickets available, which were more expensive and offered Priority Seating. This turned out to mean booths, at the top of the stairs. It was where drug lords go to discuss business in the movies. Mr. Greer and Mr. Handler sat in their booth. The distance from the stage made it feel more like they were watching a stage on television. Also, the stage was blank, so it felt like the television screen was blank. At the next booth, a man asked Mr. Handler if they were also from the industry. His girlfriend nodded, prematurely, as if Mr. Handler had already said yes. Instead Mr. Handler asked the waitress for some bourbon. So did Mr. Greer.

ASG: I was thinking about the fact that they opened up the concert by turning on the lights only onstage and playing what seemed like a full two minutes of "O Superman" before anyone came out. That's an example of a song that's completely technological and really moving to me, but I understand why to other people it sounds like . . .

DH: Like a digital watch.

ASG: Like a joke. That song doesn't sound like there's a human in the room, and yet it manages to convey some truths. It's Frankenstein's monster—something that shouldn't be human is somehow exhibiting human qualities. Metric plays music that sounds like it's a party, and yet it's all heartbreaking. I think the most positive song on *Live It Out* is the title track, pretty much the story of a woman who gets left by a guy at the last minute and decides she wants to live anyway. Which is not really optimistic.

DH: I remember the lights lowered and they started to play "O Superman," and I couldn't have devised a better way to make you happy.

It fell like an incantation over the crowd. It was completely unexpected. A glance at Mr. Greer's face showed him to be utterly happy for the first time since he was very young. He was an unrepentant Laurie Anderson fan. They played a full two minutes of the song with the lights down low: "Ah. Ah. Ah. Ah. Ah. Here come the planes. They're American planes. Made in America. Smoking or non-smoking?" All Mr. Greer and Mr. Handler could see was the setup: some speakers in a small space, a drum set, a keyboard-mike setup that looked like it would imprison whoever got into it. A little purple light over everything. For two minutes. Who knows or cares what the crowd thought? It was a beautiful robotic spell. And then the band walked on.

DH: I remember when I was fourteen I went to see a band called the Uptones. It was just a local band, and when the show was over—we were in the front—I reached up to the stage and took the piece of paper that was taped to the floor saying what songs they were going to play and in what order, because it was so exciting to me that I could own that, and I didn't even know what such a thing was called. Someone noticed it when it was taped to my wall in my bedroom and they said, "Oh you have a set list." And that's how I learned what it was called. I certainly don't have that kind of mystique about it now. So that's why I was made so happy by that show in a way I thought I couldn't be made happy by it, because now I know what a set list is.

They finished their bourbons and went down the stairs. They left their coats and umbrellas in their Priority Seating. They had to go downstairs. They had to. Mr. Greer led the way through the packed, silent crowd. The packed, silent crowd reacted the way one might expect they would if two guys, one unit older than the members of the packed, silent crowd, came down from Priority Seating and eeled their way into the middle of the room. When a young woman looked particularly sour, Mr. Handler stopped and said, "Sorry, my man's pushy." Mr. Handler is not in the habit of talking like this. If you had asked him previous to this evening, the only circumstance in which Mr. Handler could picture saying the words "my man" in sequence would be in a discussion of *My Man Godfrey*.

DH: I hear about a lot of new music from a certain Web site and today I thought, "I wonder if they've ever reviewed Metric," and they hate them!

ASG: What do they hate about them?

DH: They say it's completely derivative pop. One of the reviews compares it to the Go-Go's. "It's reheated Go-Go's."

ASG: What? I'm going to write to them. I'm going to have the whole forum write to them. I went to the Metric Web site, and one of the fan forum topics is, "How did you first learn about Metric?" Everyone's answer is

"Combat Baby." It brought me back to being fourteen. People were saying, "I heard this song, and the girl said either 'Combat Baby' or 'Come Back, Baby'; I couldn't figure it out." I remember hearing some song you liked on the radio and you had to wait for it again to find out what it really was, and it would sort of tug at you, and you would ask people about it.

DH: I remember someone told me, when I heard the song "Small Town Boy" on the radio, which was a Bronski Beat song, that it was a Sade song, so I went out and bought the album, and not only didn't it have "Small Town Boy" on it . . . but it was a Sade album. That seems like a mistake you just couldn't make nowadays. You could hear it online first.

ASG: I remember when I was in junior high, and my best friend was Peter Day, and every day I would come to school, and he would ask me about another song on the radio and whether I liked it or not. Often I didn't know the song, and if I did know it, I didn't know if I was supposed to like it or not.

DH: Was he testing you?

ASG: No, he wasn't at all. He was just interested and wanted to talk about it. His favorite band was Asia, so he had nowhere to stand. It seemed to me totally random. Like, "Cum on Feel the Noize," good song. "Total Eclipse of the Heart," bad song. Which I feel is the opposite of what's true.

DH: [laughter]

ASG: But I learned to kind of study the radio. Even though it wasn't a test, I somehow thought it was.

"Flip to the right," Ms. Haines told them. "Slip back to the left." So they did; it was a dance move and not just a political statement. Mr. Greer put his arms up in the air. Then, a little tap on the shoulder. Mr. Greer turned around and there were two young women, white T-shirts and glitter earrings. Two blinks of the eyes and: "We can't see the band when you do that." It took a few moments for this to register; it had to be shouted above the loud dance music and Ms. Haines singing for people to move around. It's difficult to be short in a space like that—Mr. Handler's wife was staying home—but if you don't stay home, isn't it about the energy and the music and everyone around you? Raising their arms? Or were they too old? Had it possibly happened: that twenty years had passed since fourteen and now the world had altered, that a singer in a small club shouting for you to dance was something everybody knew to ignore, as if it were rhetorical these days? If Ms. Haines had stepped out of her keyboard prison, walked to the edge of the stage and dove off—as she later did, arms out, at another show—who would have caught her? Without arms raised, who would have caught her? Not these two. Mr. Greer should have said: "That's rock 'n' roll, honey." But all he said was, "Sorry."

Sorry was not enough. The dance haters grew more insistent. Mr. Greer and Mr. Handler heard exasperated sighs behind them—sighs so theatrical that they could be heard over the roar of a rock 'n' roll band telling people to dance. Mr. Greer and Mr. Handler kept dancing. The people behind them kept sighing. Mr. Handler remembered mosh pits of his youth. He remembered coming home, fourteen, with blood on his T-shirt from the Fishbone concert. It was one of a number of Fishbone concerts. He remembered that his parents were not reassured by Mr. Handler's claim that it was someone else's blood. And now, between songs, people younger than Mr. Greer and Mr. Handler were informing them that if the dancing did not stop they were going to inform the manager.

DH: Why were they so mean?

ASG: Maybe they thought, "We get it: they sound like a dance band, but they're actually a thinking man's band." And *we* thought, "No, *we* get it: they sound like a dance band that sounds like it's actually a thinking man's band but they're actually a dance band and we're going to dance!"

DH: I remember an essay—I think in *Spin*—a resigned essay about growing old and still liking rock 'n' roll. It said, "How can you slam dance after you realize the world is nobody's fault?" And I think I've slam danced so much more after I realized the world is nobody's fault, actually. You can have a better time not blaming your parents and dancing really hard. And when people gave us a hard time about dancing, I just thought, "I deserve to dance." My wife was staying home because she didn't want to go, but we had agreed I would still get up early with the baby, and I was going to be a wreck. I was having to get up early in the morning for my two-year-old, and I wasn't going to be told by someone ten years younger than me, who's going to be hung over for their temp job, that I can't dance. All the youngsters should've been shaming me. They should've been out dancing *after* the show. This may be an old man argument.

ASG: It may be an old man argument.

DH: That's when you know rock 'n' roll is dead, when you go complain to the manager of a small rock club that people are dancing.

A new gentleman appeared behind Mr. Greer and Mr. Handler, and tapped them on the shoulder. Mr. Greer and Mr. Handler turned around, and the gentleman made a gesture miming a wall in front of him, as if the gentleman were trapped behind a wall. The gentleman was young and blond. He had a short, blond, spiky haircut. Mr. Greer and Mr. Handler felt old, not for the first time. The youthful gesture was inscrutable to them, so they nodded inscrutably themselves, and kept dancing. The gentleman gave Mr. Handler an insistent shove. Mr. Handler turned around and received the gesture again, and when he turned back around the man begin pressing steadily against Mr. Handler's back as if pushing him up a hill. By virtue of the laws of physics, the people in front of Mr. Greer and Mr. Handler were now aware of what was going on. Mr. Greer inquired if Mr. Handler needed help. Mr. Handler said he didn't know, as he did not understand what was going on. As a practitioner of narrative, Mr. Handler could not help imagining a context in which the gentleman pushing against Mr. Handler's back would make some sort of sense. Various scenarios of repressed desire arose off the top of Mr. Handler's head: a summer camp episode the gentleman kept telling himself hadn't actually happened, or didn't mean anything if it did, or, conversely, an unrequited locker room moment in which nothing had happened, and the gentleman wished it had. The band played on. The band played "Monster Hospital."

DH: Those "Monster Hospital" lyrics, "I fought the war and the war won": if it's not the Iraq war, what war is it?

ASG: The war inside? Maybe the jadedness of the current political scene is a replacement for the jaded angst of being fourteen.

DH: "*I* fought the war." I guess so. I mean, I bought full-page ads for Not In Our Name, and made signs, and marched downtown. And not only was the war not stopped, but those gestures were utterly disregarded, demonized, even. "But the war won." You guys got your war. It's got that cool denunciation that feels fourteen. Congratulations, you guys won, you got your war. It's better than talking about dead children.

ASG: Better to dance to, anyway.

DH: But then you couldn't dance. Then they did that thing—

ASG: I know! That Pink Floyd thing! I know!

DH: Metric!

ASG: Metric!

It was like nothing else. Months later, at a party, Mr. Greer would find himself discussing Metric with two recent college graduates who had loved the show until the Pink Floyd thing. "What was that?" they asked, rolling their eyes. It was beautiful. It was Ms. Haines curled over, murmuring about politics while the guitarist touched pedals to alter the sound of everything, echoing like in a canyon. "It's like hearing someone you love," Mr. Greer said to the young people at the party, "go on a long rant after a beer too many, about their parents and the government and something they read somewhere and got a little wrong. Don't you just love that? Hasn't that ever happened to you?" But they looked as if it never had, which was a pity. Or, as with the dancing, a case of the cools when the cools weren't called for. What was called for was this: to be into whatever was happening. You know, like when you were fourteen.

DH: I've scarcely heard any Pink Floyd, actually.

ASG: It's full of space ballads.

DH: My wife's always afraid I'm going to go through a Pink Floyd phase, because I like anything that has a robot voice. She dreads the day I get turned on to them.

ASG: Shouldn't you have gone through this phase earlier? Like fourteen?

DH: She had two younger brothers, so she's just heard more Pink Floyd than she ever wants to hear.

ASG: I think you might like it. I used to. How about that fandom about specific musicians? You know, you fantasize about some possible relationship with them? How they're gonna save you. That was definitely mine. I'd be saved.

DH: I have a really strong memory of seeing OMD opening for the Thompson Twins. One of the guys was singing and playing keyboard and it was sort of awkward—you could tell it wasn't easy for him to do that—and I remember I had this fantasy because I'd had so many piano lessons that Mr. OMD would meet me and say, "You should play, and I can just sing."

ASG: We can't have those fantasies anymore. We're writers, so if we had it now it would be helping with the lyrics. But I don't want to help with the lyrics, anyway. Because I look at the songs, and the parts of the songs aren't obviously related even.

DH: Like the part of "Empty" where she suddenly says, "I'm so glad that I'm an island." That reminds me of "Underneath the water." It's evocative, but you don't know what it's evocative of.

ASG: But it's more moving than "I am a rock, I am an island" by Paul Simon, which is a complete metaphor. Metric can sing "I'm so glad that I'm an island" without any linkage. They don't set us up, they don't take us anywhere, and it's more moving for me. And that feels more like I'm fourteen, maybe. There's some fragment of the world you can attach yourself to, but you don't have a complete picture.

When the show was over, Mr. Greer and Mr. Handler made their way back to their Priority Seating for their coats and umbrellas and decided to wait out the crowd. Someone told them they couldn't stay long. When the crowd thinned, they left. It was still pouring. They were afraid they'd never find a cab but then remembered that everyone else was so young they were undoubtedly taking public transportation. They found a cab right away.

Inside the taxi, the music was so loud Mr. Greer and Mr. Handler temporarily forgot about Metric. They asked the driver if he might turn the music down. The driver explained that the artist in question was Bryan Ferry. Mr. Greer and Mr. Handler were both vaguely familiar with Mr. Ferry's work and asked a few questions. The driver began to flip through a book of compact discs, discussing the difference between domestic and imported releases of Mr. Ferry's work. The taxi had reached Mr. Greer's home and let him out.

Alone with Mr. Handler, the driver continued to explain how difficult it was to find certain releases by Mr. Ferry, and then wandered autobiographically along the terrain the driver and Mr. Ferry had in common— mostly moments certain songs by Mr. Ferry had been on the radio in relation to the driver's love life. Finally, the driver told Mr. Handler that he simply had to hear a rare, live version of a song by Mr. Ferry of which Mr. Handler had never heard. By now they were a block from Mr. Handler's home, but the driver, without slowing down, flipped through the book and found the disc in question. Mr. Handler made the point, as gently as he could, that it was one in the morning and that the taxi was so close to Mr. Handler's home that there was no use listening. The driver insisted that this version was incredible, and put the disc into the stereo. Mr. Handler heard the applause of a crowd, and perhaps four or five quarter notes from a bass guitar. The taxi stopped at his home. Mr. Handler agreed that this version was incredible.

Everyone loves something.

Contributors

John Albert grew up in the suburbs of Los Angeles. As a teenager he co-founded the cross-dressing "death rock" band Christian Death, then played drums in a low-rent version of a punk band, Bad Religion. He has written articles on surfing, pop music, crime, robots, and the Hell's Angels, among others. His book *Wrecking Crew* (Scribner), chronicling the true-life adventures of his amateur baseball team comprised of junkies, gambling addicts, transvestites, and washed-up rock stars, is being made into a film by Paramount Pictures.

Mike Albo is a writer and performer who lives and loves in Brooklyn. His first novel, *Hornito*, came out in 2000 from HarperCollins. He collaborated with his longtime friend Virginia Heffernan for his next novel, *The Underminer: The Best Friend Who Casually Destroys Your Life*, which was published in 2005 from Bloomsbury. He's performed numerous solo shows, including *Spray*, *Please Everything Burst*, and *My Price Point*, all also co-written with Ms. Heffernan. Check out www.mikealbo.com and finger his chakras for upcoming shows, his spaced-out blog, performance clips, and recent writing.

Bruce Bauman is the author of the novel *And The Word Was*. His work has appeared in numerous magazines and anthologies. He is senior editor of *Black Clock* magazine.

Thomas Beller is the author of a collection of stories, *Seduction Theory*, and a novel, *The Sleep-Over Artist*, which was a *New York Times* Notable Book and a *Los Angeles Times* Best Book of 2000. His most recent book is a collection of personal essays, *How To Be a Man: Scenes From a Protracted Boyhood*, many of which first appeared in *The New Yorker* and *The New York Times*. He is a founder and editor of *Open City Magazine and Books*, and creator of the Web site, *Mr. Beller's Neighborhood*.

Arion Berger is a writer and editor who lives in the Washington, DC, area.

Marc Bojanowski is the author of the novel *The Dog Fighter* (Morrow, 2004).

Rebecca Brown is the author of many books, including *The Last Time I Saw You*, *The End of Youth*, and *The Terrible Girls*, all with City Lights. She has also written a play and the libretto for a dance opera. She lives in Seattle, teaches at Goddard College in Vermont, and is the Artistic Director of Literature at Centrum in Washington state (centrum.org).

Richard Burgin is the author of twelve books, including the novel *Ghost Quartet* (recently translated into Russian) and the story collections *The Conference on Beautiful Moments* and *The Identity Club: New and Selected Stories and Songs*, which includes a CD of twenty of Burgin's best songs and pieces. Five of Burgin's stories have won Pushcart Prizes and one other was reprinted in *The Best American Mystery Stories 2005*. He is a professor of English and communication at Saint Louis University, where he continues to edit *Boulevard*, the internationally distributed literary journal he founded twenty-two years ago.

Kevin Canty has written three novels (*Into the Great Wide Open*, *Nine Below Zero*, and *Winslow In Love*) and two short story collections (*A Stranger in This World* and *Honeymoon*). His essays and stories have been published in *The New Yorker*, *Esquire*, *GQ*, *Vogue*, *Tin House*, and many other places. He lives in Missoula, Montana, where he teaches in the MFA program at the University of Montana and plays lead guitar in the Pleasure Kings.

Ron Carlson grew up on the west side of Salt Lake City. He is the author of eight books of fiction, most recently his selected stories, *A Kind of Flying*. His novel *Five Skies* will be published in 2007. He teaches at Arizona State University.

Tracy Chevalier is the author of the best-selling novel *Girl with a Pearl Earring*, as well as three others. Her new novel, about the English painter/poet William Blake, will be published in early 2007. She has lived in England for twenty years, and has a husband and son who sound like Alastair Cooke.

Max Allan Collins, a Mystery Writers of America "Edgar" nominee in both fiction and nonfiction categories, has earned fourteen Private Eye Writers of America "Shamus" nominations for his historical thrillers, winning for his Nathan Heller novels, *True Detective* (1983) and *Stolen Away* (1991). His graphic novel *Road to Perdition* is the basis of the Academy Award–winning film starring Tom Hanks; prose sequels, *Road to Purgatory* and *Road to Paradise*, were published by Morrow in 2004 and 2005. His many comics credits include *Dick Tracy*, *Ms. Tree*, *Batman*, and *CSI: Crime Scene Investigation*, based on the hit TV series for which he has also written video games, jigsaw puzzles, and an internationally best-selling series of novels. An independent filmmaker in his native Iowa, his latest indie feature, *Eliot Ness: An Untouchable Life* (2005), is based on his Edgar-nominated play. He and his writer wife, Barbara, frequently collaborate, sometimes under the name Barbara Allan.

Elizabeth Crane is the author of two collections of short stories from Little, Brown, *When the Messenger is Hot* and *All This Heavenly Glory*. She received the Chicago Public Library 21st Century Award, granted by the Chicago Public Library Foundation, in October 2003. A New York City native, Crane lives in Chicago with her husband and teaches writing at Northwestern University and the University of Chicago.

Charles R. Cross is the author of five books, including 2005's *Room Full of Mirrors: A Biography of Jimi Hendrix*, published by Hyperion in the United States and Hodder in the United Kingdom. His 2001 release, *Heavier Than Heaven: The Biography of Kurt Cobain* (Hyperion/Hodder), was a *New York Times* best-seller. In 2002, *Heavier Than Heaven* won the ASCAP Timothy White Award for outstanding biography. Cross's other books include the national best-seller *Backstreets: Springsteen, the Man and His Music* (Harmony, 1989), *Led Zeppelin: Heaven and Hell* (Harmony, 1992), and *Nevermind: The Classic Album* (Schirmer, 1998).

Alice Elliott Dark is the author of the novel *Think of England*, and two books of short stories, *In the Gloaming* and *Naked to the Waist*. Her work has appeared in such publications as *The New Yorker*, *Harper's*, *Redbook*, *DoubleTake*, and *The New York Times*. The short story "In the Gloaming" has been widely anthologized, adapted to two film versions, and was chosen by John Updike for inclusion in *Best American Short Stories of the Century*.

Jennifer Egan is the author of *The Invisible Circus*, which was released as a feature film by Fine Line in 2001, *Emerald City and Other Stories*, *Look at Me*, which was nominated for the National Book Award in 2001, and most recently *The Keep*. Her nonfiction articles appear frequently in *The New York Times Magazine*.

Maggie Estep has published six books, including *Hex*, a *New York Times* Notable Book of 2003. She has contributed to various magazines and anthologies, including *Brooklyn Noir*, *Hard Boiled Brooklyn*, and *The Best American Erotica*. She lives in Brooklyn, New York.

Nick Flynn's most recent book is *Another Bullshit Night in Suck City*, a memoir about his father and homelessness, which won the PEN/Martha Albrand Award and has been translated into eleven languages. He lives in Texas and New York.

David Gates is the author of the novels *Jernigan* and *Preston Falls*, and of the short story collection *The Wonders of the Invisible World*.

Gary Giddins wrote *The Village Voice*'s "Weather Bird" column for thirty years. His eight books—including *Weather Bird* and, most recently, *Natural Selection*—and three documentary films have garnered unparalleled recognition for jazz, including a National Book Critics Circle Award in Criticism, two Ralph J. Gleason Music Book Awards, six ASCAP Deems Taylor Awards, a Guggenheim, and a Peabody. He lives in New York City.

Andrew Sean Greer is the author of a collection of short stories, *How It Was for Me*, and two novels, *The Path of Minor Planets* and *The Confessions of Max Tivoli*, a national best-seller. He has been featured on *The Today Show Book Club* and is the recipient of the Northern California Book Award, the California Book Award, the New York Public Library Young Lions Award, and a Fellowship from the National Endowment for the Arts. His fourth book, *The Ballad of Pearlie Cook*, will be out from Farrar, Straus and Giroux in 2007.

Daniel Handler is the author of the novels *The Basic Eight*, *Watch Your Mouth*, and *Adverbs*, and, as Lemony Snicket, a sequence of novels for children collectively entitled *A Series of Unfortunate Events*. He lives in San Francisco with his wife and child.

John Haskell is the author of the short story collection *I Am Not Jackson Pollock* (Farrar, Straus and Giroux, 2003) and the novel *American Purgatorio*

(Farrar, Straus and Giroux, 2005). He was born in San Diego and now lives in Brooklyn.

Samantha Hunt is the author of two novels, *The Seas* and *The Invention of Everything Else*.

Heidi Julavits is the author of three novels, most recently *The Uses of Enchantment*. She is a founding editor of *The Believer*. She lives in New York City and Maine.

Karen Karbo is the author of three novels and a memoir, all of which were named *New York Times* Notable Books. She's a frequent contributor to *Outside, Entertainment Weekly,* and *The New York Times.* She lives in Portland, Oregon, where she avoids listening to the Eagles.

Chuck Klosterman is the author of *Fargo Rock City: A Heavy Metal Odyssey in Rural North Dakota; Sex, Drugs, and Cocoa Puffs: A Low Culture Manifesto; Killing Yourself to Live: 85% of a True Story;* and *Chuck Klosterman IV.* He has written for *Esquire, GQ, Spin, The New York Times Magazine, The Washington Post, The Believer,* and ESPN. He lives in New York City.

Sean Manning lives in New York. His writing has appeared in the *New York Press, The Brooklyn Rail,* and *BlackBook.*

Rick Moody's most recent novel is *The Diviners.* His band, the Wingdale Community Singers, released their eponymously titled debut on Plain Recordings in 2005.

Lydia Millet is the author of five novels, including *My Happy Life,* which won the PEN/USA Award for Fiction in 2003. Her sixth, *How the Dead Dream,* will be published by Soft Skull Press in 2007.

Thurston Moore is a founding member of radical avant rockers Sonic Youth. He plays concerts, goes to concerts, puts on concerts, and is looking forward to the next . . . concert.

Paul Muldoon's main collections of poetry are *New Weather* (1973), *Mules* (1977), *Why Brownlee Left* (1980), *Quoof* (1983), *Meeting The British* (1987), *Madoc: A Mystery* (1990), *The Annals of Chile* (1994), *Hay* (1998), *Poems 1968–1998* (2001), and *Moy Sand and Gravel* (2002), for which he won the 2003 Pulitzer Prize. His most recent collection is *Horse Latitudes* (2006).

Marc Nesbitt is the author of *Gigantic* and currently lives in New York.

Carl Newman is the leader of the New Pornographers. In 2004, he released *Slow Wonder* (Matador), a solo album.

Sigrid Nunez's fifth novel, *The Last of Her Kind* (Farrar, Straus and Giroux), was published in January 2006. A new edition of her third novel, *Mitz: The Marmoset of Bloomsbury*, will be published by Soft Skull Press in spring 2007.

Diana Ossana, born and raised in an Italian American family in St. Louis, Missouri, has written two novels, more than a dozen screenplays, and numerous essays. She most recently co-wrote and produced the feature film *Brokeback Mountain*, and was awarded, along with Larry McMurtry, an Academy Award for Best Adapted Screenplay. She spends her time in Texas, Arizona, and South Dakota.

Harvey Pekar is primarily known for his *American Splendor* comic books and the film of the same name based on them. However, since 1959, he has been writing for nationally and internationally distributed jazz publications, including *The Jazz Review*, *Metronome*, *Down Beat*, *The Jazz Journal*, *The Jazz Monthly*, and *Coda*.

Robert Polito directs the graduate writing program at The New School. His books include the poetry collection *Doubles*, *A Reader's Guide to James Merrill's The Changing Light at Sandover*, and *Savage Art: A Biography of Jim Thompson*, for which he received the National Book Critics Circle Award. He has edited *Crime Novels: American Noir of the 1930s and 1940s*, *Crime Novels: American Noir of the 1950s*, and *The Selected Poems of Kenneth Fearing*, all for the Library of America, and editions of Dashiell Hammett and James M. Cain for Everyman Library. He lives in New Paltz and New York City.

Jon Raymond is the author of *The Half-Life* (Bloomsbury, 2004) and *Old Joy*, a short fiction that was recently adapted into a feature film. He is an associate editor at *Tin House*, and his writing has appeared in *Artforum*, *Bookforum*, *Plazm*, and other periodicals. He lives in Portland, Oregon.

Ishmael Reed's latest projects are *New and Collected Poems, 1964–2006* (Carroll & Graf) and *"Bad Mouth" Conjure 3*, produced by Kip Hanrahan's American Clave Records and featuring David Murray and Billy Bang.

David Ritz has written biographies of, among others, Ray Charles, Marvin Gaye, and B.B. King. He's currently co-authoring books with Scott Weiland and Grandmaster Flash.

Luc Sante's books include *Low Life* and *The Factory of Facts*. He opened for Tricky in Central Park (summer, 2000), so he knows firsthand what it's like to be booed by thousands of people.

Gene Santoro is the author of several books, including *Myself When I Am Real: The Life and Music of Charles Mingus* and *Highway 61 Revisited: The Tangled Roots of American Music*. His essays and features have appeared in many publications, such as *The New York Times, The New Yorker, The Atlantic Monthly, New York, The New York Post, The Village Voice, 7 Days, Discover, Taxi, The Nation, Spin, Rolling Stone, Pulse, Down Beat*, and *Billboard*. He covers music for the *New York Daily News* and is a columnist at *Chamber Music*. His work has been widely anthologized.

Dani Shapiro's most recent books include *Family History* (Knopf, 2003) and the best-selling memoir *Slow Motion*, for which she co-wrote the screenplay along with her husband, screenwriter Michael Maren, for Sony/Phoenix Pictures and Reese Witherspoon. Her short stories and essays have appeared in *The New Yorker, Granta, Tin House, Elle, Bookforum, Oprah*, and *Ploughshares*, among others, and have been broadcast on National Public Radio. Her books have been translated into seven languages. She lives with her husband and young son in Litchfield County, Connecticut. Her new novel, *Black & White*, will be published by Knopf in April.

Jerry Stahl is the author of the memoir *Permanent Midnight* and the novels *Perv—A Love Story, Plainclothes Naked*, and *I, Fatty*.

Susan Straight's sixth novel, *A Million Nightingales*, was published in 2006 by Pantheon. She has written for *The New York Times Magazine, Harper's, The Los Angeles Times Magazine, Salon, The Nation, Zoetrope All-Story*, and others. She still lives in Riverside, California, and still listens to Parliament.

Lynne Tillman is a novelist, short story writer, and essayist. Her latest novel, *American Genius, A Comedy*, was published in October 2006 by Soft Skull Press. In 2006, she received a Guggenheim Fellowship in fiction.

Holly George-Warren has contributed to more than forty books about popular music. The editor of *Farm Aid: A Song for America*, she is co-editor of *The Rolling Stone Encyclopedia of Rock & Roll*, *Martin Scorsese Presents the Blues: A Musical Journey*, and *The Appalachians: America's First and Last Frontier*. She has written for *The New York Times*, *The Village Voice*, *Rolling Stone*, *Mojo*, *The Oxford American*, and *The Journal of Country Music*, among other publications. Her biography of Gene Autry will be published by Oxford University Press in 2007.

Robert Burke Warren is a writer, teacher, and musician. His alter ego is "rock of all ages" troubadour Uncle Rock. He has toured the world as a bass player, performed as Buddy Holly in London's West End, written songs with Rosanne Cash and Wanda Jackson, and been a stay-at-home dad. He lives in the Catskill Mountains of Upstate New York with his wife Holly George-Warren and their son Jack. More information at www.robertbwarren.com.

Linda Yablonsky is the author of *The Story of Junk: A Novel*, and an art critic based in New York, where she is a regular contributor to *Bloomberg News*, *The New York Times*, and *Art News*, among several other publications. She was founding program director and producer of WPS1.org, the Internet radio station from P.S.1/MoMA, and is currently completing a new novel.

Acknowledgments

The editor thanks the following people for their help and encouragement:

Ben Schafer
Monster Magnet
Irving Plaza
New York City
May 5, 1999

Jim Fitzgerald
Jimi Hendrix
Regis University Fieldhouse
Denver, Colorado
February 14, 1968

Anne Garrett
Green Day
SECC
Glasgow, Scotland
December 10, 2000

Vanessa White Wolf
Phish
Big Cypress Reservation
The Florida Everglades
December 31, 1999

Susan Manning
The Rolling Stones
Gund Arena
Cleveland, Ohio
April 1, 1999

Glenn Dixon
Pavement
9:30 Club
Washington, DC
June 17, 1992

Alex Lange
Fishbone
Lupo's Heartbreak Hotel
Providence, Rhode Island
1987

Dan Migdal
Big Day Out
RAS Showgrounds
Melbourne, Australia
January 28, 2002

Bob Clark
Stone Temple Pilots
Nautica Stage
Cleveland, Ohio
June 30, 2000

David Wilson
The Replacements/Elvis Costello
Madison Square Garden
New York City
May 22, 1991

Lissa Warren
Toad the Wet Sprocket
Millett Hall at Miami University
Oxford, Ohio
1993

Beth Ferraro
Ben Harper & the Innocent
    Criminals
9:30 Club
Washington, DC
July 25, 2005

Lori Hobkirk
John Denver
Red Rocks Amphitheatre
Morrison, Colorado
August 14, 1973

Credits